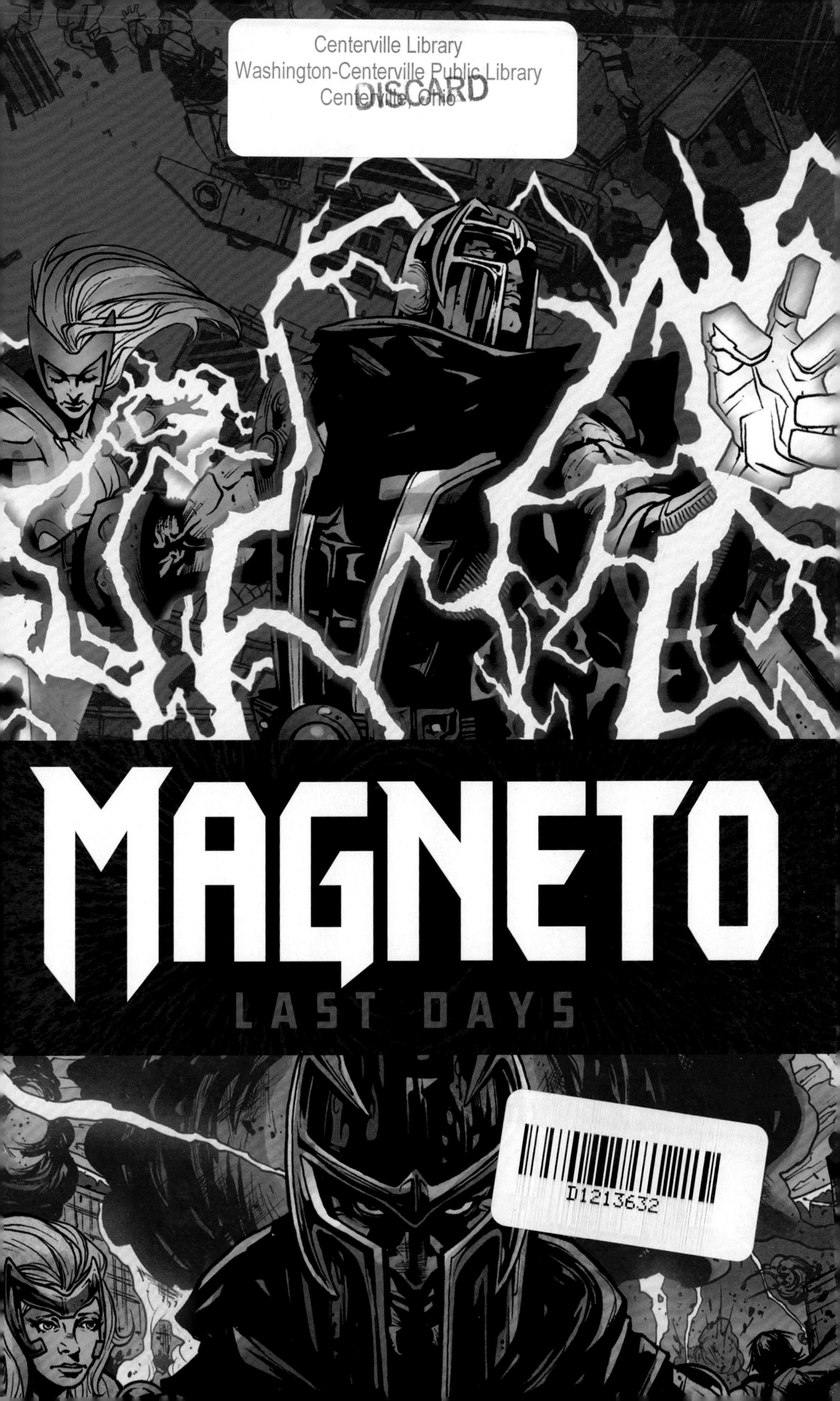
MAGNETO
LAST DAYS

COLLECTION EDITOR: **JENNIFER GRÜNWALD**
ASSISTANT EDITOR: **SARAH BRUNSTAD**
ASSOCIATE MANAGING EDITOR: **ALEX STARBUCK**
EDITOR, SPECIAL PROJECTS: **MARK D. BEAZLEY**
SENIOR EDITOR, SPECIAL PROJECTS: **JEFF YOUNGQUIST**
SVP PRINT, SALES & MARKETING: **DAVID GABRIEL**
BOOK DESIGNER: **ADAM DEL RE**

EDITOR IN CHIEF: **AXEL ALONSO**
CHIEF CREATIVE OFFICER: **JOE QUESADA**
PUBLISHER: **DAN BUCKLEY**
EXECUTIVE PRODUCER: **ALAN FINE**

MAGNETO VOL. 4: LAST DAYS. Contains material originally published in magazine form as MAGNETO #18-21 and X-MEN #50-51. First printing 2015. ISBN# 978-0-7851-9805-5. Published by MARVEL WORLDWIDE, INC., a subsidiary of MARVEL ENTERTAINMENT, LLC. OFFICE OF PUBLICATION: 135 West 50th Street, New York, NY 10020. Copyright © 2015 MARVEL No similarity between any of the names, characters, persons, and/or institutions in this magazine with those of any living or dead person or institution is intended, and any such similarity which may exist is purely coincidental. **Printed in Canada.** ALAN FINE, President, Marvel Entertainment; DAN BUCKLEY, President, TV, Publishing and Brand Management; JOE QUESADA, Chief Creative Officer; TOM BREVOORT, SVP of Publishing; DAVID BOGART, SVP of Operations & Procurement, Publishing; C.B. CEBULSKI, VP of International Development & Brand Management; DAVID GABRIEL, SVP Print, Sales & Marketing; JIM O'KEEFE, VP of Operations & Logistics; DAN CARR, Executive Director of Publishing Technology; SUSAN CRESPI, Editorial Operations Manager; ALEX MORALES, Publishing Operations Manager; STAN LEE, Chairman Emeritus. For information regarding advertising in Marvel Comics or on Marvel. com, please contact Jonathan Rheingold, VP of Custom Solutions & Ad Sales, at jrheingold@marvel.com. For Marvel subscription inquiries, please call 800-217-9158. **Manufactured between 8/21/2015 and 9/28/2015 by SOLISCO PRINTERS, SCOTT, QC, CANADA.**

10 9 8 7 6 5 4 3 2 1

MAGNETO

LAST DAYS

WRITER:	**CULLEN BUNN**
ARTISTS:	**PAUL DAVIDSON** (#18–20) & **GABRIEL HERNANDEZ WALTA** (#21)
COLOR ARTISTS:	**PAUL MOUNTS** (#18–20) & **JORDIE BELLAIRE** (#21)
LETTERER:	**VC's CORY PETIT**
COVER ART:	**DAVID YARDIN**
ASSISTANT EDITORS:	**CHRISTINA HARRINGTON** & **XANDER JAROWEY**
EDITOR:	**DANIEL KETCHUM**
X-MEN GROUP EDITOR:	**MIKE MARTS**
MAGNETO CREATED BY	**STAN LEE** & **JACK KIRBY**

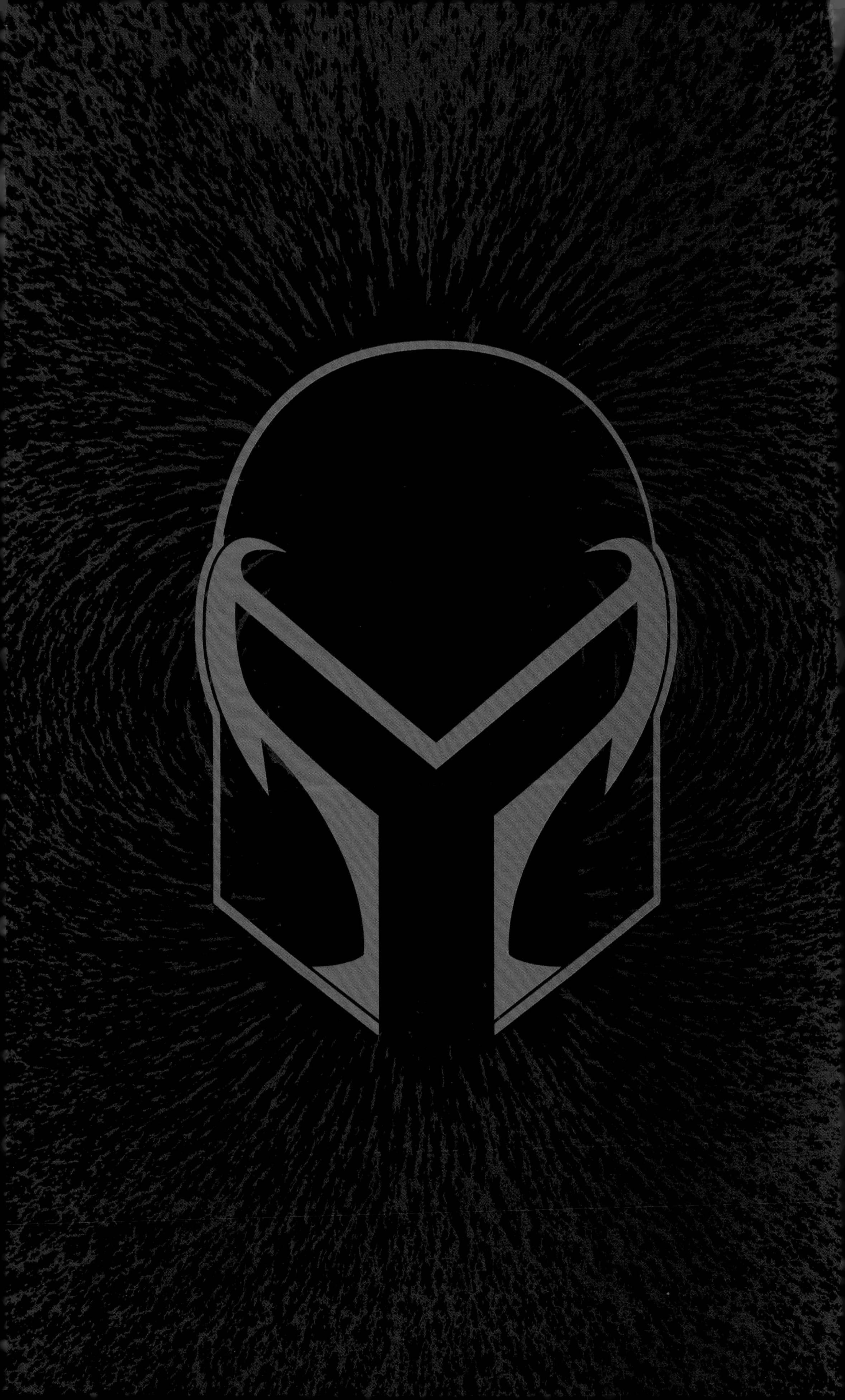

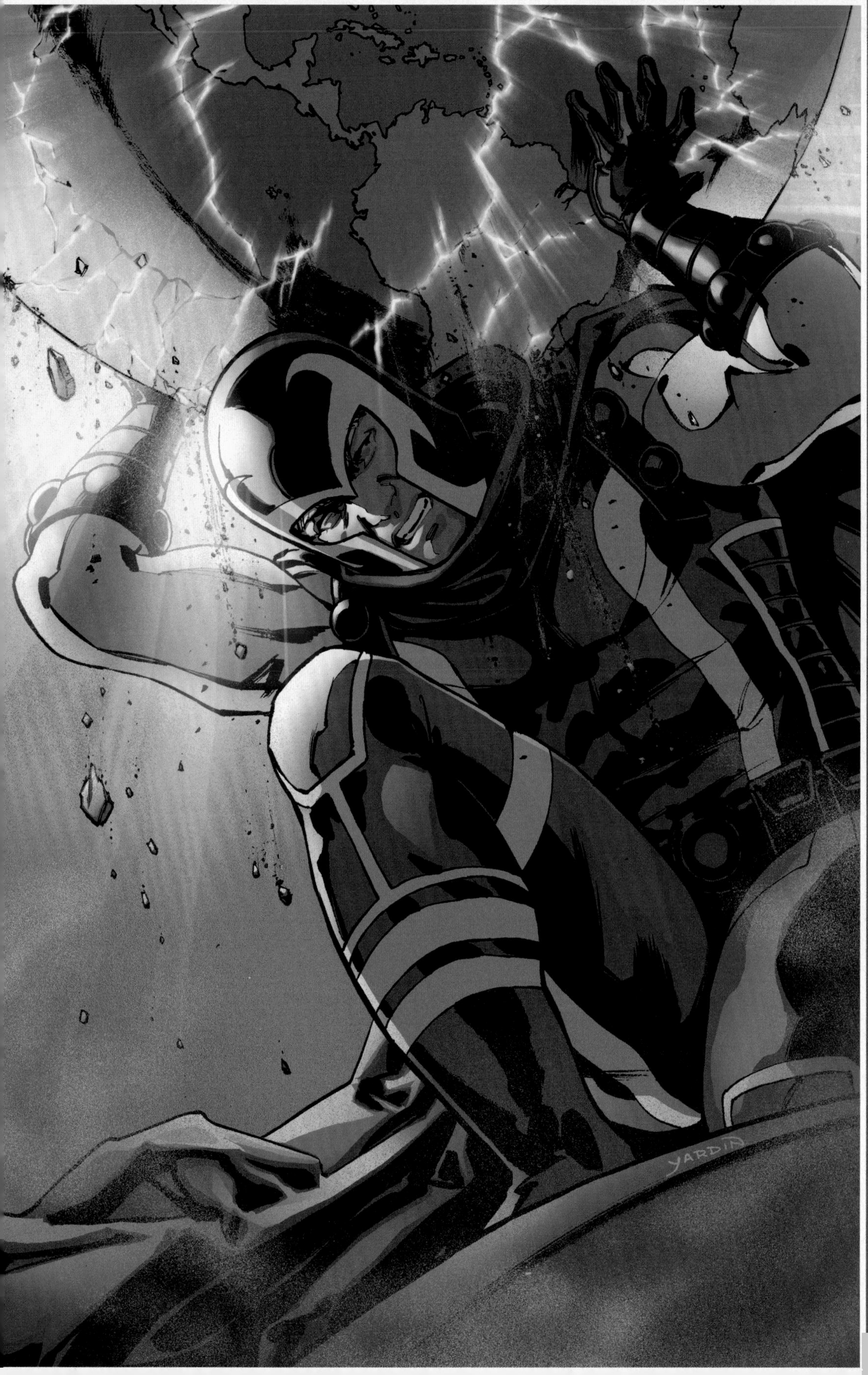
YARDIN

MAGNETO

ASSUMING THE MANTLE OF "PROTECTOR OF MUTANTKIND" ONCE MORE,
MAGNETO HAS TAKEN TO WORKING AS A LONE VIGILANTE, EXACTING
REVENGE ON THE PERPETRATORS OF ANTI-MUTANT CRIMES.

MAGNETO HAS DEDICATED HIS LIFE TO ENSURING A FUTURE FOR MUTANTS,
BUT IN DOING SO HE HAS FOUND HIMSELF ESTRANGED FROM THOSE HE
CARES FOR MOST, SETTING HIM APART EVEN FROM HIS DAUGHTER,
LORNA DANE, THE MUTANT KNOWN AS POLARIS.

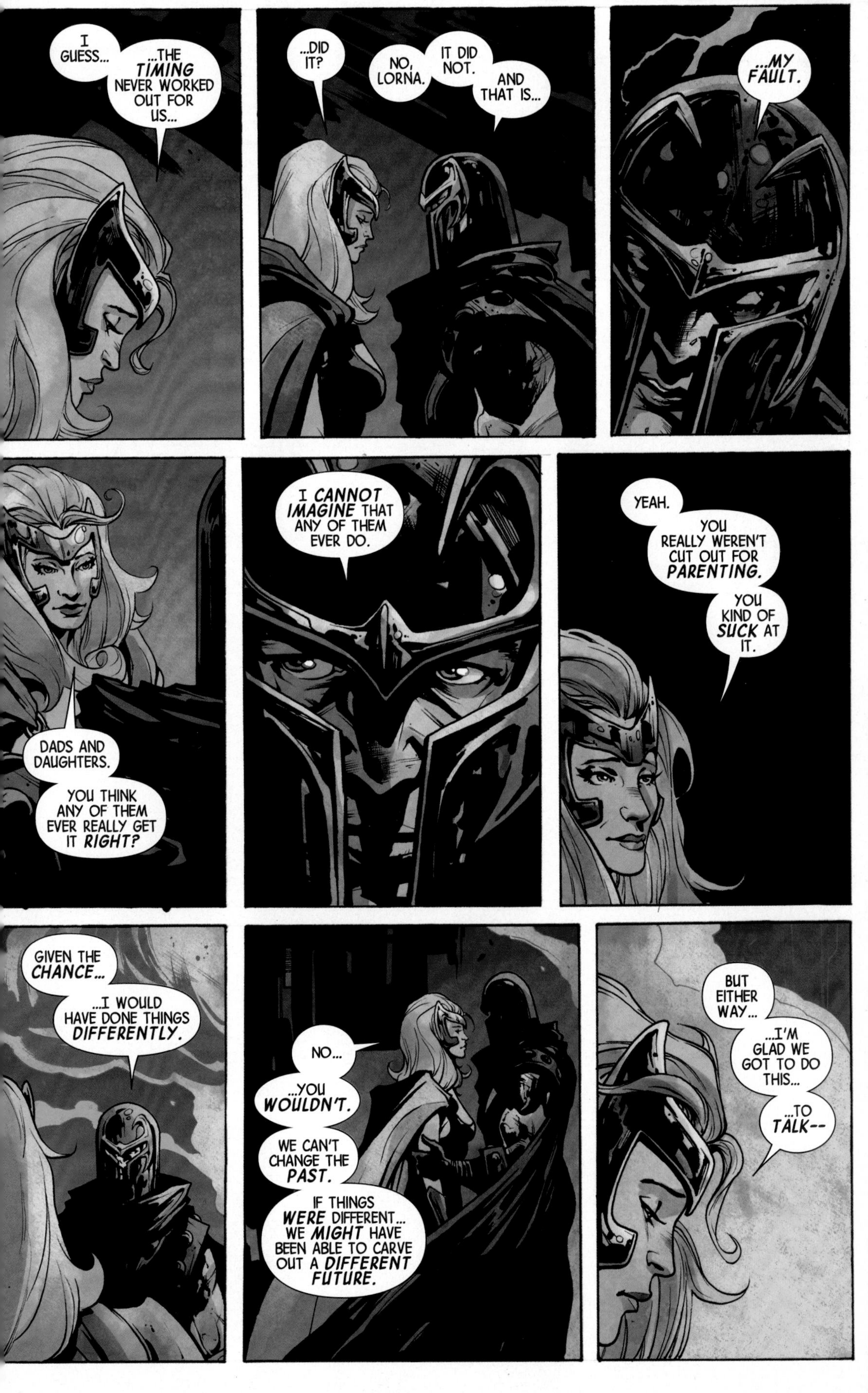
I GUESS...
...THE TIMING NEVER WORKED OUT FOR US...
...DID IT?
NO, LORNA.
IT DID NOT.
AND THAT IS...
...MY FAULT.
DADS AND DAUGHTERS.
YOU THINK ANY OF THEM EVER REALLY GET IT RIGHT?
I CANNOT IMAGINE THAT ANY OF THEM EVER DO.
YEAH.
YOU REALLY WEREN'T CUT OUT FOR PARENTING.
YOU KIND OF SUCK AT IT.
GIVEN THE CHANCE...
...I WOULD HAVE DONE THINGS DIFFERENTLY.
NO...
...YOU WOULDN'T.
WE CAN'T CHANGE THE PAST.
IF THINGS WERE DIFFERENT... WE MIGHT HAVE BEEN ABLE TO CARVE OUT A DIFFERENT FUTURE.
BUT EITHER WAY...
...I'M GLAD WE GOT TO DO THIS...
...TO TALK--

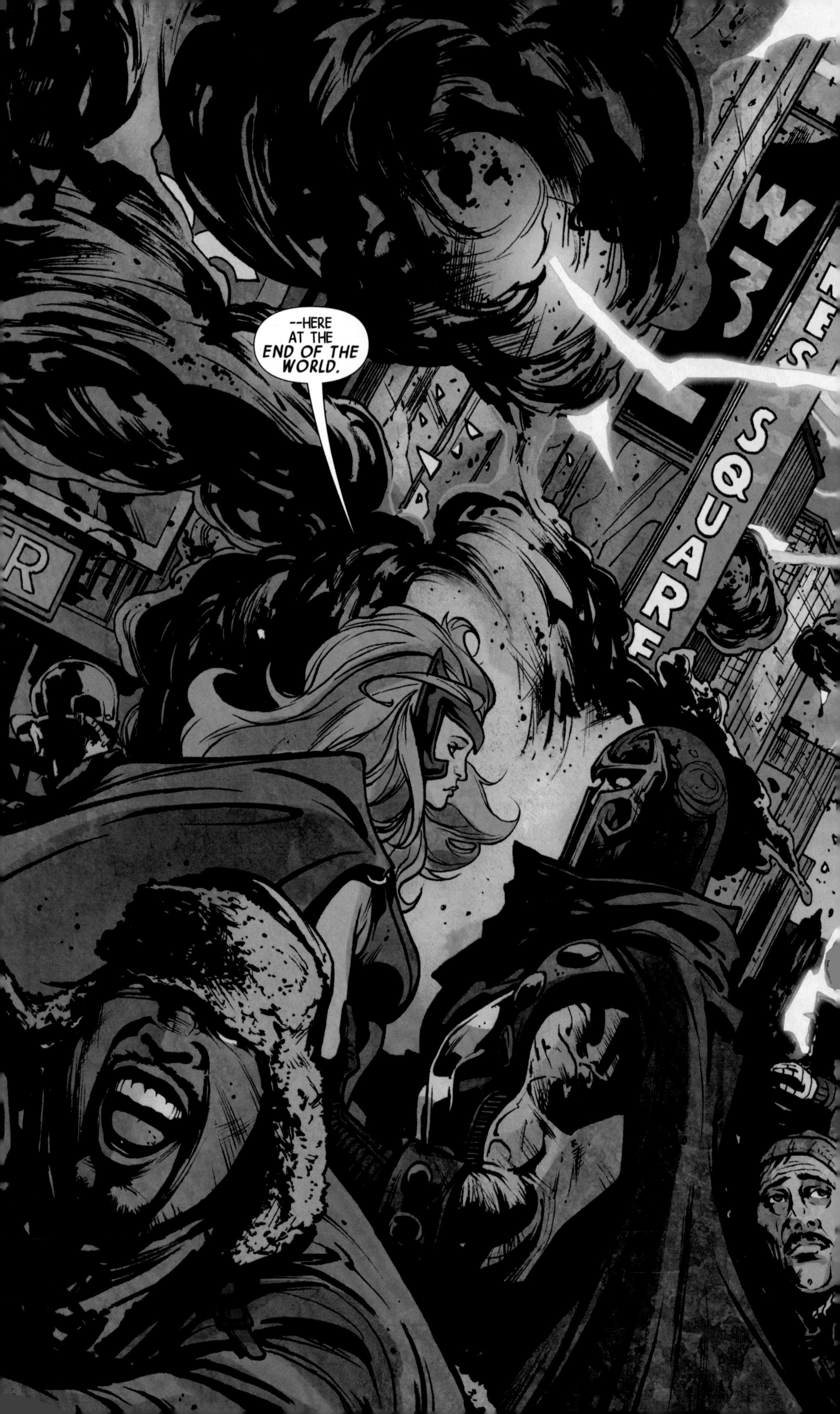
--HERE AT THE END OF THE WORLD.
SQUARE

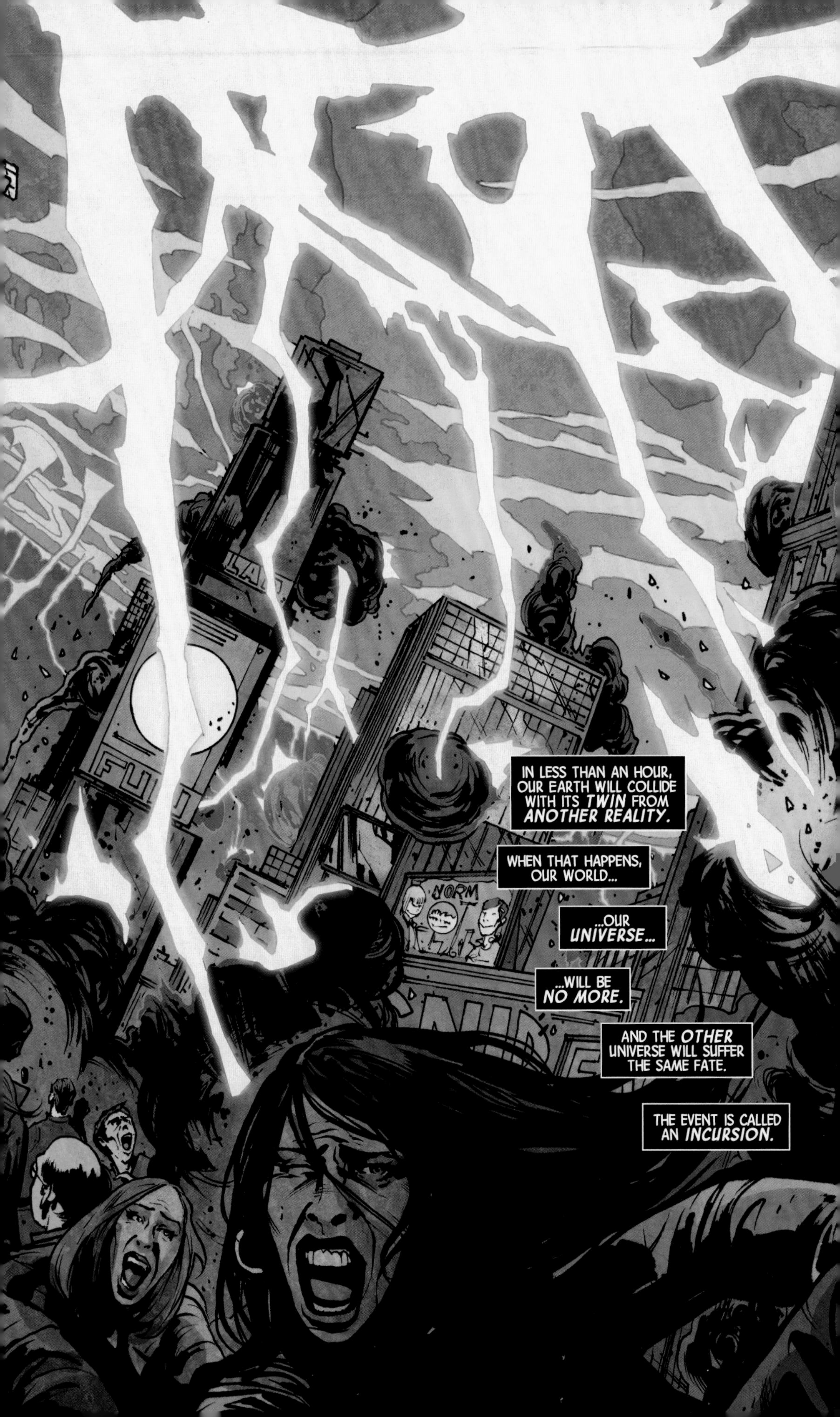
IN LESS THAN AN HOUR, OUR EARTH WILL COLLIDE WITH ITS TWIN FROM ANOTHER REALITY.
WHEN THAT HAPPENS, OUR WORLD...
...OUR UNIVERSE...
...WILL BE NO MORE.
AND THE OTHER UNIVERSE WILL SUFFER THE SAME FATE.
THE EVENT IS CALLED AN INCURSION.

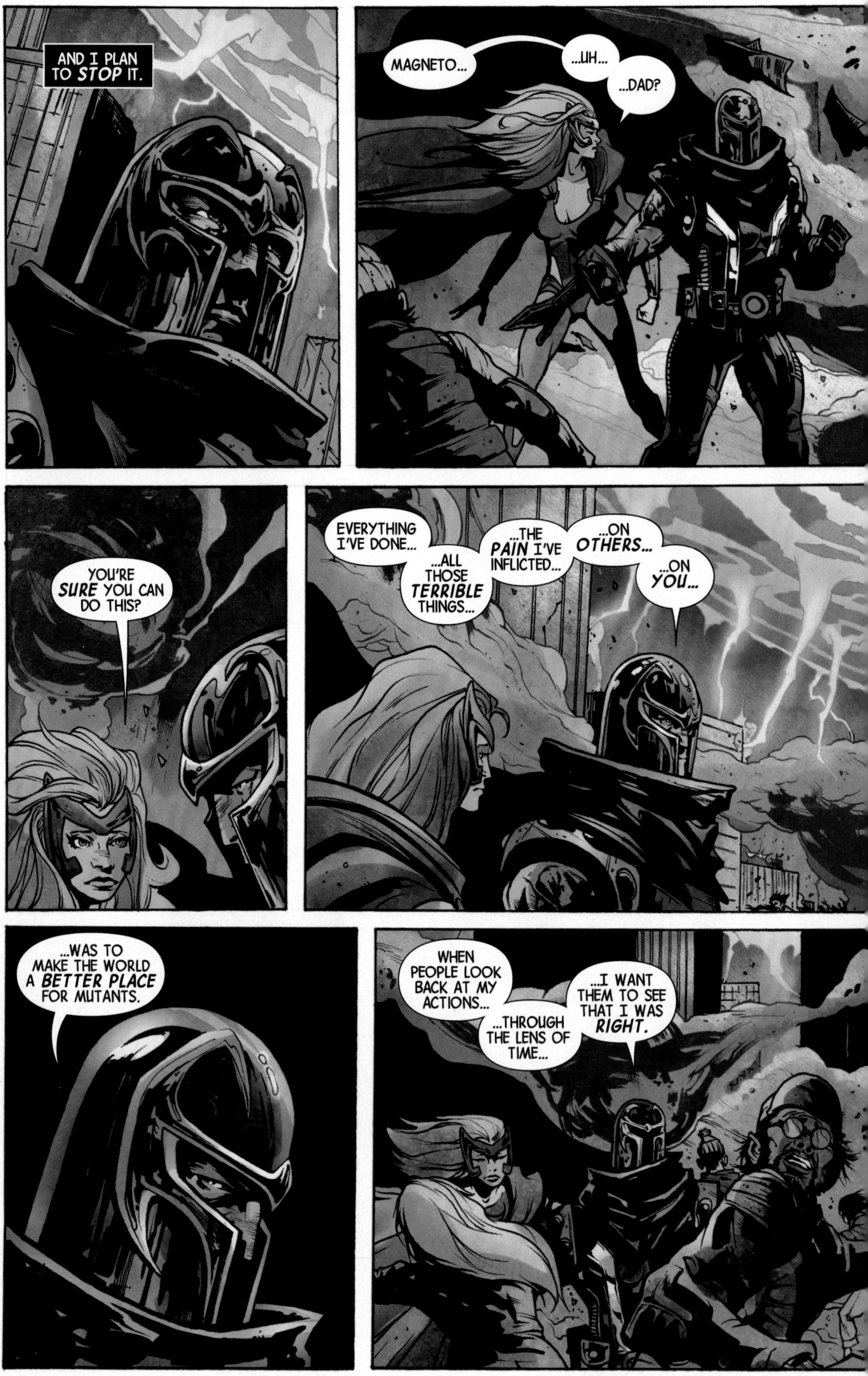
AND I PLAN TO STOP IT.
MAGNETO...
...UH...
...DAD?
YOU'RE SURE YOU CAN DO THIS?
EVERYTHING I'VE DONE...
...ALL THOSE TERRIBLE THINGS...
...THE PAIN I'VE INFLICTED...
...ON OTHERS...
...ON YOU...
...WAS TO MAKE THE WORLD A BETTER PLACE FOR MUTANTS.
WHEN PEOPLE LOOK BACK AT MY ACTIONS...
...THROUGH THE LENS OF TIME...
...I WANT THEM TO SEE THAT I WAS RIGHT.

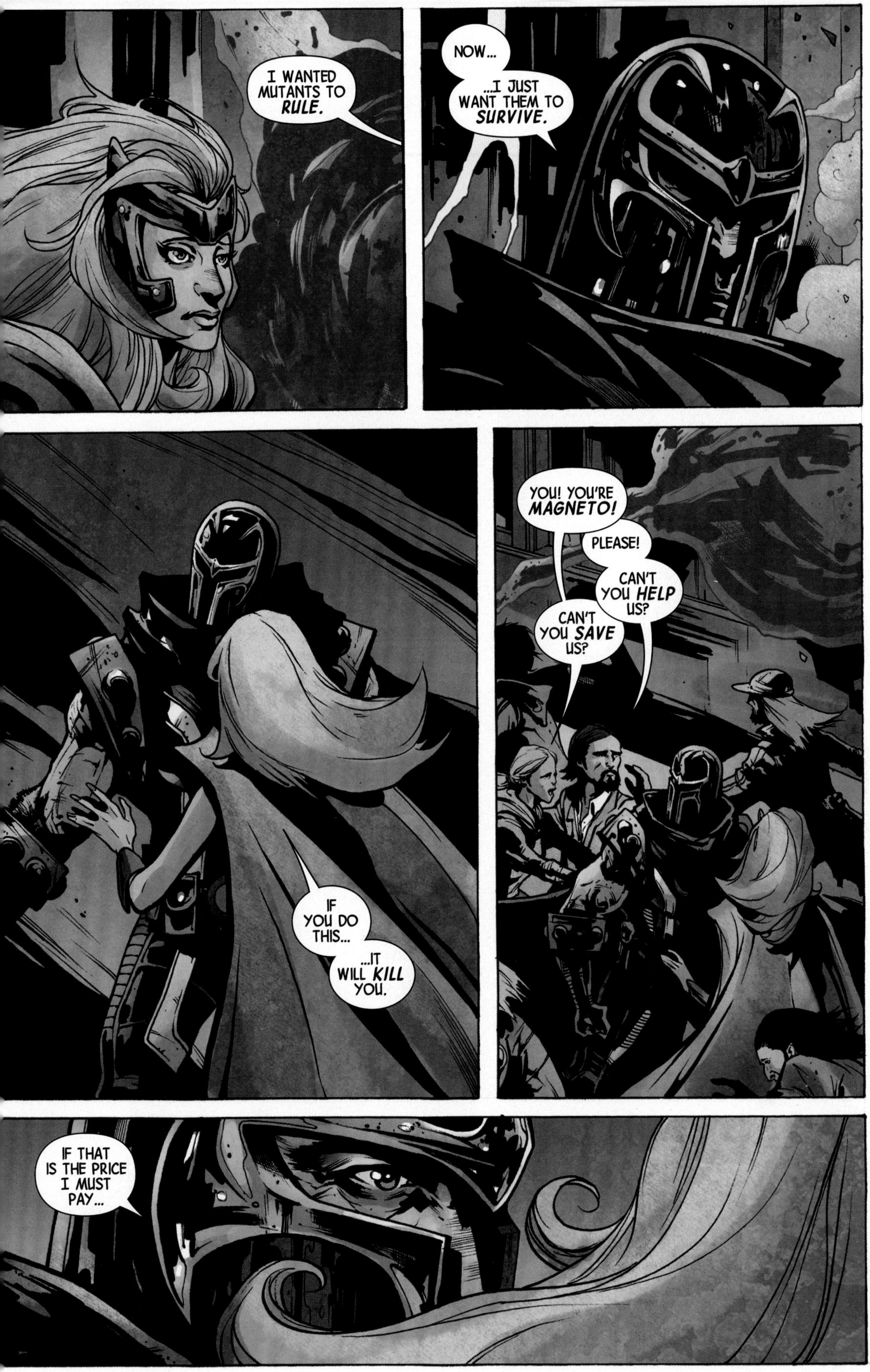
I WANTED MUTANTS TO RULE.
NOW...
...I JUST WANT THEM TO SURVIVE.
IF YOU DO THIS...
...IT WILL KILL YOU.
YOU! YOU'RE MAGNETO!
PLEASE!
CAN'T YOU HELP US?
CAN'T YOU SAVE US?
IF THAT IS THE PRICE I MUST PAY...

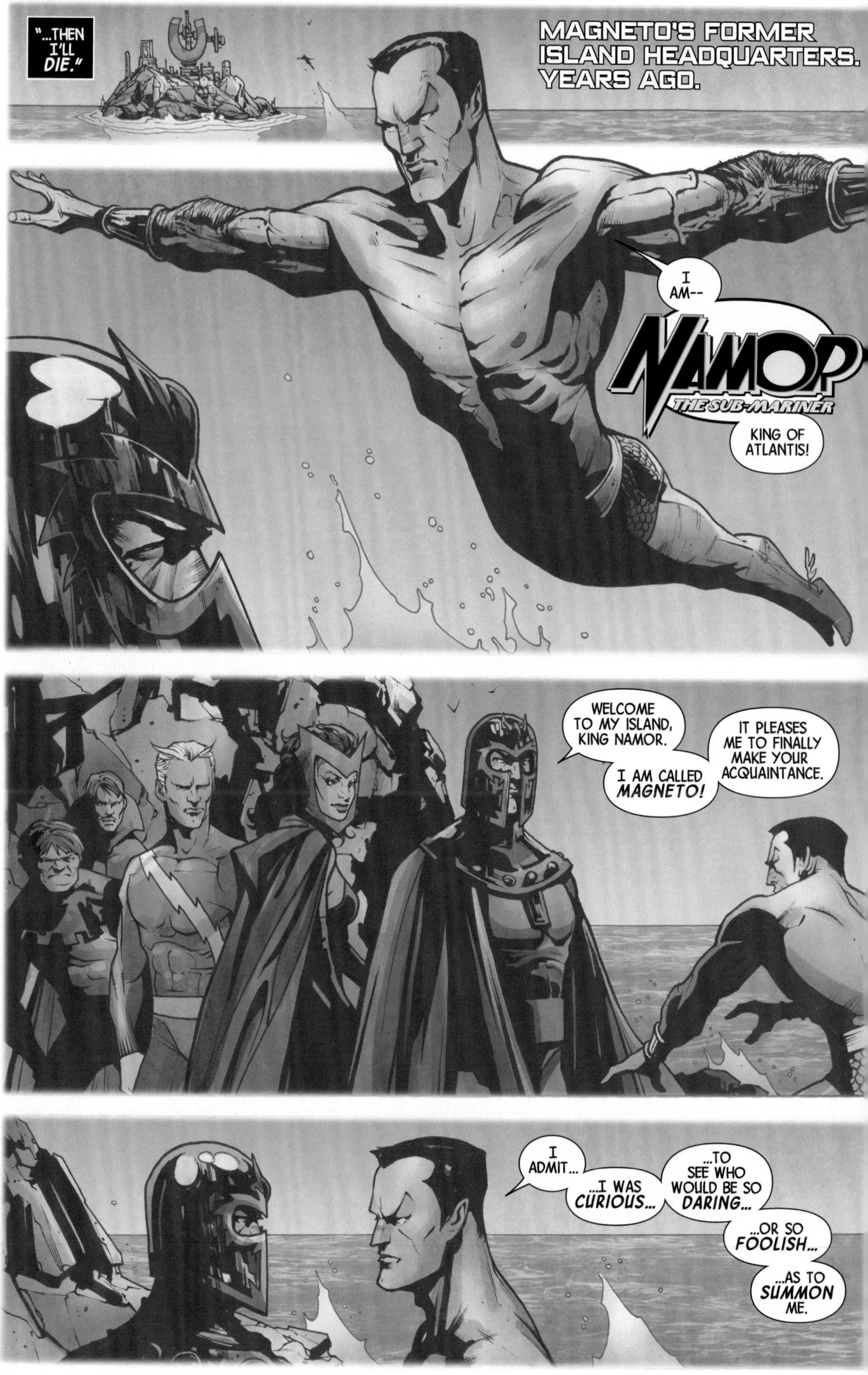
"...THEN I'LL DIE."
MAGNETO'S FORMER ISLAND HEADQUARTERS. YEARS AGO.
I AM--
NAMOR THE SUB-MARINER
KING OF ATLANTIS!
WELCOME TO MY ISLAND, KING NAMOR.
I AM CALLED MAGNETO!
IT PLEASES ME TO FINALLY MAKE YOUR ACQUAINTANCE.
I ADMIT...
...I WAS CURIOUS...
...TO SEE WHO WOULD BE SO DARING...
...OR SO FOOLISH...
...AS TO SUMMON ME.

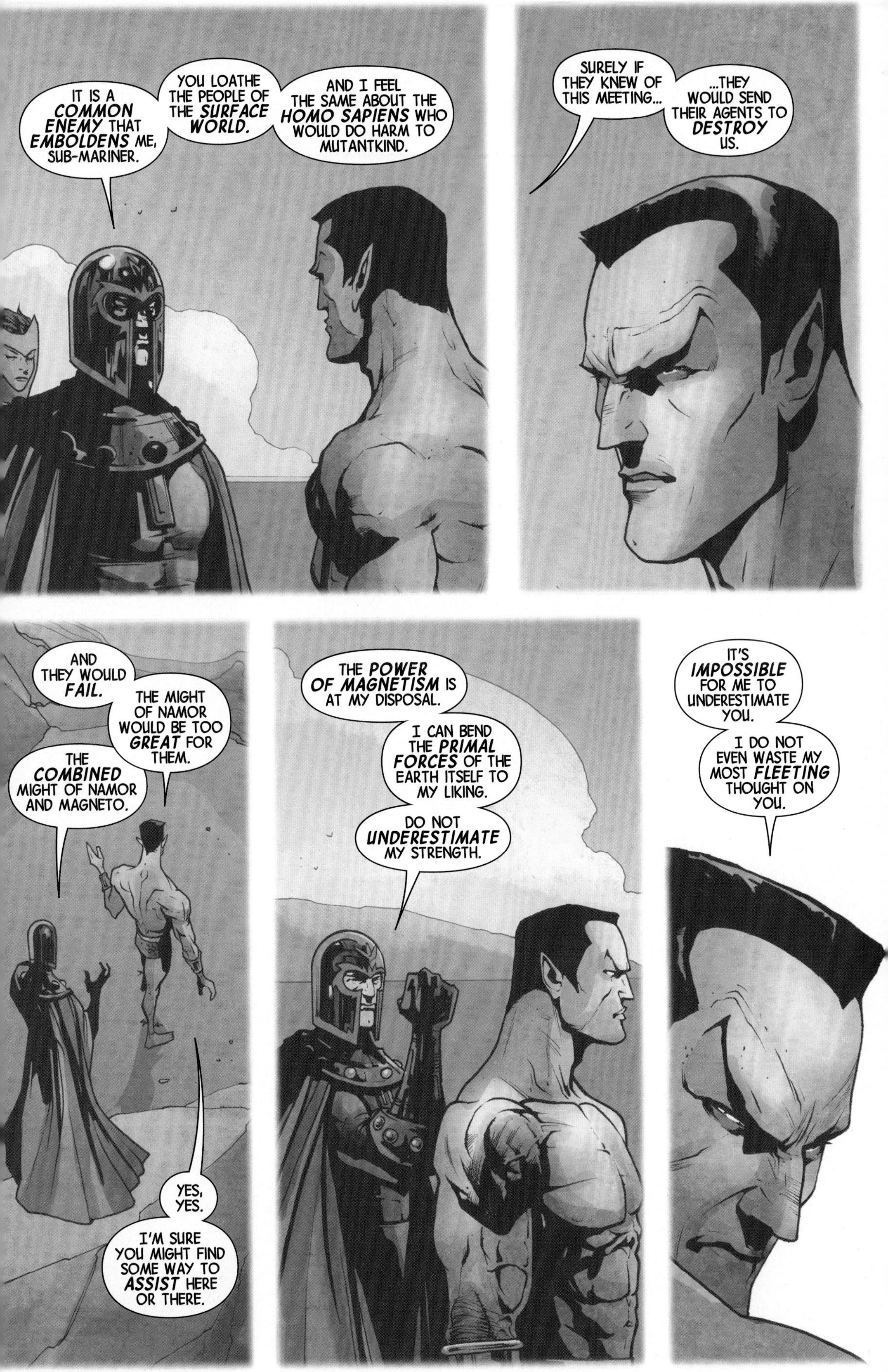
IT IS A COMMON ENEMY THAT EMBOLDENS ME, SUB-MARINER.
YOU LOATHE THE PEOPLE OF THE SURFACE WORLD.
AND I FEEL THE SAME ABOUT THE HOMO SAPIENS WHO WOULD DO HARM TO MUTANTKIND.
SURELY IF THEY KNEW OF THIS MEETING...
...THEY WOULD SEND THEIR AGENTS TO DESTROY US.
AND THEY WOULD FAIL.
THE MIGHT OF NAMOR WOULD BE TOO GREAT FOR THEM.
THE COMBINED MIGHT OF NAMOR AND MAGNETO.
YES, YES.
I'M SURE YOU MIGHT FIND SOME WAY TO ASSIST HERE OR THERE.
THE POWER OF MAGNETISM IS AT MY DISPOSAL.
I CAN BEND THE PRIMAL FORCES OF THE EARTH ITSELF TO MY LIKING.
DO NOT UNDERESTIMATE MY STRENGTH.
IT'S IMPOSSIBLE FOR ME TO UNDERESTIMATE YOU.
I DO NOT EVEN WASTE MY MOST FLEETING THOUGHT ON YOU.

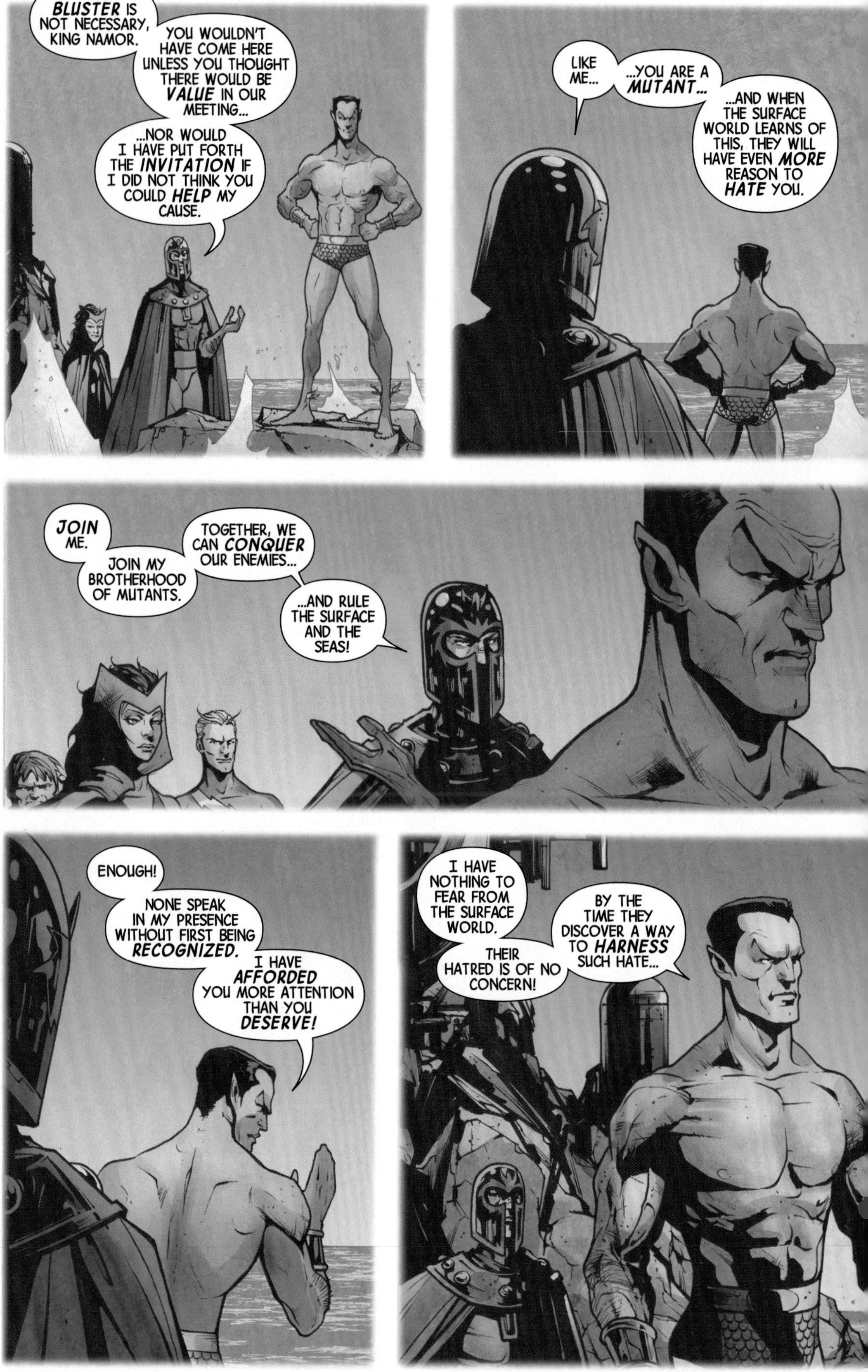
YOUR BLUSTER IS NOT NECESSARY, KING NAMOR.
YOU WOULDN'T HAVE COME HERE UNLESS YOU THOUGHT THERE WOULD BE VALUE IN OUR MEETING...
...NOR WOULD I HAVE PUT FORTH THE INVITATION IF I DID NOT THINK YOU COULD HELP MY CAUSE.
LIKE ME...
...YOU ARE A MUTANT...
...AND WHEN THE SURFACE WORLD LEARNS OF THIS, THEY WILL HAVE EVEN MORE REASON TO HATE YOU.
JOIN ME.
JOIN MY BROTHERHOOD OF MUTANTS.
TOGETHER, WE CAN CONQUER OUR ENEMIES...
...AND RULE THE SURFACE AND THE SEAS!
ENOUGH!
NONE SPEAK IN MY PRESENCE WITHOUT FIRST BEING RECOGNIZED.
I HAVE AFFORDED YOU MORE ATTENTION THAN YOU DESERVE!
I HAVE NOTHING TO FEAR FROM THE SURFACE WORLD.
THEIR HATRED IS OF NO CONCERN!
BY THE TIME THEY DISCOVER A WAY TO HARNESS SUCH HATE...

"...THEIR CIVILIZATION WILL BE NAUGHT BUT DUST!"

BEFORE YOU DO THIS...

...I SHOULD TELL YOU...

...WHAT YOU WERE DOING ON GENOSHA...

...I WOULD HAVE LIKED TO HAVE SEEN WHERE THAT WENT THIS TIME.

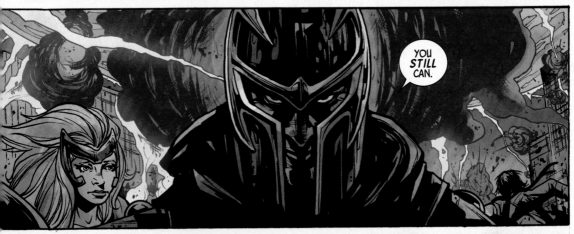

YOU STILL CAN.

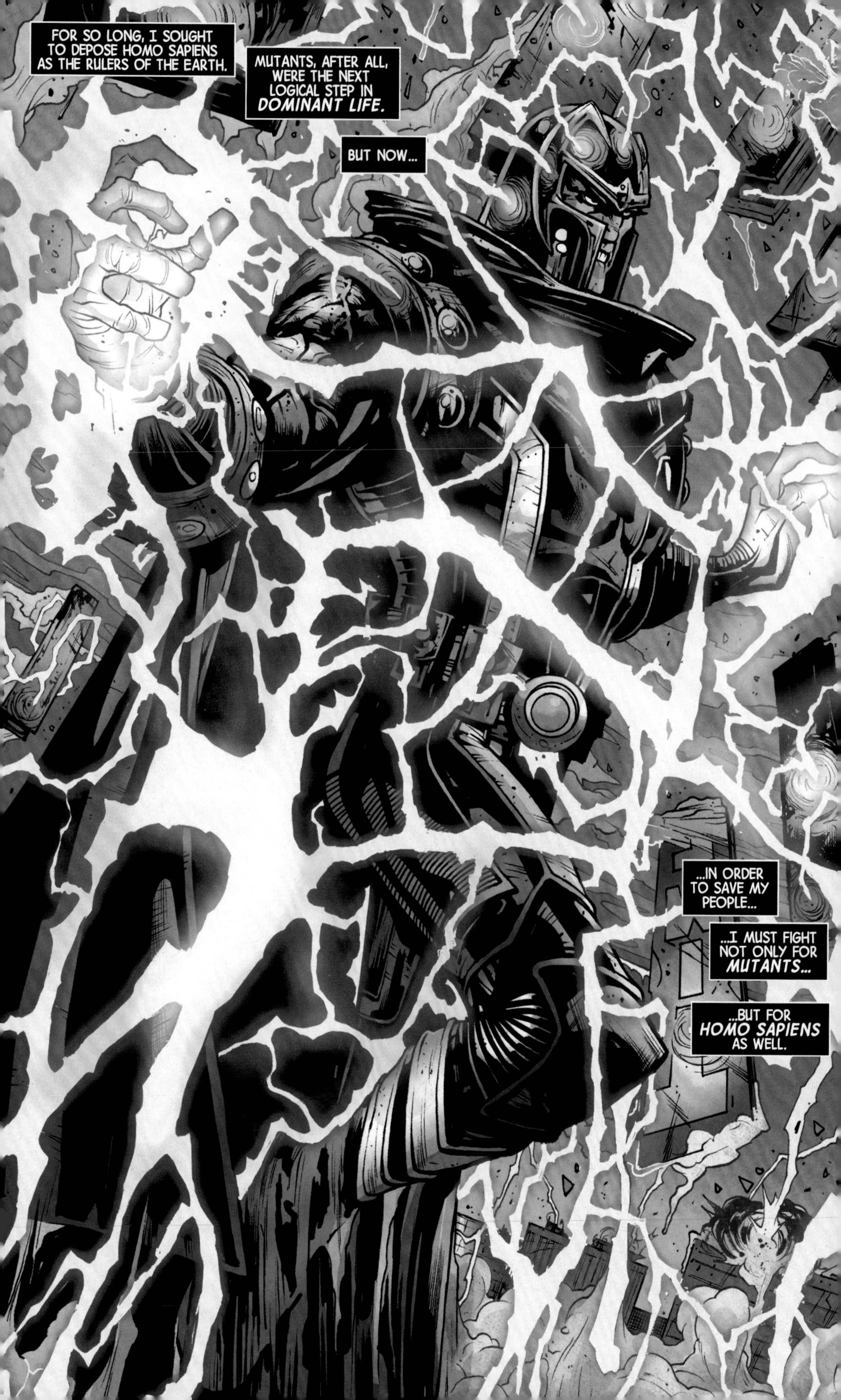
FOR SO LONG, I SOUGHT TO DEPOSE HOMO SAPIENS AS THE RULERS OF THE EARTH.
MUTANTS, AFTER ALL, WERE THE NEXT LOGICAL STEP IN *DOMINANT LIFE.*
BUT NOW...
...IN ORDER TO SAVE MY PEOPLE...
...I MUST FIGHT NOT ONLY FOR *MUTANTS...*
...BUT FOR *HOMO SAPIENS* AS WELL.

THIS IS *UNFAMILIAR TERRITORY* FOR US ALL.

FOR *POLARIS*, IT MIGHT FEEL AS IF SHE IS LOOKING AT HER FATHER FOR THE *FIRST TIME*.

FOR THE *MARAUDERS*...

...THE WORLD MIGHT FEEL AS IF IT HAS BEEN TURNED *UPSIDE DOWN*.

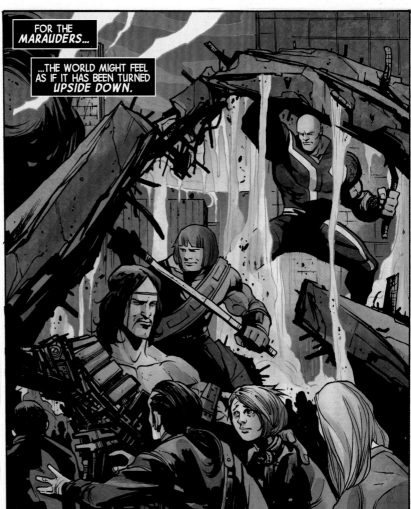

THEY ARE CONDITIONED TO WREAK *HAVOC*...

...TO *TERRIFY*...

...TO *KILL*...

...BUT NOW THEY FIND THEMSELVES *RESCUING* OTHERS.

ADMIT IT, *MALICE*...

...YOU'VE *MISSED* THIS!

RIPTIDE... IT TAKES *EVERYTHING* I'VE GOT TO KEEP FROM TEARING YOU IN HALF.

CALLING ME "MALICE" DOESN'T DO *ANYTHING* TO *STRENGTHEN* MY RESOLVE.

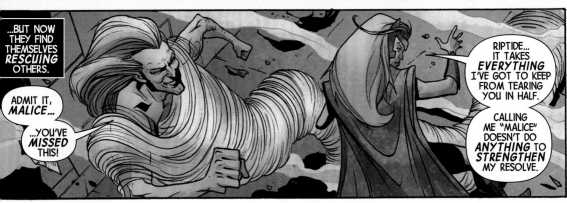

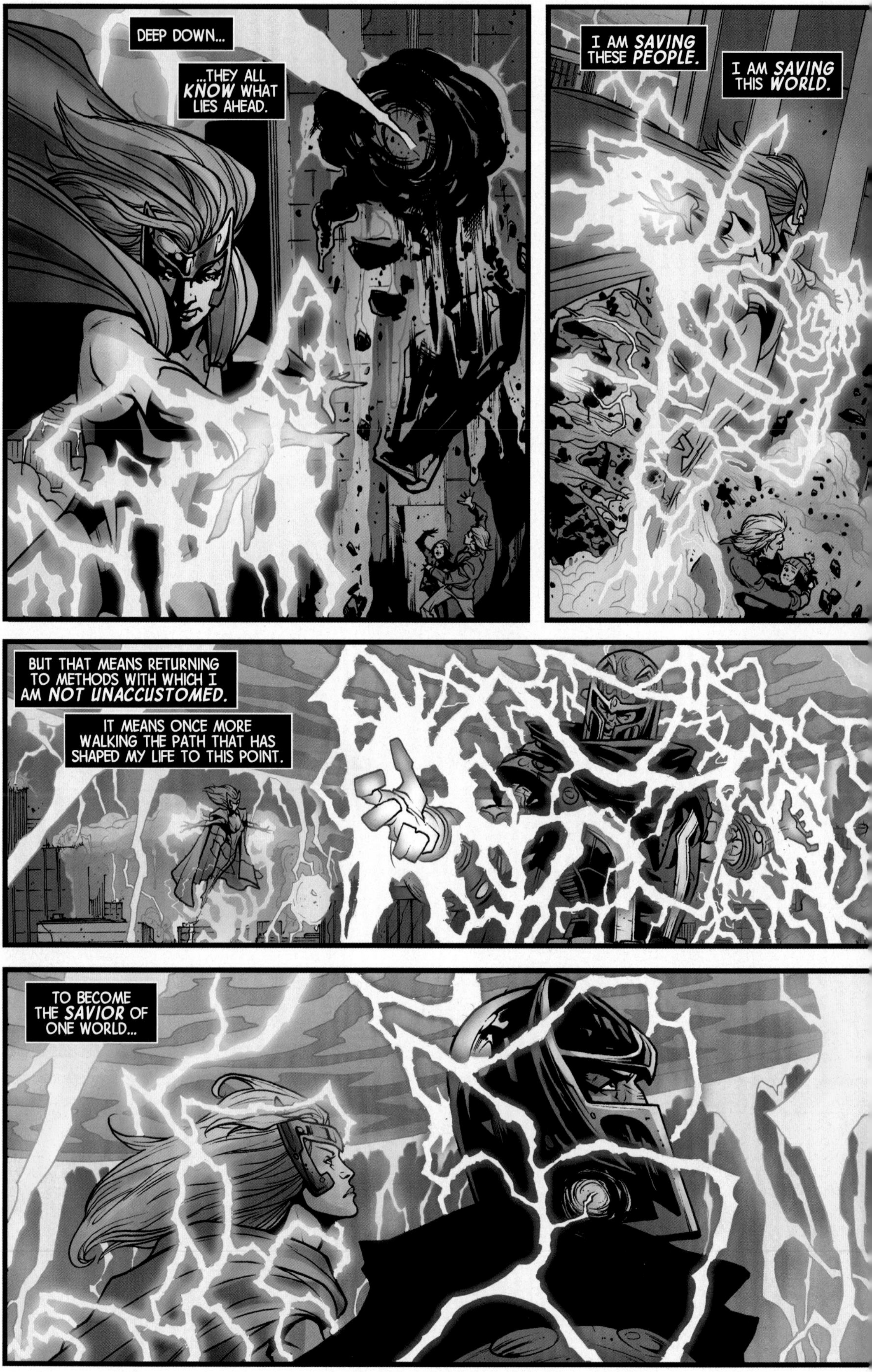
DEEP DOWN...
...THEY ALL KNOW WHAT LIES AHEAD.
I AM SAVING THESE PEOPLE.
I AM SAVING THIS WORLD.
BUT THAT MEANS RETURNING TO METHODS WITH WHICH I AM NOT UNACCUSTOMED.
IT MEANS ONCE MORE WALKING THE PATH THAT HAS SHAPED MY LIFE TO THIS POINT.
TO BECOME THE SAVIOR OF ONE WORLD...

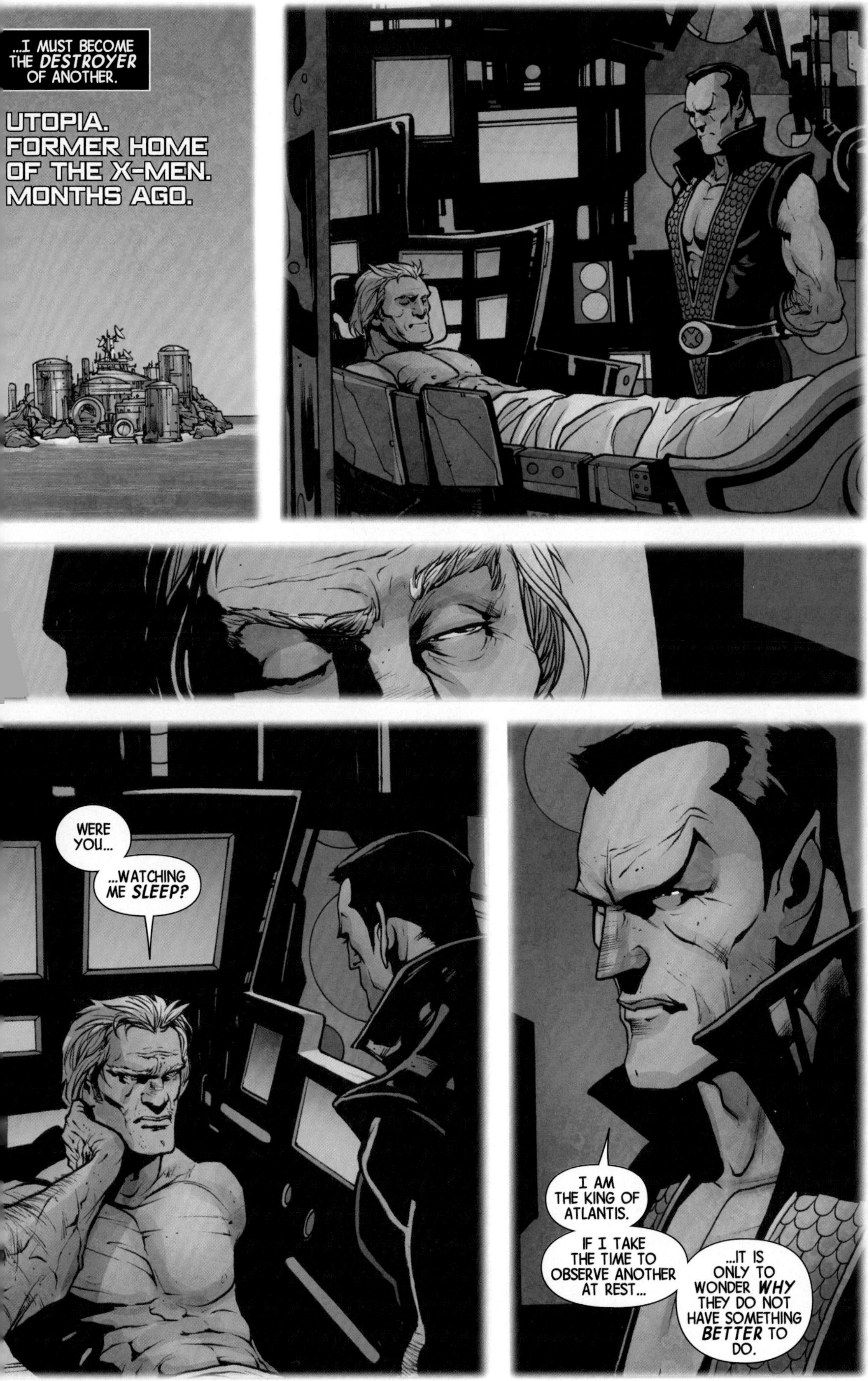

...I MUST BECOME THE *DESTROYER* OF ANOTHER.
UTOPIA. FORMER HOME OF THE X-MEN. MONTHS AGO.
WERE YOU...
...WATCHING ME *SLEEP?*
I AM THE KING OF ATLANTIS.
IF I TAKE THE TIME TO OBSERVE ANOTHER AT REST...
...IT IS ONLY TO WONDER *WHY* THEY DO NOT HAVE SOMETHING *BETTER* TO DO.

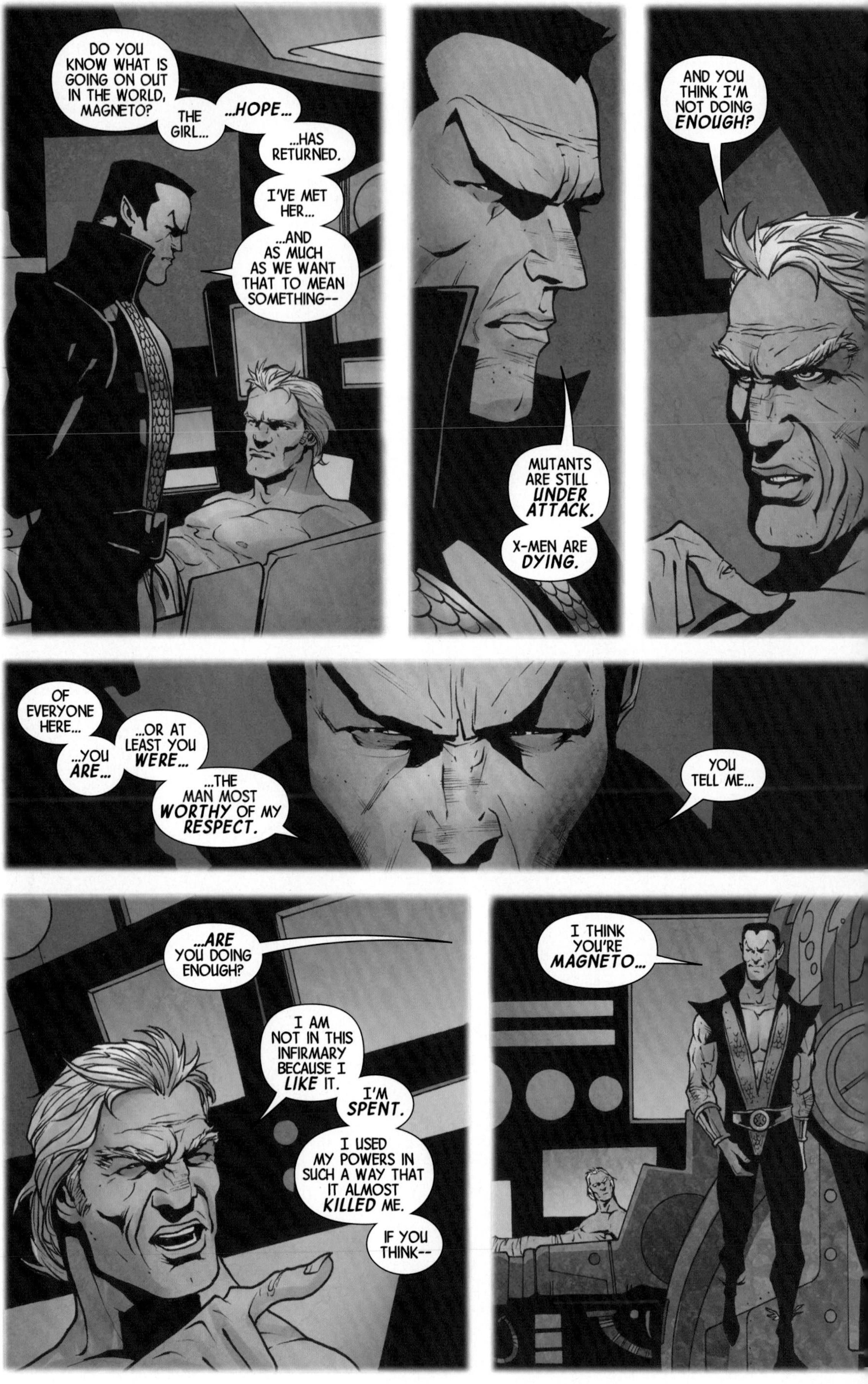
DO YOU KNOW WHAT IS GOING ON OUT IN THE WORLD, MAGNETO?
THE GIRL...
...HOPE...
...HAS RETURNED.
I'VE MET HER...
...AND AS MUCH AS WE WANT THAT TO MEAN SOMETHING--
MUTANTS ARE STILL UNDER ATTACK.
X-MEN ARE DYING.
AND YOU THINK I'M NOT DOING ENOUGH?
OF EVERYONE HERE...
...YOU ARE...
...OR AT LEAST YOU WERE...
...THE MAN MOST WORTHY OF MY RESPECT.
YOU TELL ME...
...ARE YOU DOING ENOUGH?
I AM NOT IN THIS INFIRMARY BECAUSE I LIKE IT.
I'M SPENT.
I USED MY POWERS IN SUCH A WAY THAT IT ALMOST KILLED ME.
IF YOU THINK--
I THINK YOU'RE MAGNETO...

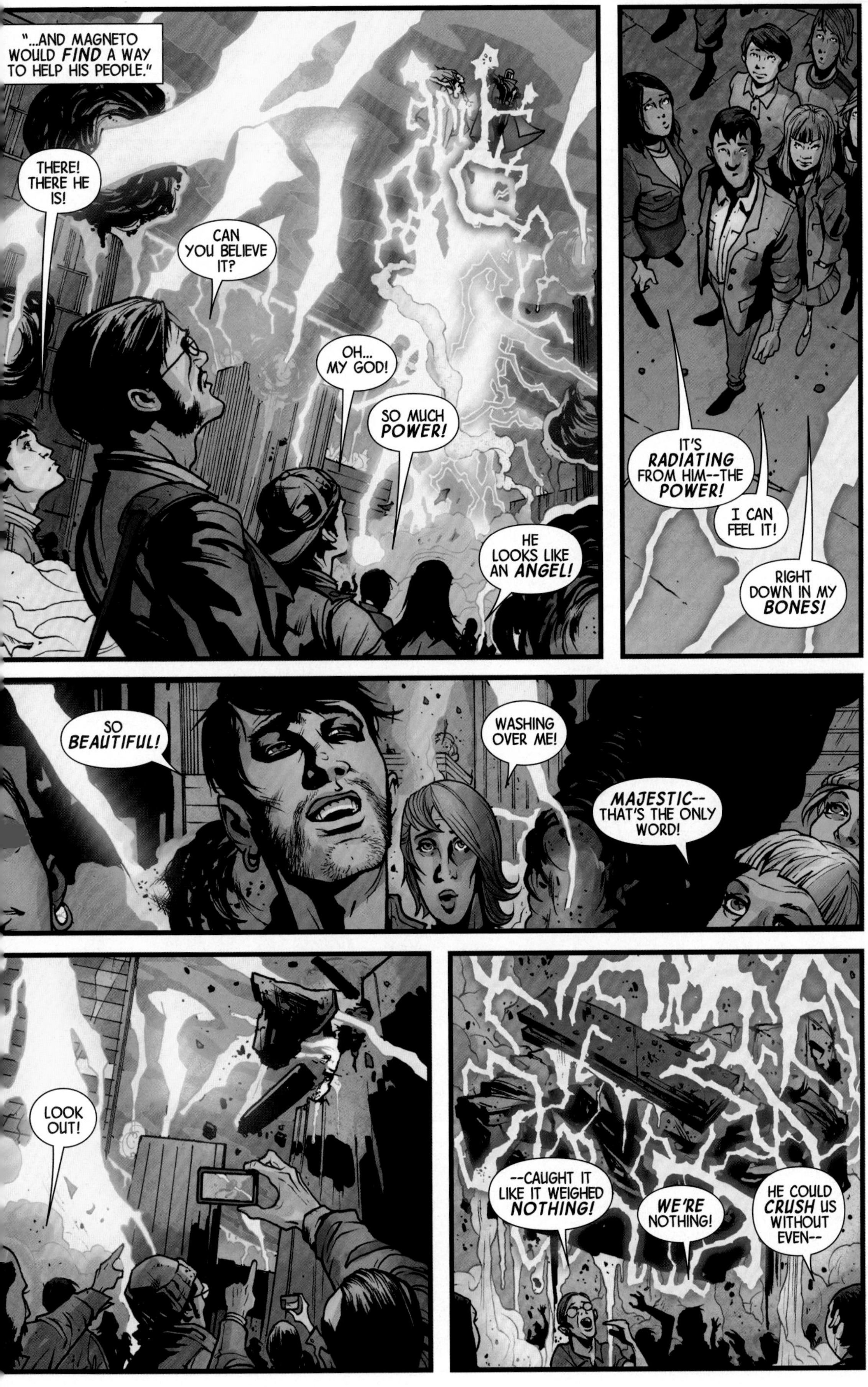
"...AND MAGNETO WOULD FIND A WAY TO HELP HIS PEOPLE."
THERE! THERE HE IS!
CAN YOU BELIEVE IT?
OH... MY GOD!
SO MUCH POWER!
HE LOOKS LIKE AN ANGEL!
IT'S RADIATING FROM HIM--THE POWER!
I CAN FEEL IT!
RIGHT DOWN IN MY BONES!
SO BEAUTIFUL!
WASHING OVER ME!
MAJESTIC--THAT'S THE ONLY WORD!
LOOK OUT!
--CAUGHT IT LIKE IT WEIGHED NOTHING!
WE'RE NOTHING!
HE COULD CRUSH US WITHOUT EVEN--

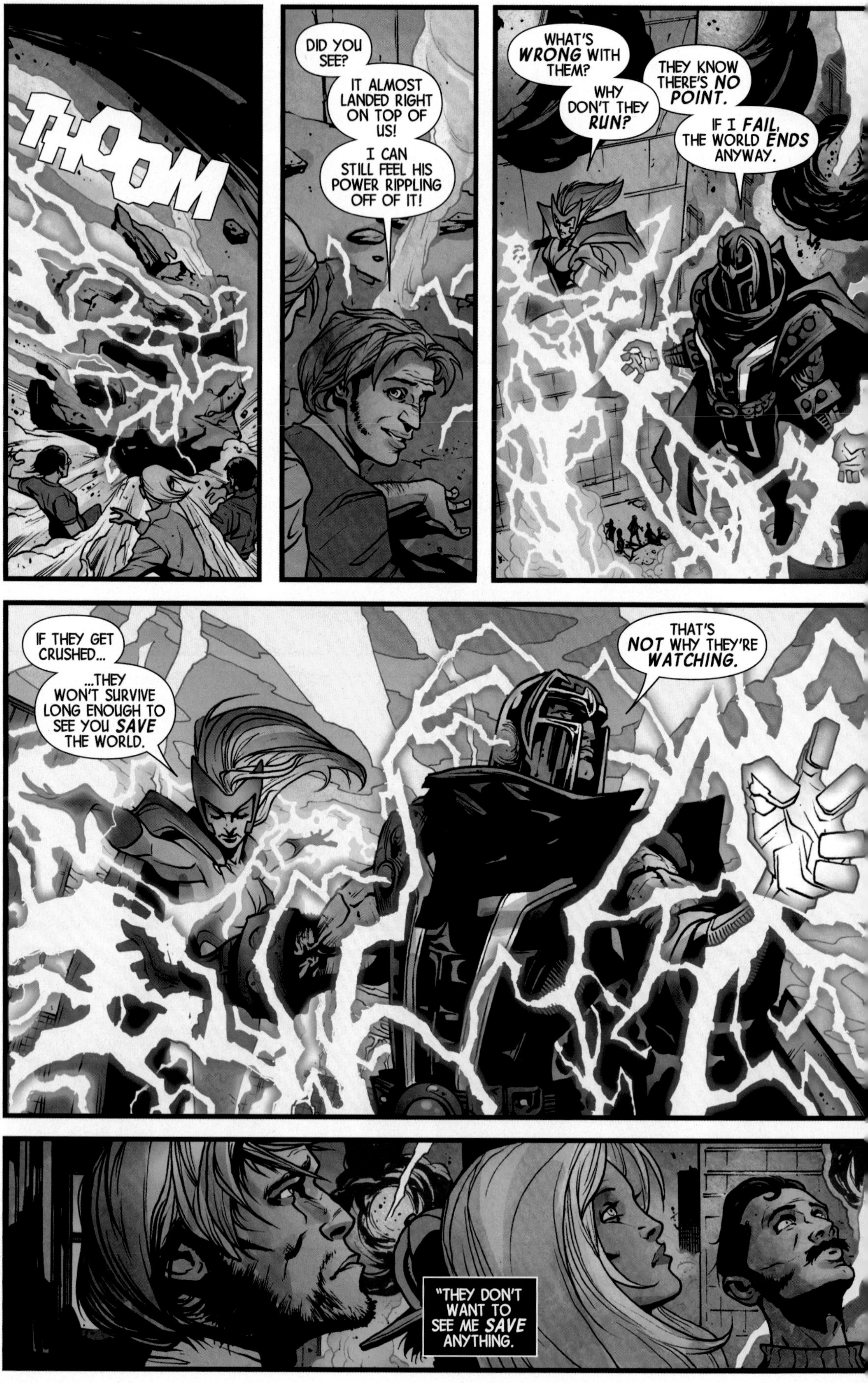

THOOM
DID YOU SEE?
IT ALMOST LANDED RIGHT ON TOP OF US!
I CAN STILL FEEL HIS POWER RIPPLING OFF OF IT!
WHAT'S WRONG WITH THEM?
WHY DON'T THEY RUN?
THEY KNOW THERE'S NO POINT.
IF I FAIL, THE WORLD ENDS ANYWAY.
IF THEY GET CRUSHED...
...THEY WON'T SURVIVE LONG ENOUGH TO SEE YOU SAVE THE WORLD.
THAT'S NOT WHY THEY'RE WATCHING.
"THEY DON'T WANT TO SEE ME SAVE ANYTHING.

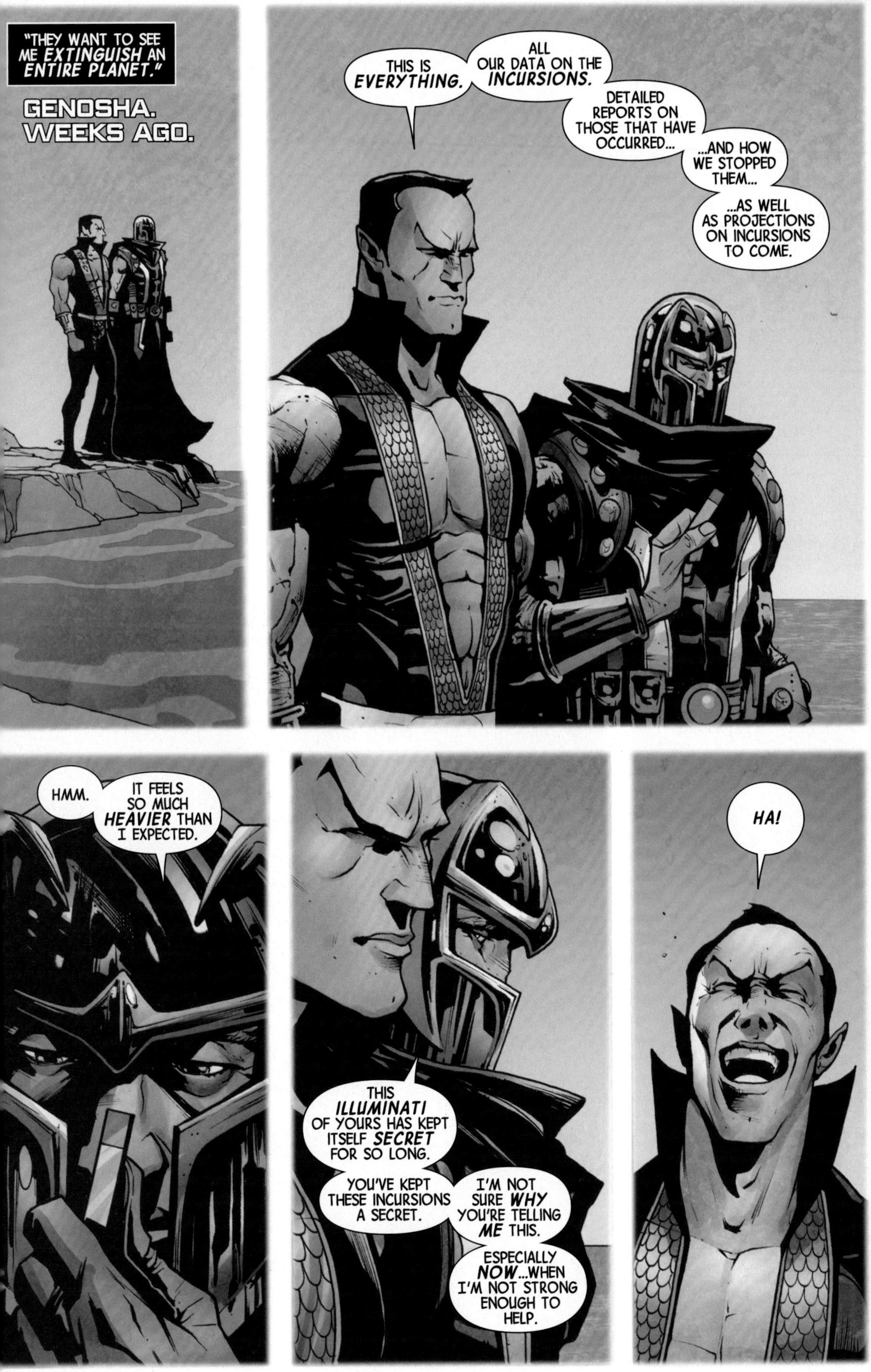
"THEY WANT TO SEE ME EXTINGUISH AN ENTIRE PLANET."
GENOSHA. WEEKS AGO.
THIS IS EVERYTHING.
ALL OUR DATA ON THE INCURSIONS.
DETAILED REPORTS ON THOSE THAT HAVE OCCURRED...
...AND HOW WE STOPPED THEM...
...AS WELL AS PROJECTIONS ON INCURSIONS TO COME.
HMM.
IT FEELS SO MUCH HEAVIER THAN I EXPECTED.
THIS ILLUMINATI OF YOURS HAS KEPT ITSELF SECRET FOR SO LONG.
YOU'VE KEPT THESE INCURSIONS A SECRET.
I'M NOT SURE WHY YOU'RE TELLING ME THIS.
ESPECIALLY NOW...WHEN I'M NOT STRONG ENOUGH TO HELP.
HA!

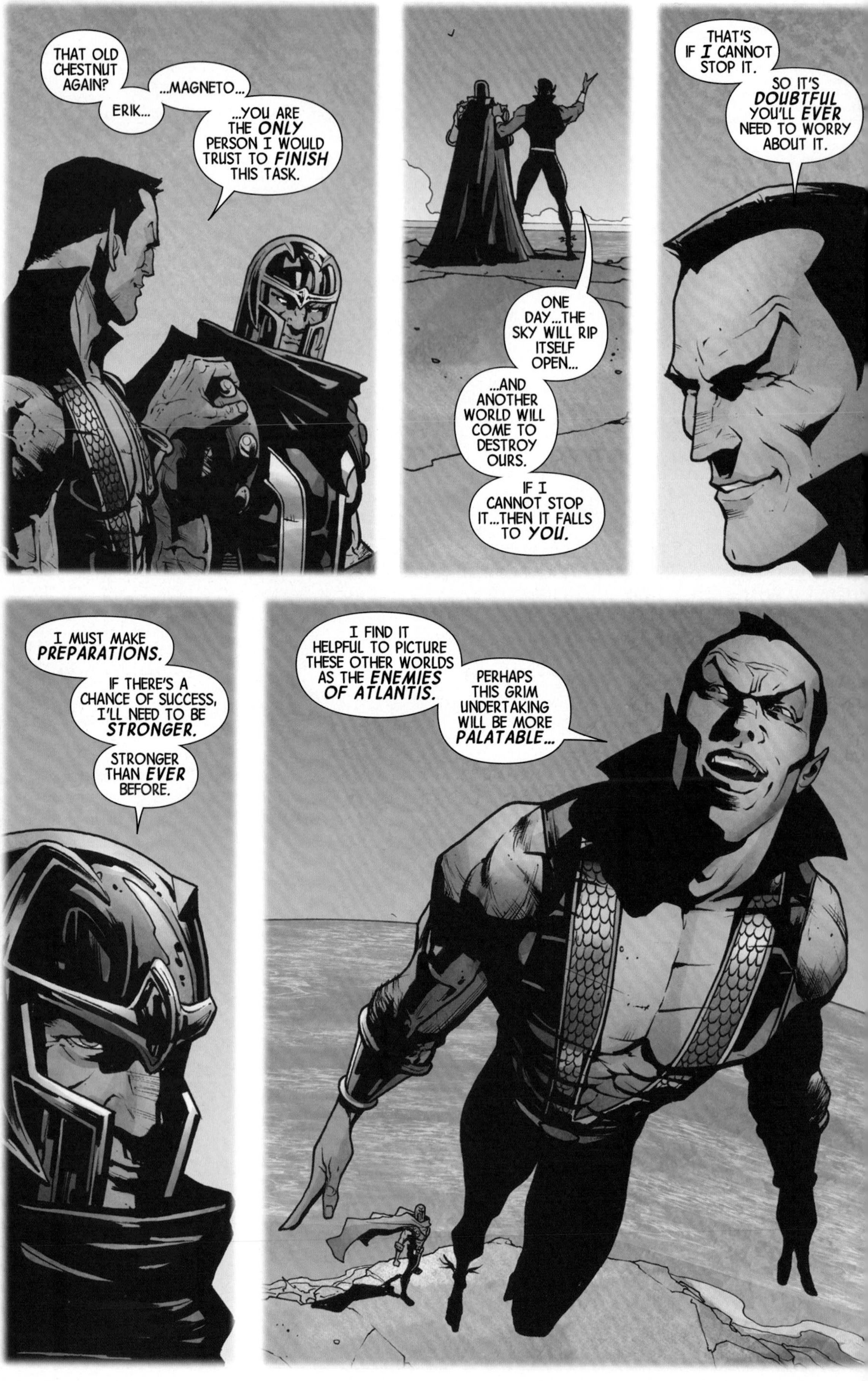
THAT OLD CHESTNUT AGAIN?
ERIK...
...MAGNETO...
...YOU ARE THE ONLY PERSON I WOULD TRUST TO FINISH THIS TASK.
ONE DAY...THE SKY WILL RIP ITSELF OPEN...
...AND ANOTHER WORLD WILL COME TO DESTROY OURS.
IF I CANNOT STOP IT...THEN IT FALLS TO YOU.
THAT'S IF I CANNOT STOP IT.
SO IT'S DOUBTFUL YOU'LL EVER NEED TO WORRY ABOUT IT.
I MUST MAKE PREPARATIONS.
IF THERE'S A CHANCE OF SUCCESS, I'LL NEED TO BE STRONGER.
STRONGER THAN EVER BEFORE.
I FIND IT HELPFUL TO PICTURE THESE OTHER WORLDS AS THE ENEMIES OF ATLANTIS.
PERHAPS THIS GRIM UNDERTAKING WILL BE MORE PALATABLE...

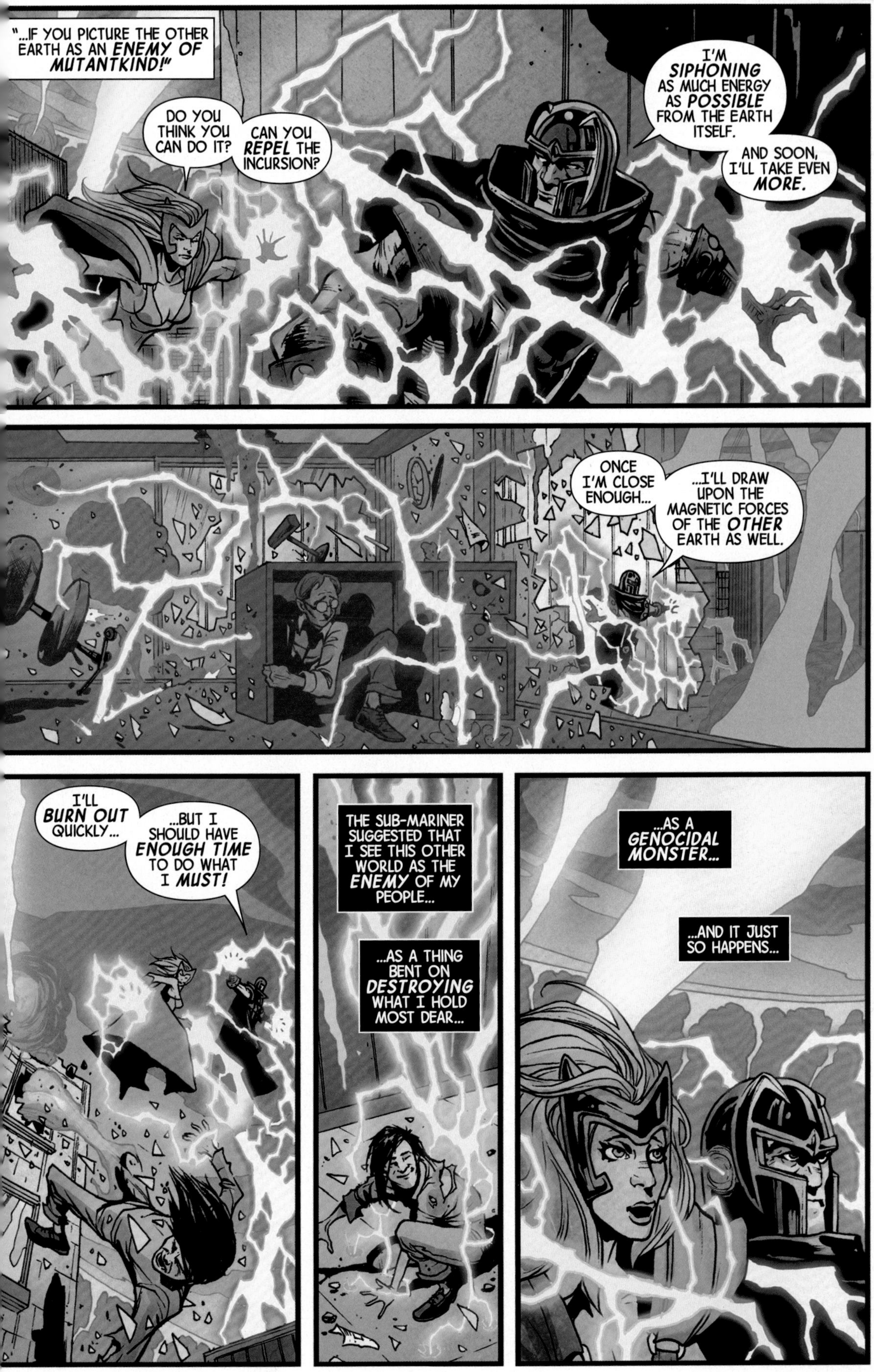
"...IF YOU PICTURE THE OTHER EARTH AS AN ENEMY OF MUTANTKIND!"
DO YOU THINK YOU CAN DO IT?
CAN YOU REPEL THE INCURSION?
I'M SIPHONING AS MUCH ENERGY AS POSSIBLE FROM THE EARTH ITSELF.
AND SOON, I'LL TAKE EVEN MORE.
ONCE I'M CLOSE ENOUGH...
...I'LL DRAW UPON THE MAGNETIC FORCES OF THE OTHER EARTH AS WELL.
I'LL BURN OUT QUICKLY...
...BUT I SHOULD HAVE ENOUGH TIME TO DO WHAT I MUST!
THE SUB-MARINER SUGGESTED THAT I SEE THIS OTHER WORLD AS THE ENEMY OF MY PEOPLE...
...AS A THING BENT ON DESTROYING WHAT I HOLD MOST DEAR...
...AS A GENOCIDAL MONSTER...
...AND IT JUST SO HAPPENS...

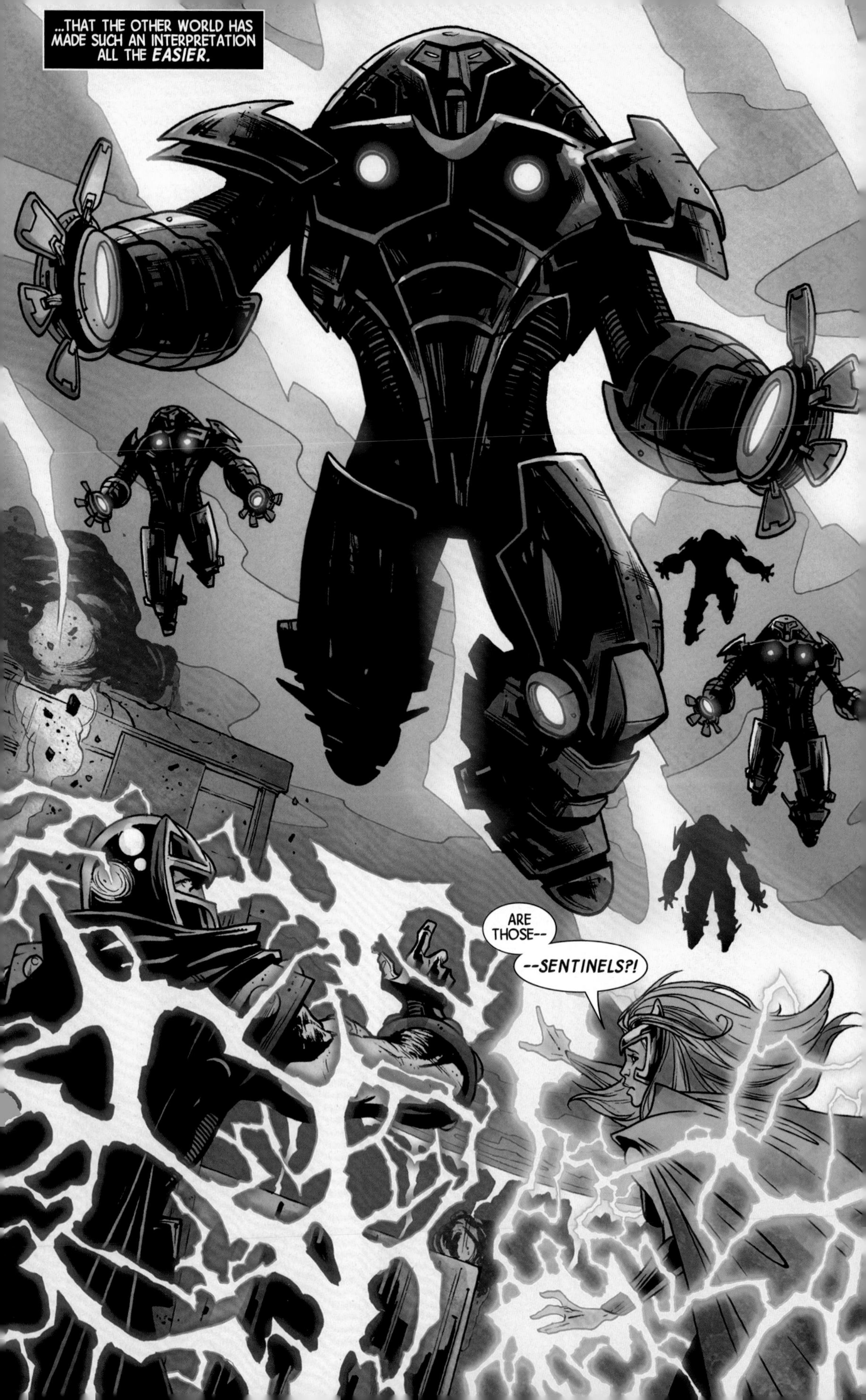
...THAT THE OTHER WORLD HAS MADE SUCH AN INTERPRETATION ALL THE EASIER.
ARE THOSE--
--SENTINELS?!

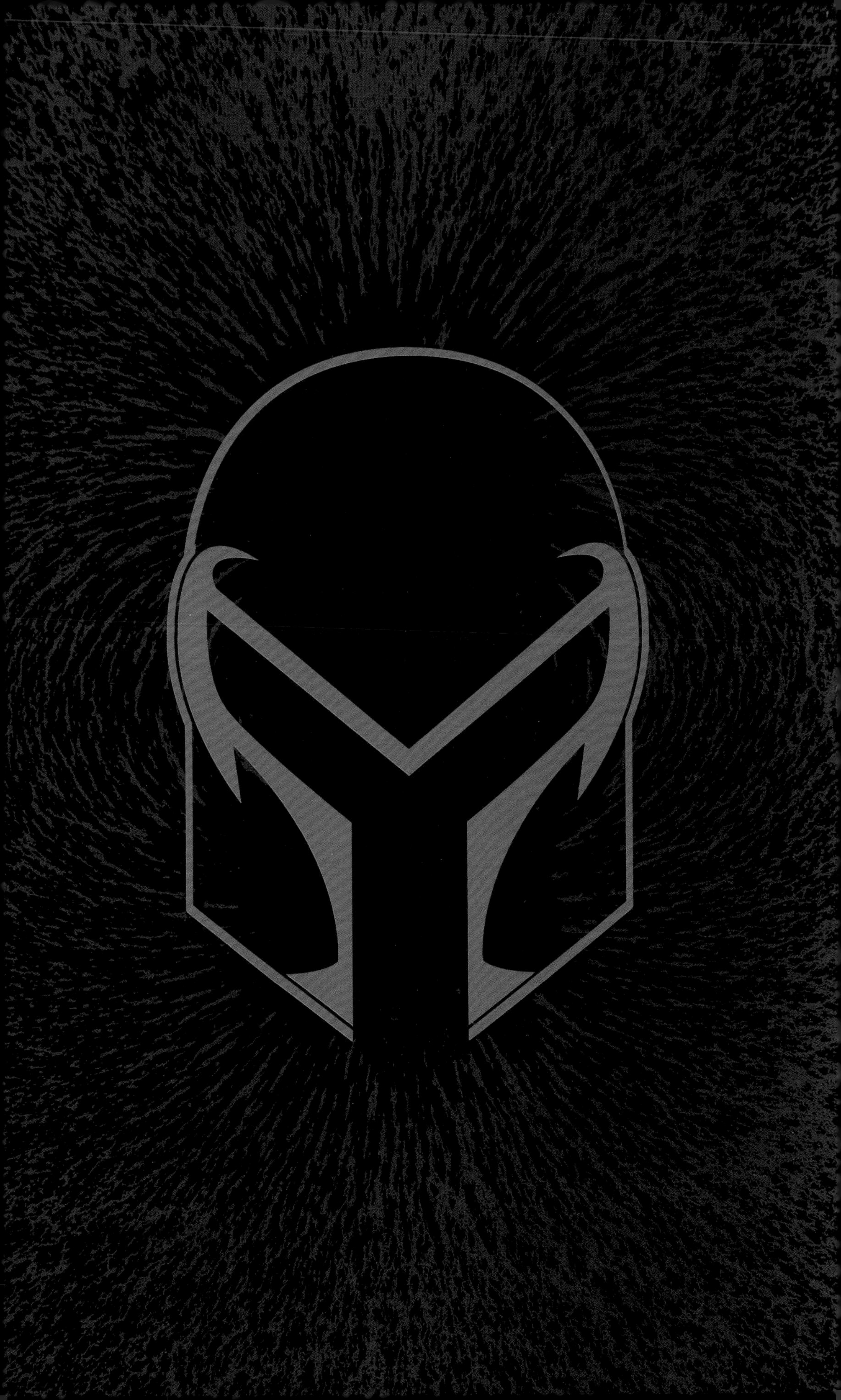

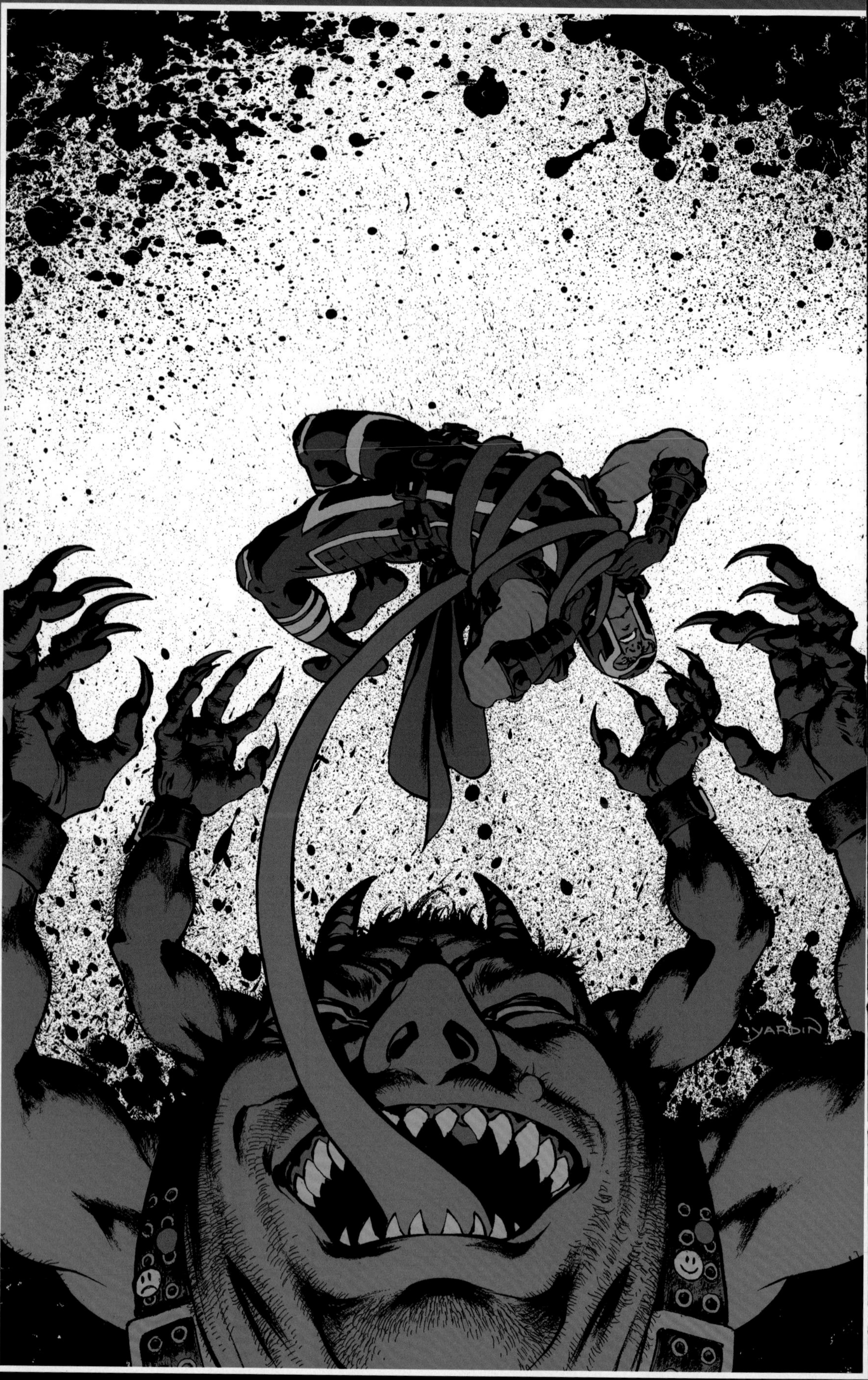
YARDIN

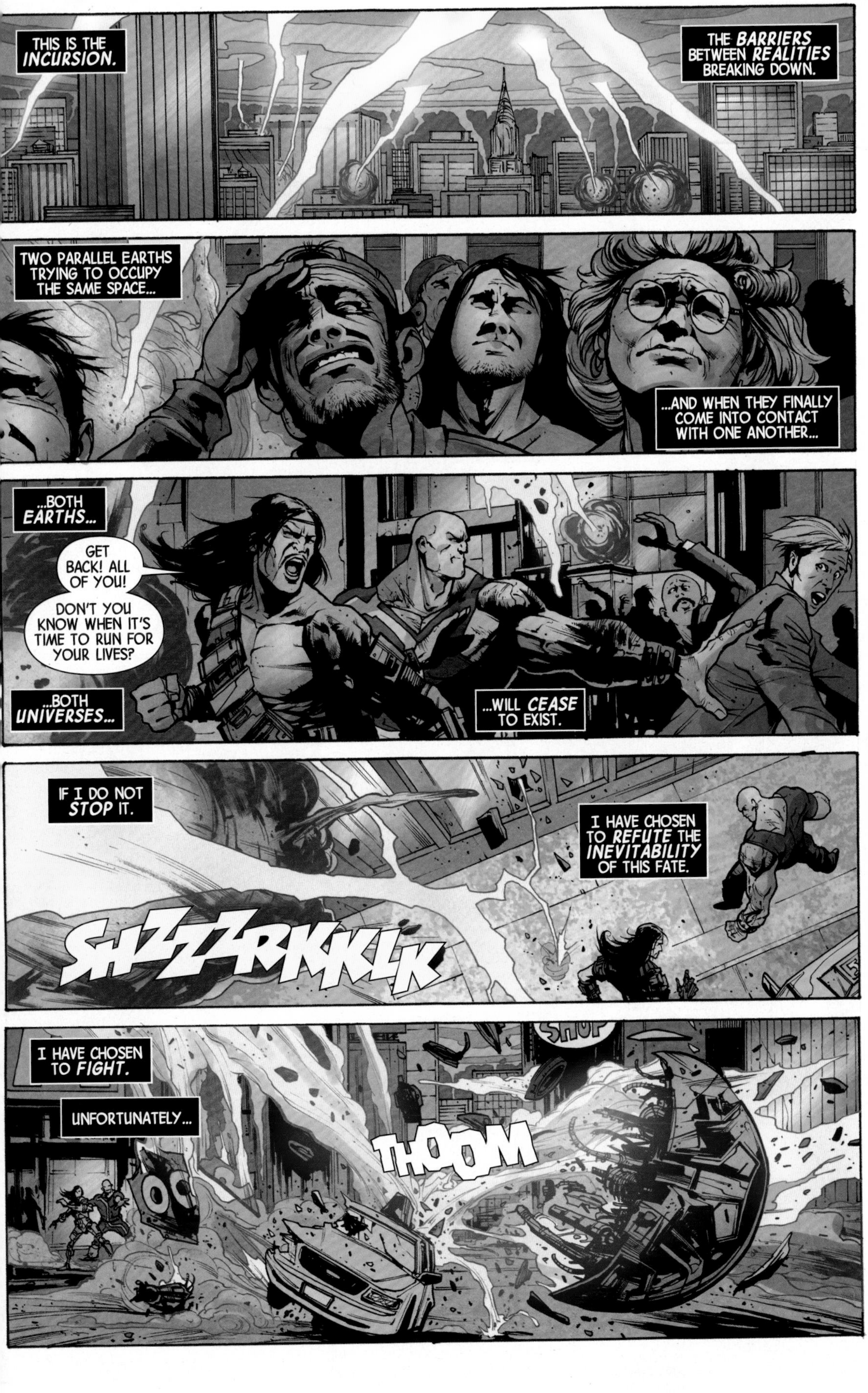
THIS IS THE INCURSION.
THE BARRIERS BETWEEN REALITIES BREAKING DOWN.
TWO PARALLEL EARTHS TRYING TO OCCUPY THE SAME SPACE...
...AND WHEN THEY FINALLY COME INTO CONTACT WITH ONE ANOTHER...
...BOTH EARTHS...
GET BACK! ALL OF YOU!
DON'T YOU KNOW WHEN IT'S TIME TO RUN FOR YOUR LIVES?
...BOTH UNIVERSES...
...WILL CEASE TO EXIST.
IF I DO NOT STOP IT.
I HAVE CHOSEN TO REFUTE THE INEVITABILITY OF THIS FATE.
SHZZZRKKKLK
I HAVE CHOSEN TO FIGHT.
UNFORTUNATELY...
SHOP
THOOOM

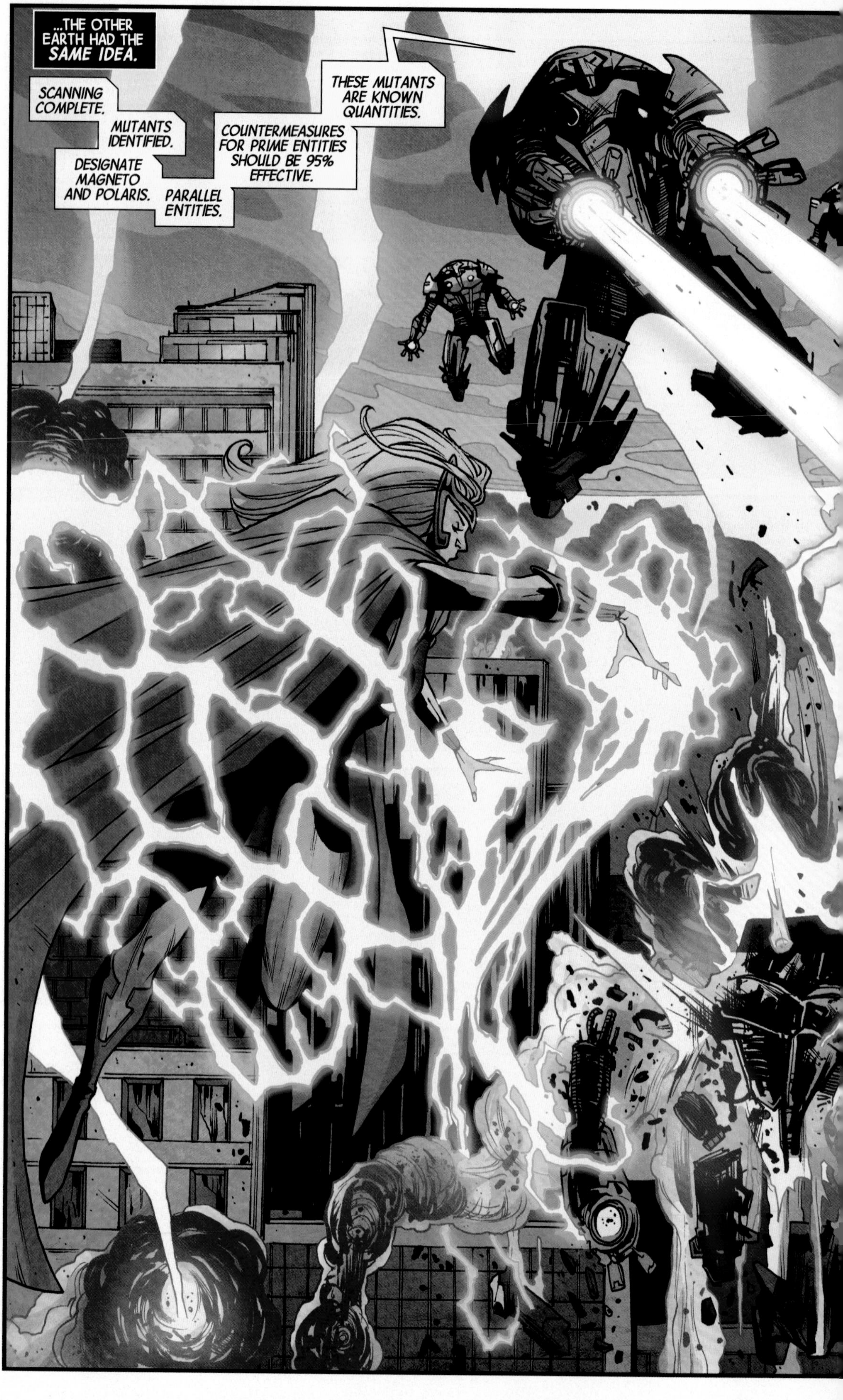
...THE OTHER EARTH HAD THE *SAME IDEA.*
SCANNING COMPLETE.
MUTANTS IDENTIFIED.
DESIGNATE MAGNETO AND POLARIS.
PARALLEL ENTITIES.
COUNTERMEASURES FOR PRIME ENTITIES SHOULD BE 95% EFFECTIVE.
THESE MUTANTS ARE KNOWN QUANTITIES.

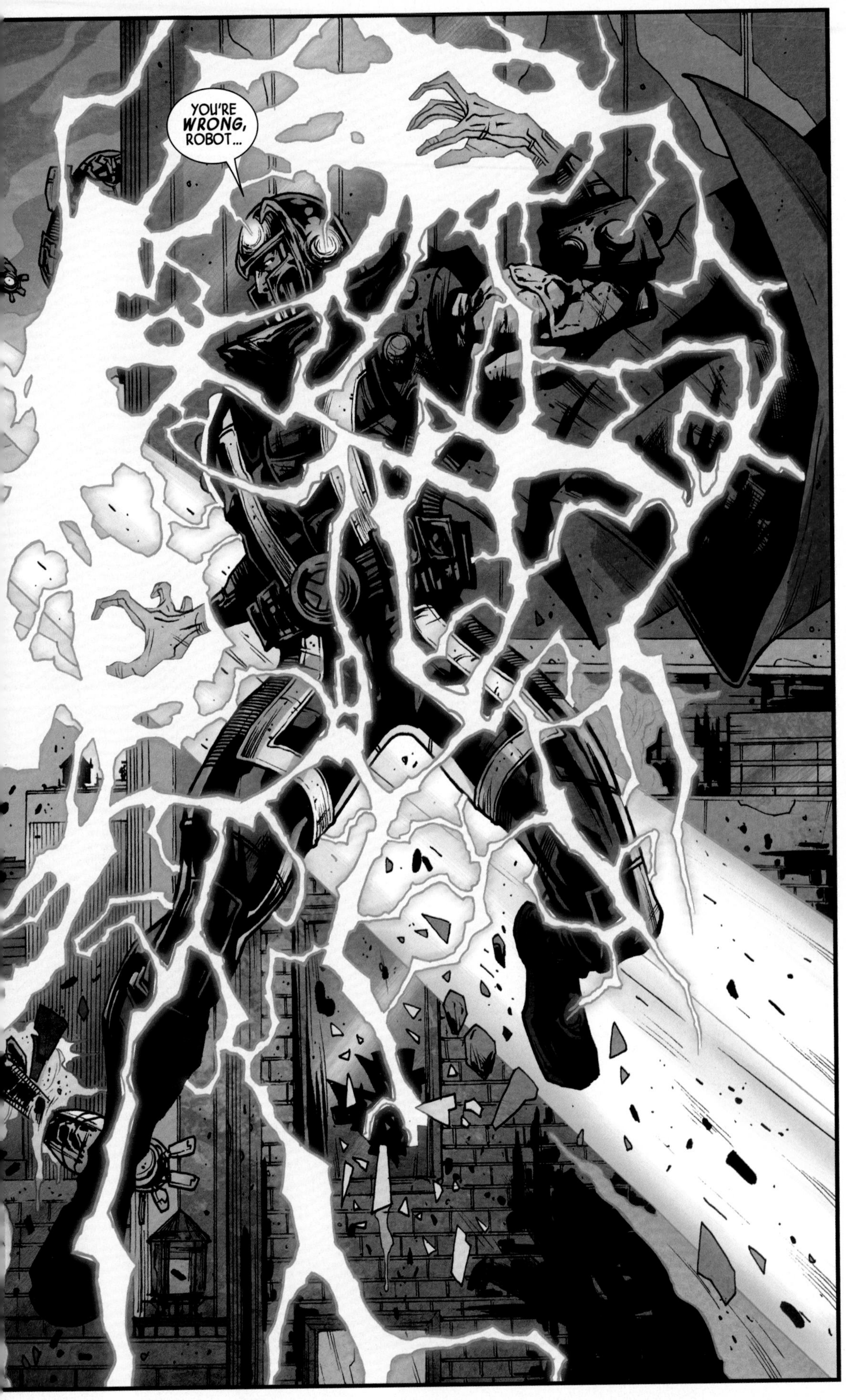
YOU'RE WRONG, ROBOT...

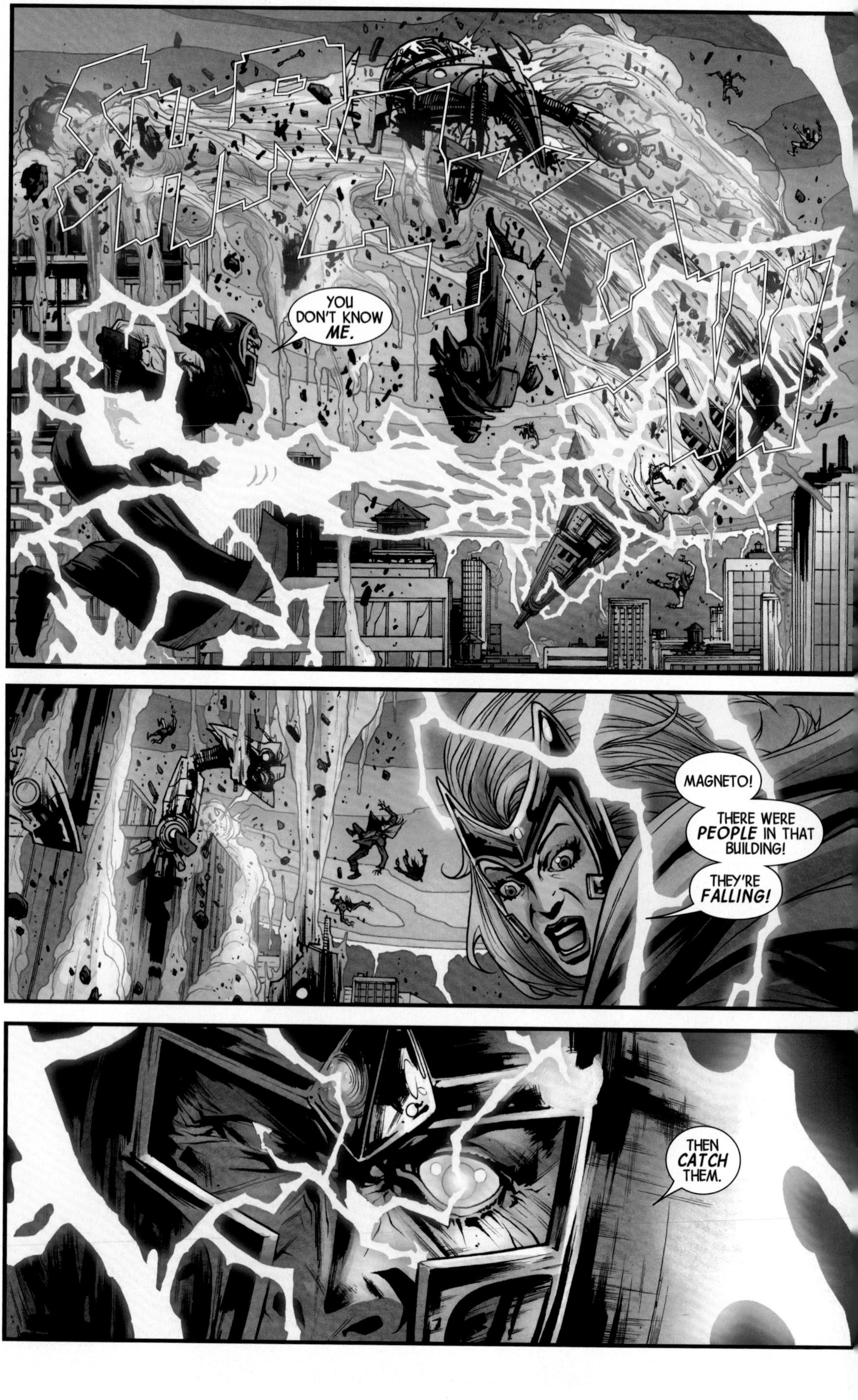
YOU DON'T KNOW *ME.*
MAGNETO!
THERE WERE *PEOPLE* IN THAT BUILDING!
THEY'RE *FALLING!*
THEN *CATCH* THEM.

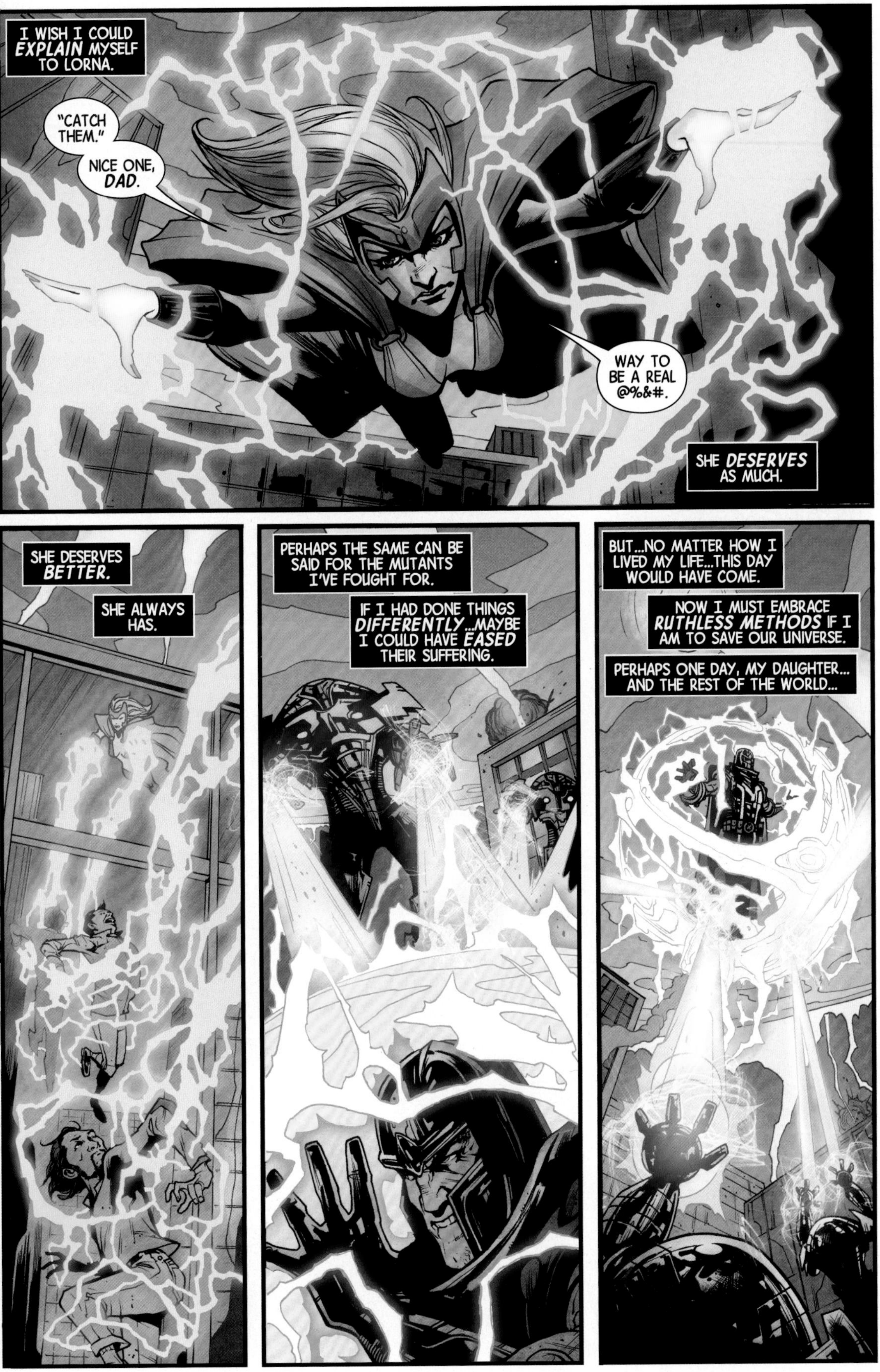
I WISH I COULD EXPLAIN MYSELF TO LORNA.
"CATCH THEM."
NICE ONE, DAD.
WAY TO BE A REAL @%&#.
SHE DESERVES AS MUCH.
SHE DESERVES BETTER.
SHE ALWAYS HAS.
PERHAPS THE SAME CAN BE SAID FOR THE MUTANTS I'VE FOUGHT FOR.
IF I HAD DONE THINGS DIFFERENTLY...MAYBE I COULD HAVE EASED THEIR SUFFERING.
BUT...NO MATTER HOW I LIVED MY LIFE...THIS DAY WOULD HAVE COME.
NOW I MUST EMBRACE RUTHLESS METHODS IF I AM TO SAVE OUR UNIVERSE.
PERHAPS ONE DAY, MY DAUGHTER... AND THE REST OF THE WORLD...

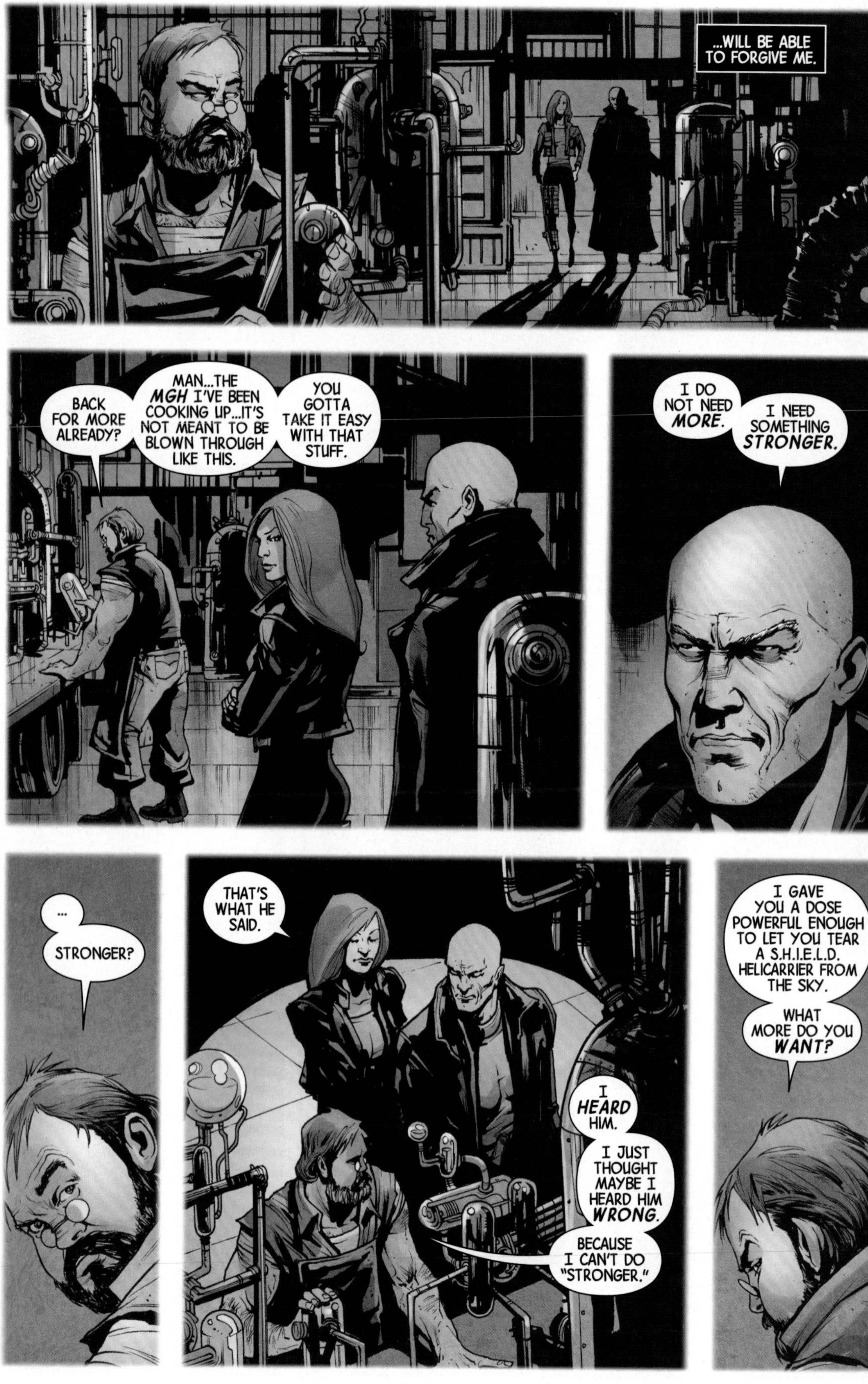

...WILL BE ABLE TO FORGIVE ME.
BACK FOR MORE ALREADY?
MAN...THE MGH I'VE BEEN COOKING UP...IT'S NOT MEANT TO BE BLOWN THROUGH LIKE THIS.
YOU GOTTA TAKE IT EASY WITH THAT STUFF.
I DO NOT NEED MORE.
I NEED SOMETHING STRONGER.
...
STRONGER?
THAT'S WHAT HE SAID.
I HEARD HIM.
I JUST THOUGHT MAYBE I HEARD HIM WRONG.
BECAUSE I CAN'T DO "STRONGER."
I GAVE YOU A DOSE POWERFUL ENOUGH TO LET YOU TEAR A S.H.I.E.L.D. HELICARRIER FROM THE SKY.
WHAT MORE DO YOU WANT?

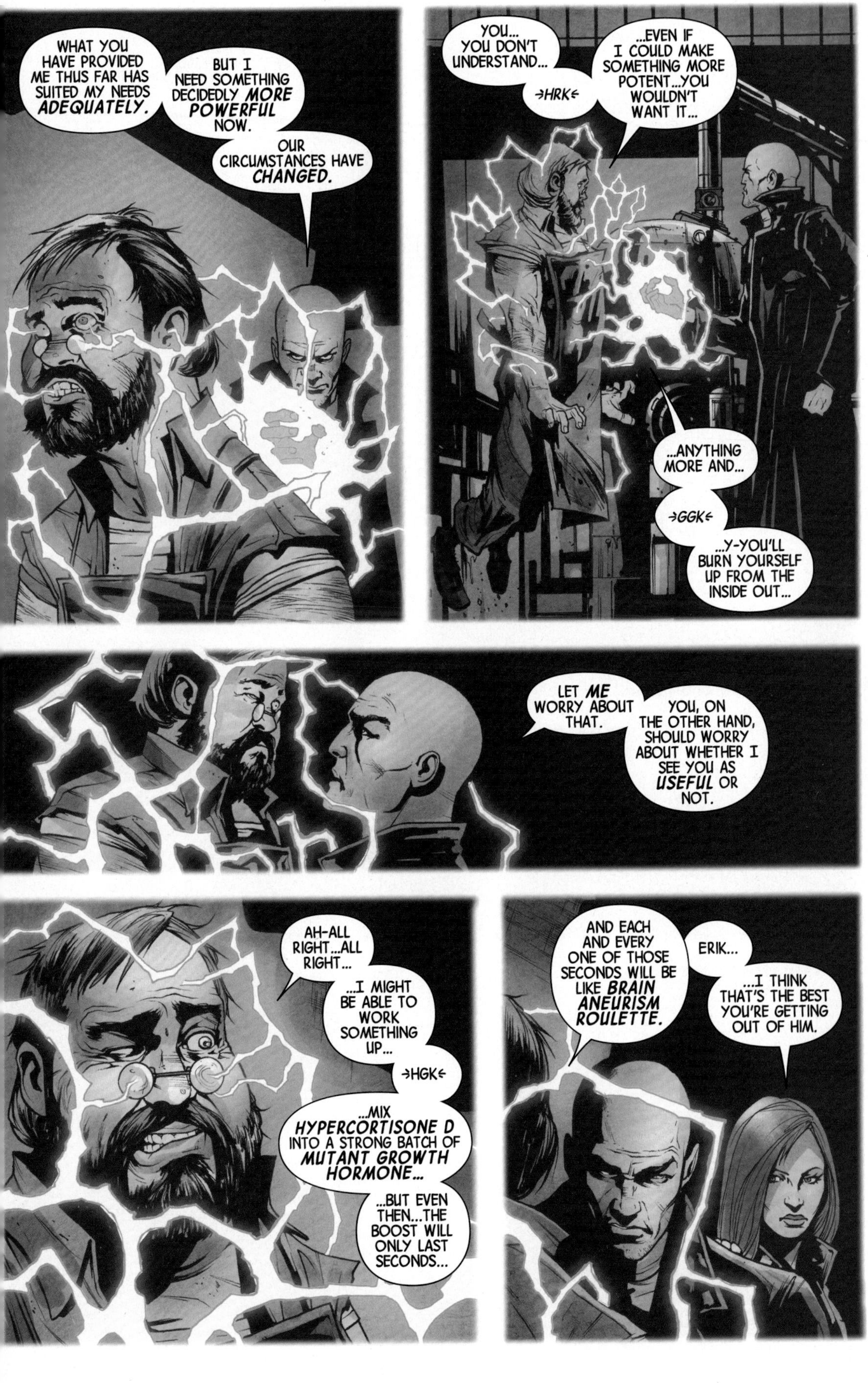
WHAT YOU HAVE PROVIDED ME THUS FAR HAS SUITED MY NEEDS ADEQUATELY.
BUT I NEED SOMETHING DECIDEDLY MORE POWERFUL NOW.
OUR CIRCUMSTANCES HAVE CHANGED.
YOU... YOU DON'T UNDERSTAND...
→HRK←
...EVEN IF I COULD MAKE SOMETHING MORE POTENT...YOU WOULDN'T WANT IT...
...ANYTHING MORE AND...
→GGK←
...Y-YOU'LL BURN YOURSELF UP FROM THE INSIDE OUT...
LET ME WORRY ABOUT THAT.
YOU, ON THE OTHER HAND, SHOULD WORRY ABOUT WHETHER I SEE YOU AS USEFUL OR NOT.
AH-ALL RIGHT...ALL RIGHT...
...I MIGHT BE ABLE TO WORK SOMETHING UP...
→HGK←
...MIX HYPERCORTISONE D INTO A STRONG BATCH OF MUTANT GROWTH HORMONE...
...BUT EVEN THEN...THE BOOST WILL ONLY LAST SECONDS...
AND EACH AND EVERY ONE OF THOSE SECONDS WILL BE LIKE BRAIN ANEURISM ROULETTE.
ERIK...
...I THINK THAT'S THE BEST YOU'RE GETTING OUT OF HIM.

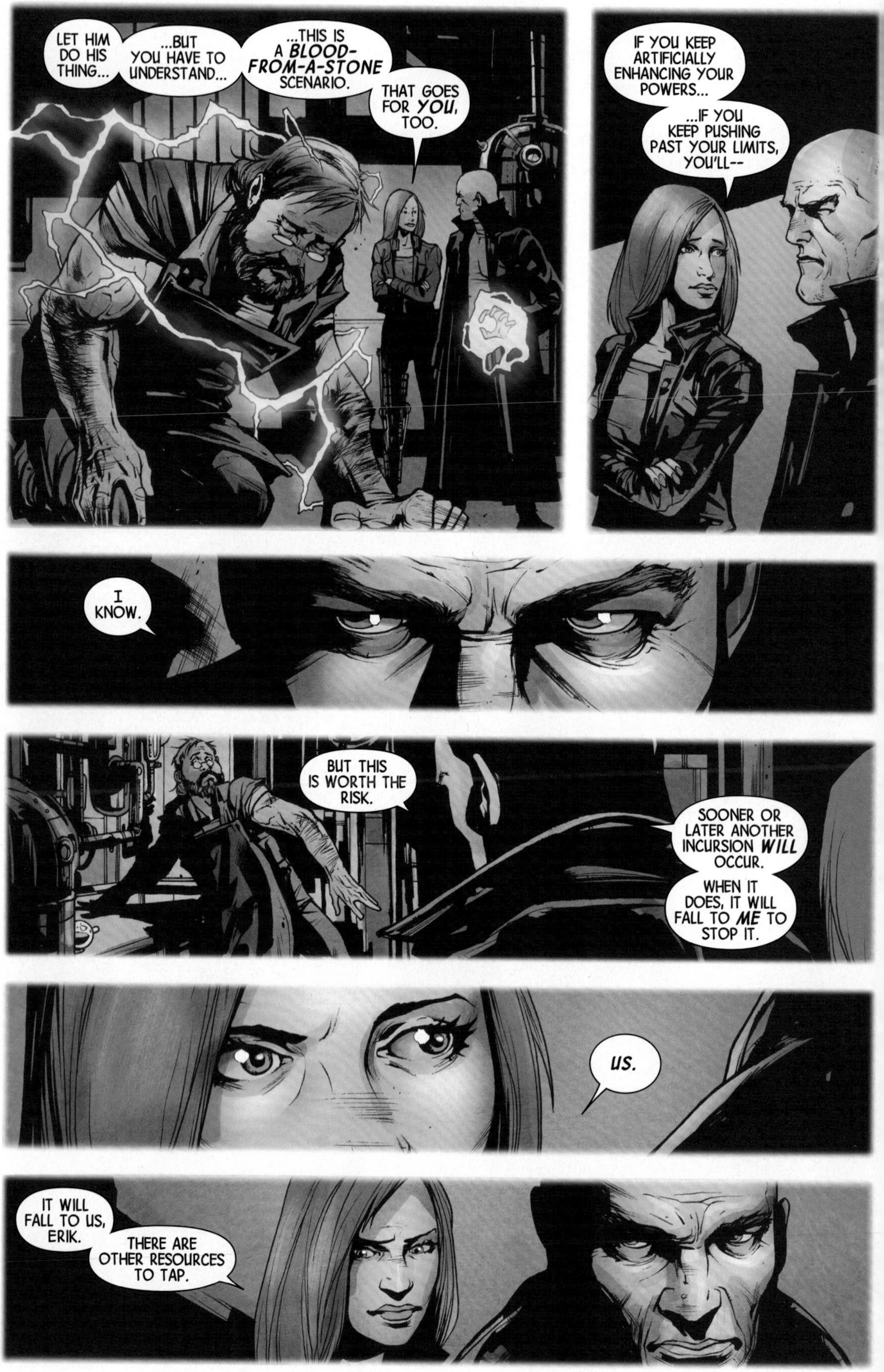
LET HIM DO HIS THING...
...BUT YOU HAVE TO UNDERSTAND...
...THIS IS A BLOOD-FROM-A-STONE SCENARIO.
THAT GOES FOR YOU, TOO.
IF YOU KEEP ARTIFICIALLY ENHANCING YOUR POWERS...
...IF YOU KEEP PUSHING PAST YOUR LIMITS, YOU'LL--
I KNOW.
BUT THIS IS WORTH THE RISK.
SOONER OR LATER ANOTHER INCURSION WILL OCCUR.
WHEN IT DOES, IT WILL FALL TO ME TO STOP IT.
US.
IT WILL FALL TO US, ERIK.
THERE ARE OTHER RESOURCES TO TAP.

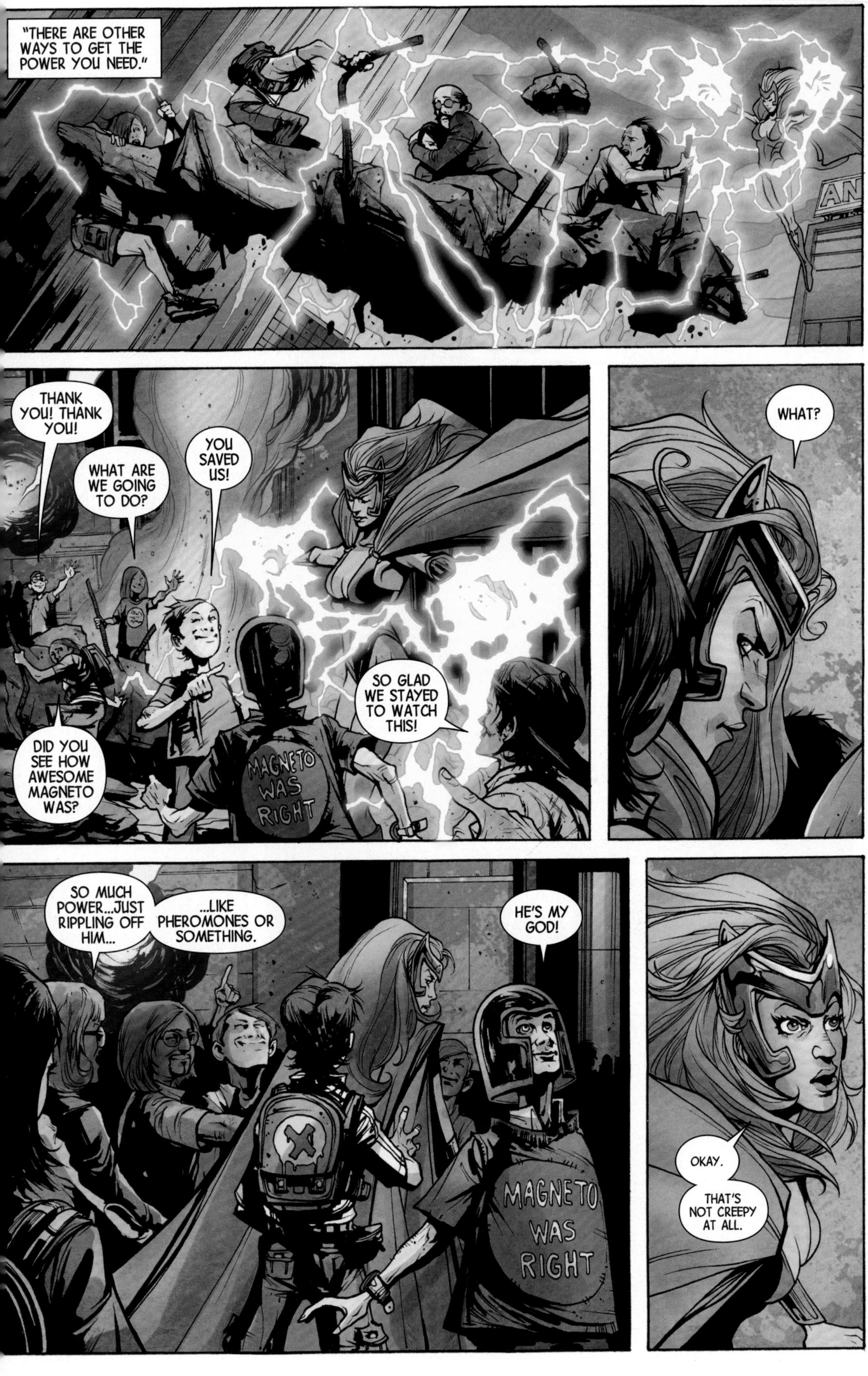
"THERE ARE OTHER WAYS TO GET THE POWER YOU NEED."
THANK YOU! THANK YOU!
WHAT ARE WE GOING TO DO?
YOU SAVED US!
SO GLAD WE STAYED TO WATCH THIS!
DID YOU SEE HOW AWESOME MAGNETO WAS?
MAGNETO WAS RIGHT
WHAT?
SO MUCH POWER...JUST RIPPLING OFF HIM...
...LIKE PHEROMONES OR SOMETHING.
HE'S MY GOD!
MAGNETO WAS RIGHT
OKAY.
THAT'S NOT CREEPY AT ALL.

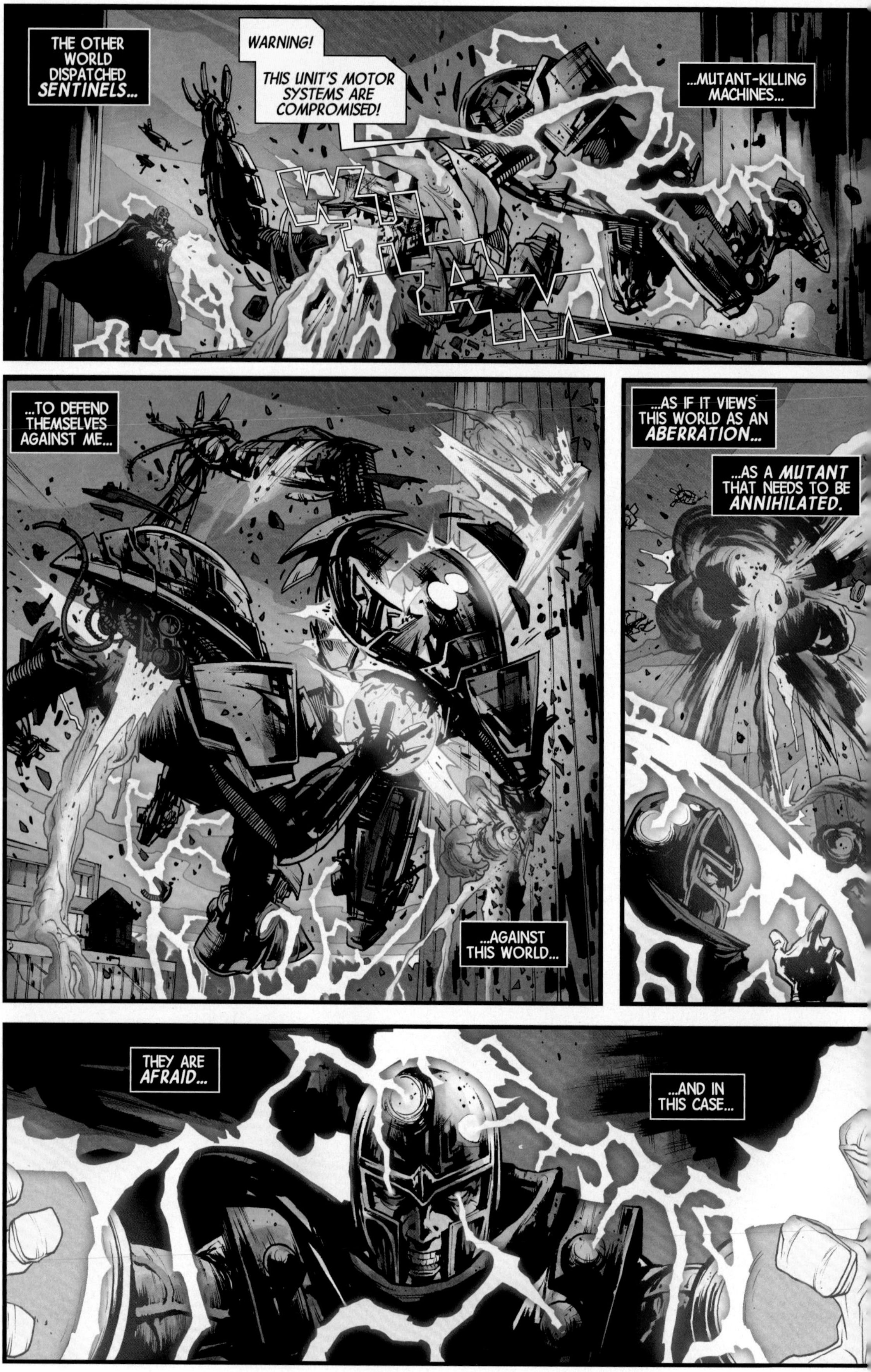

THE OTHER WORLD DISPATCHED SENTINELS...
WARNING!
THIS UNIT'S MOTOR SYSTEMS ARE COMPROMISED!
...MUTANT-KILLING MACHINES...
WHAM
...TO DEFEND THEMSELVES AGAINST ME...
...AGAINST THIS WORLD...
...AS IF IT VIEWS THIS WORLD AS AN ABERRATION...
...AS A MUTANT THAT NEEDS TO BE ANNIHILATED.
THEY ARE AFRAID...
...AND IN THIS CASE...

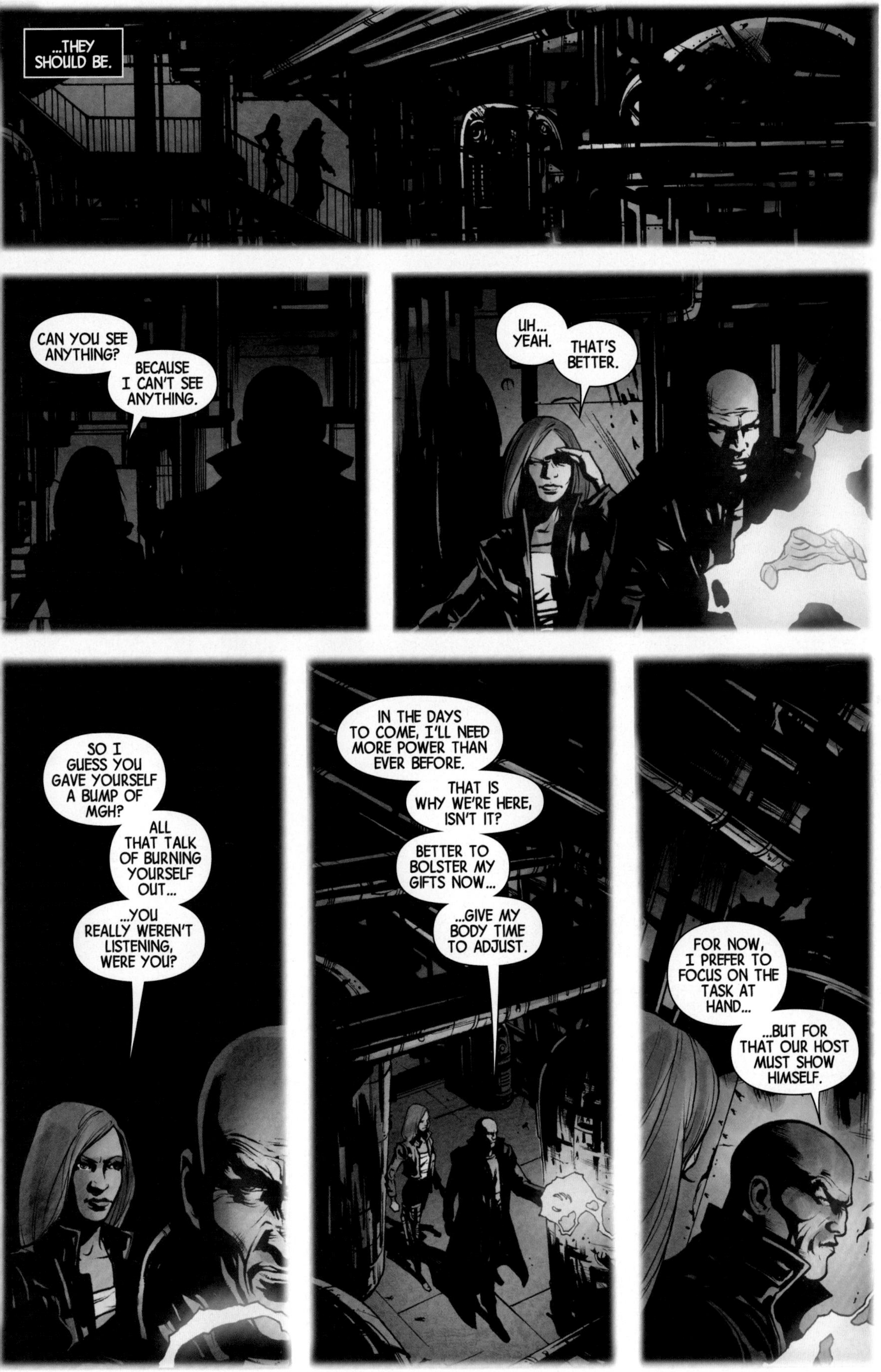

...THEY SHOULD BE.
CAN YOU SEE ANYTHING?
BECAUSE I CAN'T SEE ANYTHING.
UH... YEAH.
THAT'S BETTER.
SO I GUESS YOU GAVE YOURSELF A BUMP OF MGH?
ALL THAT TALK OF BURNING YOURSELF OUT...
...YOU REALLY WEREN'T LISTENING, WERE YOU?
IN THE DAYS TO COME, I'LL NEED MORE POWER THAN EVER BEFORE.
THAT IS WHY WE'RE HERE, ISN'T IT?
BETTER TO BOLSTER MY GIFTS NOW...
...GIVE MY BODY TIME TO ADJUST.
FOR NOW, I PREFER TO FOCUS ON THE TASK AT HAND...
...BUT FOR THAT OUR HOST MUST SHOW HIMSELF.

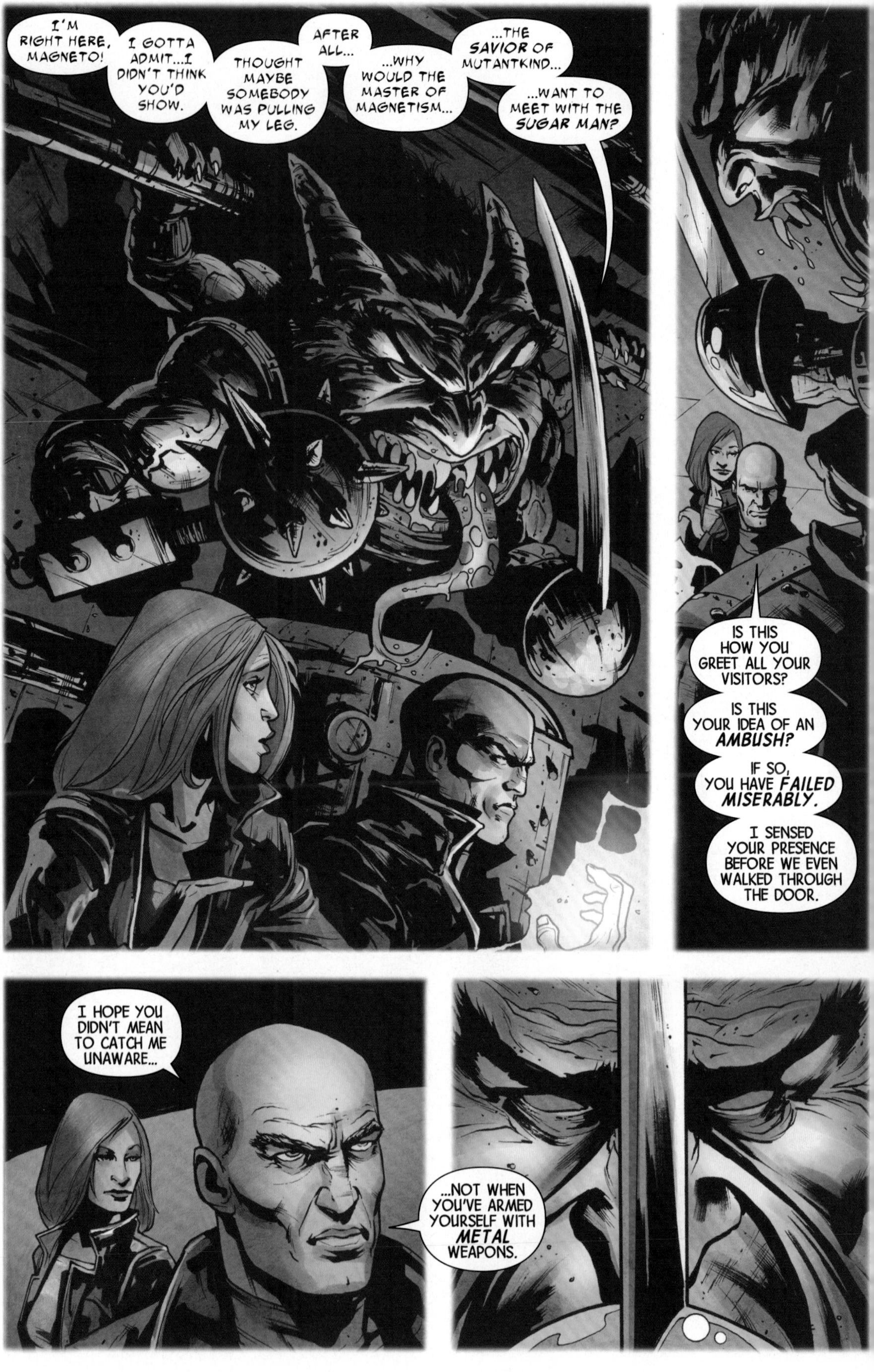
I'M RIGHT HERE, MAGNETO!
I GOTTA ADMIT...I DIDN'T THINK YOU'D SHOW.
THOUGHT MAYBE SOMEBODY WAS PULLING MY LEG.
AFTER ALL...
...WHY WOULD THE MASTER OF MAGNETISM...
...THE SAVIOR OF MUTANTKIND...
...WANT TO MEET WITH THE SUGAR MAN?
IS THIS HOW YOU GREET ALL YOUR VISITORS?
IS THIS YOUR IDEA OF AN AMBUSH?
IF SO, YOU HAVE FAILED MISERABLY.
I SENSED YOUR PRESENCE BEFORE WE EVEN WALKED THROUGH THE DOOR.
I HOPE YOU DIDN'T MEAN TO CATCH ME UNAWARE...
...NOT WHEN YOU'VE ARMED YOURSELF WITH METAL WEAPONS.

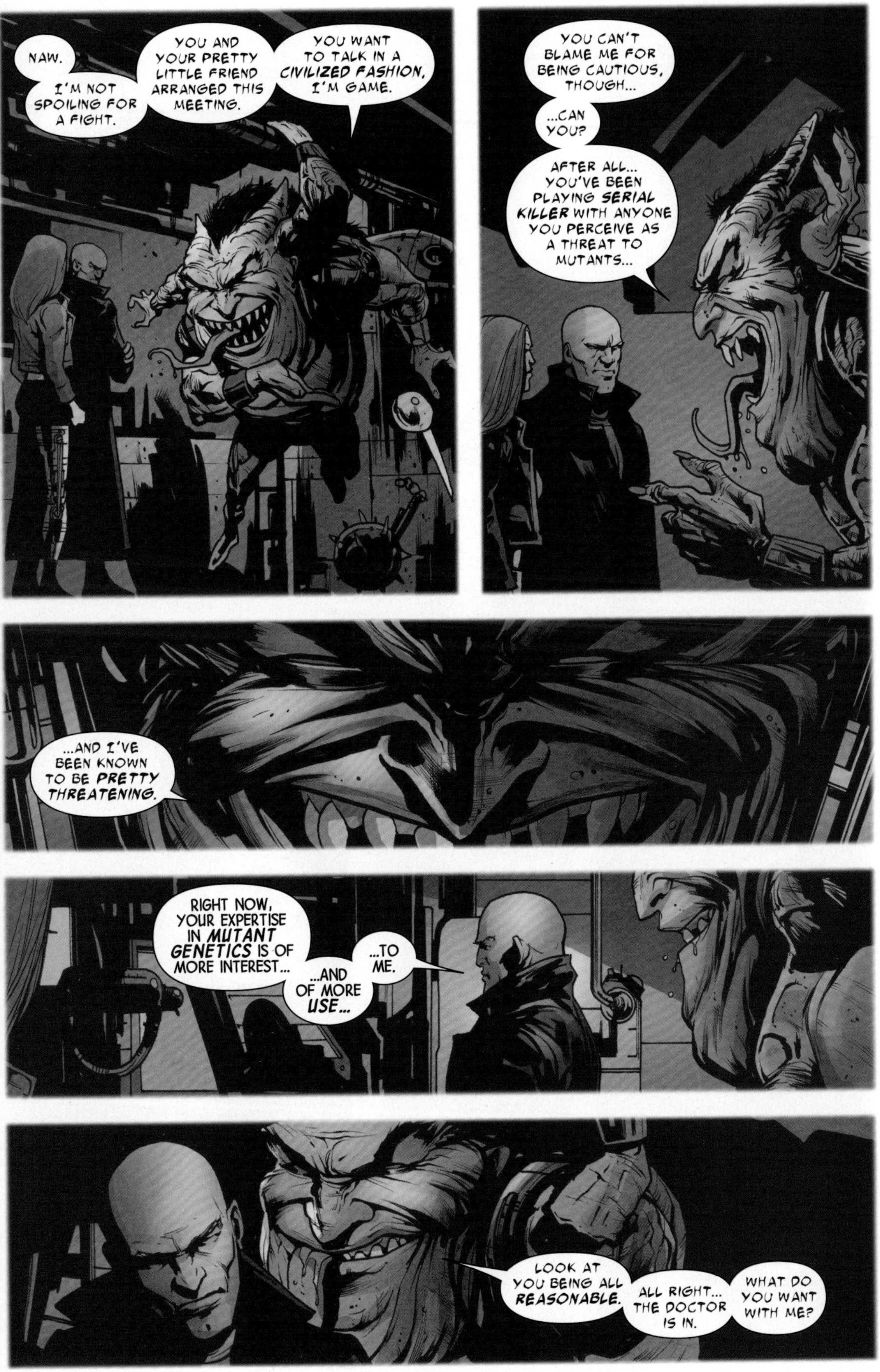
NAW.
I'M NOT SPOILING FOR A FIGHT.
YOU AND YOUR PRETTY LITTLE FRIEND ARRANGED THIS MEETING.
YOU WANT TO TALK IN A CIVILIZED FASHION, I'M GAME.
YOU CAN'T BLAME ME FOR BEING CAUTIOUS, THOUGH...
...CAN YOU?
AFTER ALL... YOU'VE BEEN PLAYING SERIAL KILLER WITH ANYONE YOU PERCEIVE AS A THREAT TO MUTANTS...
...AND I'VE BEEN KNOWN TO BE PRETTY THREATENING.
RIGHT NOW, YOUR EXPERTISE IN MUTANT GENETICS IS OF MORE INTEREST...
...AND OF MORE USE...
...TO ME.
LOOK AT YOU BEING ALL REASONABLE.
ALL RIGHT... THE DOCTOR IS IN.
WHAT DO YOU WANT WITH ME?

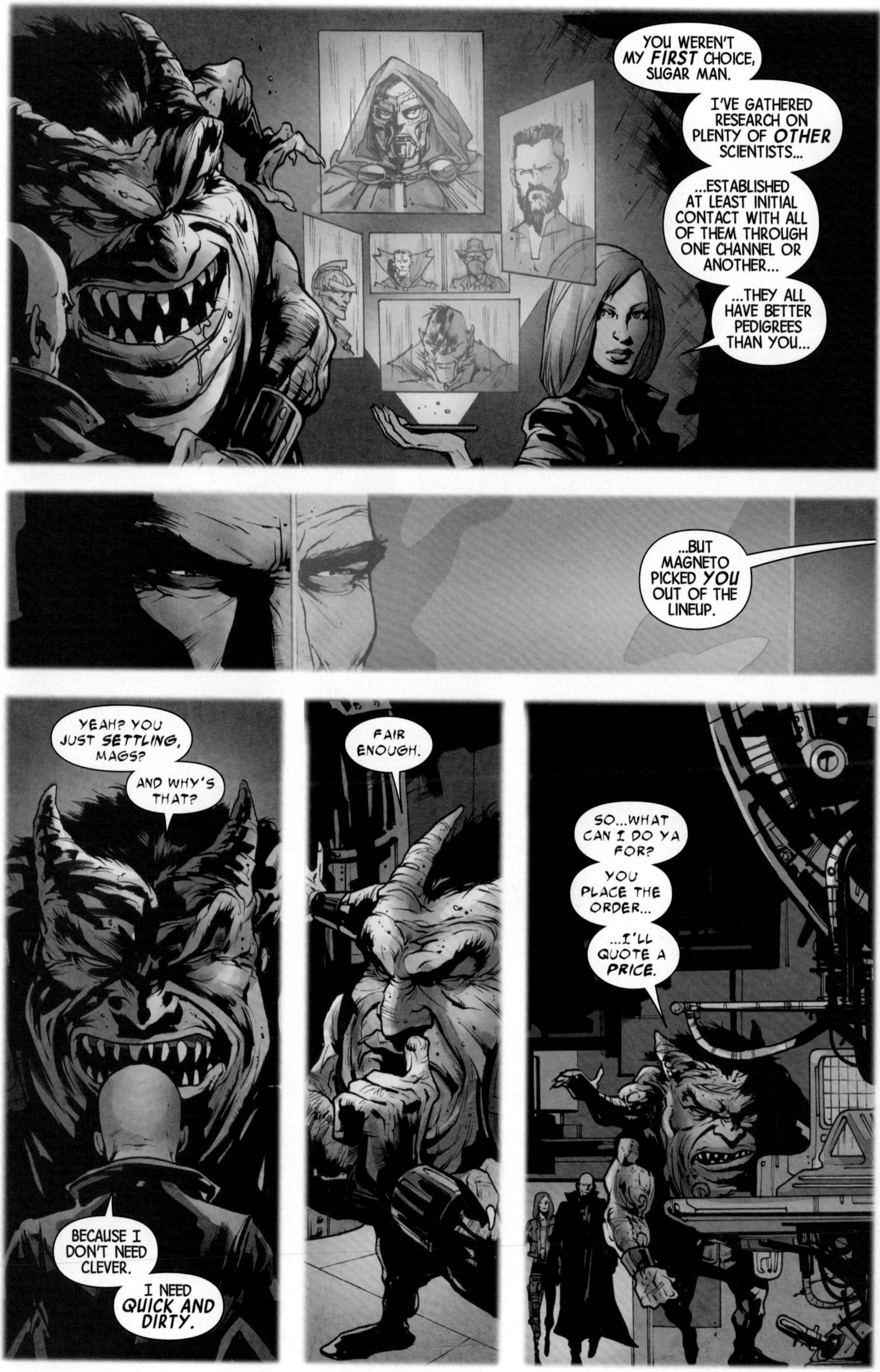
YOU WEREN'T MY FIRST CHOICE, SUGAR MAN.
I'VE GATHERED RESEARCH ON PLENTY OF OTHER SCIENTISTS...
...ESTABLISHED AT LEAST INITIAL CONTACT WITH ALL OF THEM THROUGH ONE CHANNEL OR ANOTHER...
...THEY ALL HAVE BETTER PEDIGREES THAN YOU...
...BUT MAGNETO PICKED YOU OUT OF THE LINEUP.
YEAH? YOU JUST SETTLING, MAGS?
AND WHY'S THAT?
BECAUSE I DON'T NEED CLEVER.
I NEED QUICK AND DIRTY.
FAIR ENOUGH.
SO...WHAT CAN I DO YA FOR?
YOU PLACE THE ORDER...
...I'LL QUOTE A PRICE.

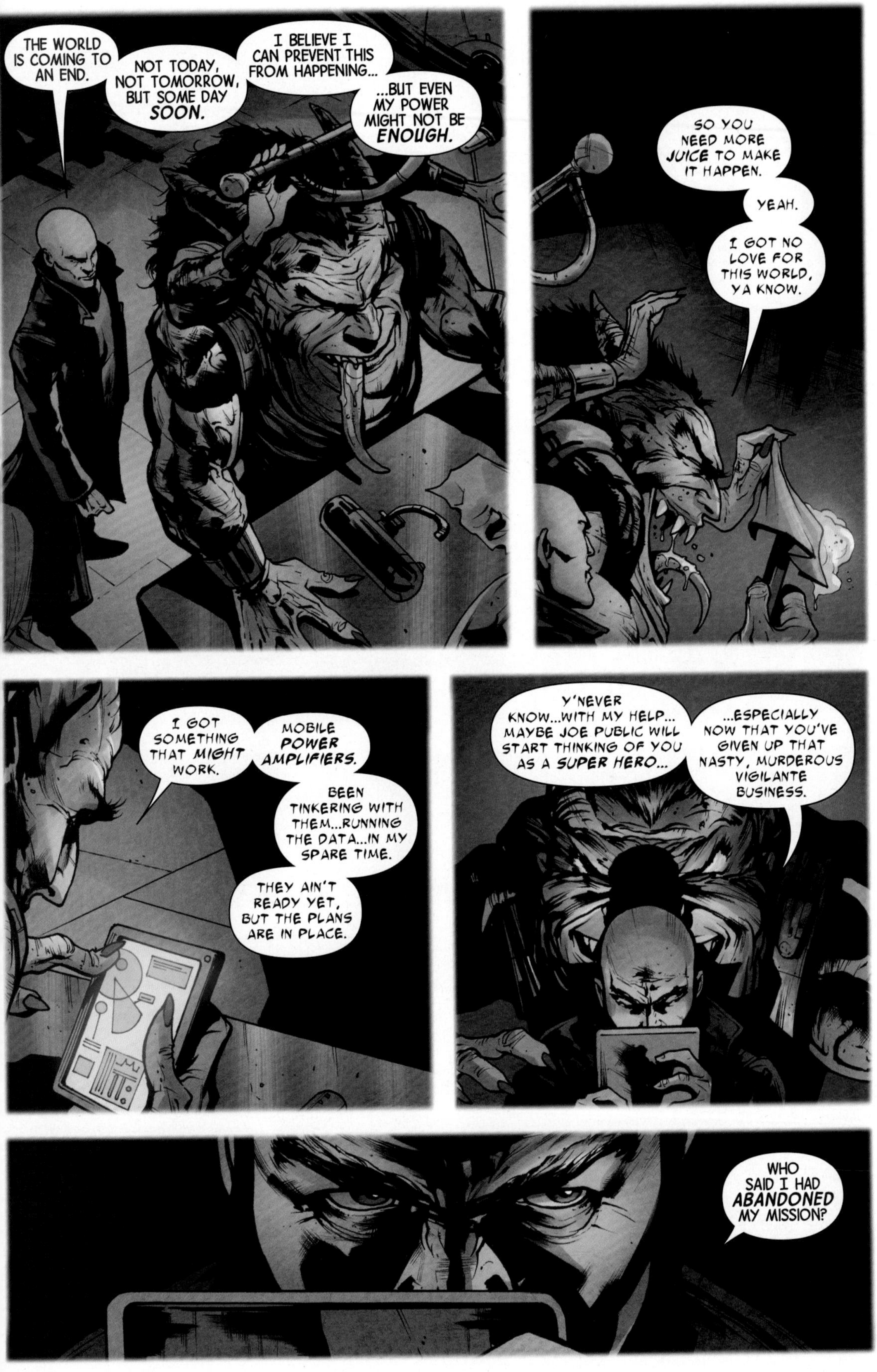
THE WORLD IS COMING TO AN END.
NOT TODAY, NOT TOMORROW, BUT SOME DAY SOON.
I BELIEVE I CAN PREVENT THIS FROM HAPPENING...
...BUT EVEN MY POWER MIGHT NOT BE ENOUGH.
SO YOU NEED MORE JUICE TO MAKE IT HAPPEN.
YEAH.
I GOT NO LOVE FOR THIS WORLD, YA KNOW.
I GOT SOMETHING THAT MIGHT WORK.
MOBILE POWER AMPLIFIERS.
BEEN TINKERING WITH THEM...RUNNING THE DATA...IN MY SPARE TIME.
THEY AIN'T READY YET, BUT THE PLANS ARE IN PLACE.
Y'NEVER KNOW...WITH MY HELP... MAYBE JOE PUBLIC WILL START THINKING OF YOU AS A SUPER HERO...
...ESPECIALLY NOW THAT YOU'VE GIVEN UP THAT NASTY, MURDEROUS VIGILANTE BUSINESS.
WHO SAID I HAD ABANDONED MY MISSION?

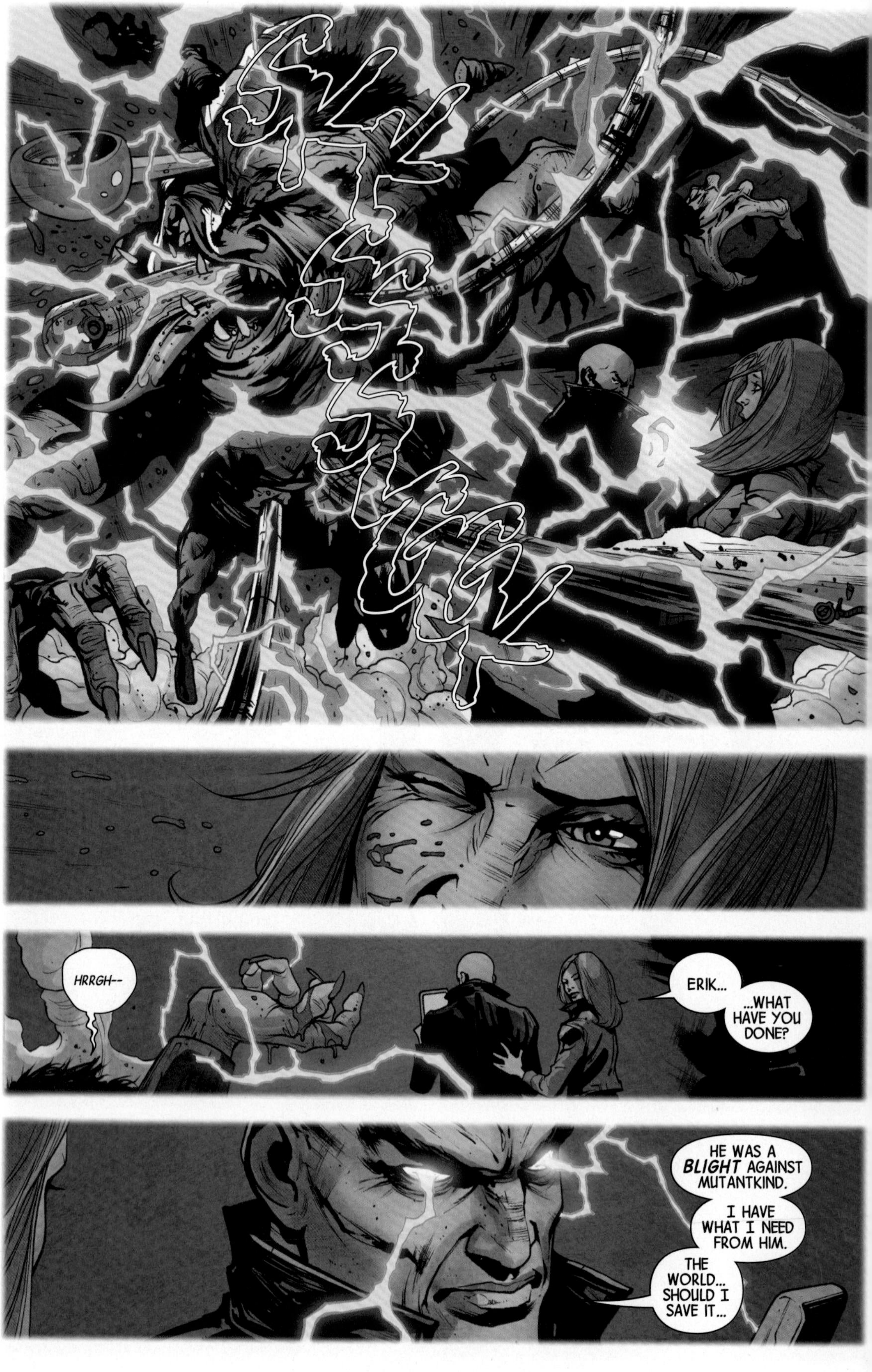
HRRGH--
ERIK...
...WHAT HAVE YOU DONE?
HE WAS A BLIGHT AGAINST MUTANTKIND.
I HAVE WHAT I NEED FROM HIM.
THE WORLD... SHOULD I SAVE IT...

"...IS *BETTER OFF* WITHOUT HIS ILK."

SO MUCH POWER.

THERE'S NO WAY...

...HE CAN MAINTAIN THAT.

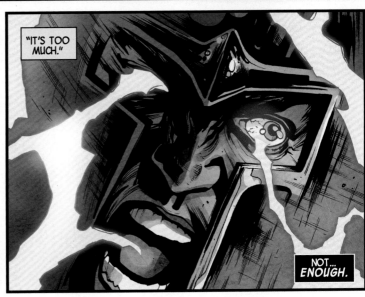

"IT'S TOO MUCH."

NOT... ENOUGH.

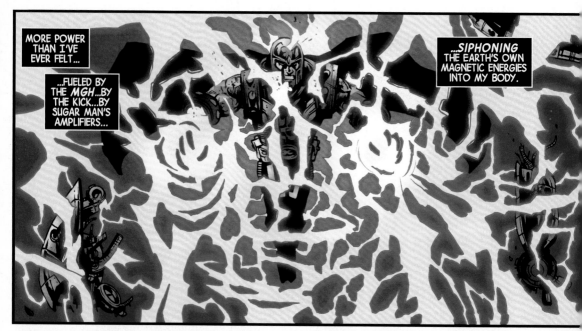

MORE POWER THAN I'VE EVER FELT...

...FUELED BY THE *MGH*...BY THE KICK...BY SUGAR MAN'S AMPLIFIERS...

...*SIPHONING* THE EARTH'S OWN MAGNETIC ENERGIES INTO MY BODY.

IT IS MORE POWER THAN I'VE *EVER* CHANNELED.

BUT IT IS *NOT* ENOUGH.

AND YET...

...IT IS *TOO GREAT* AT THE SAME TIME.

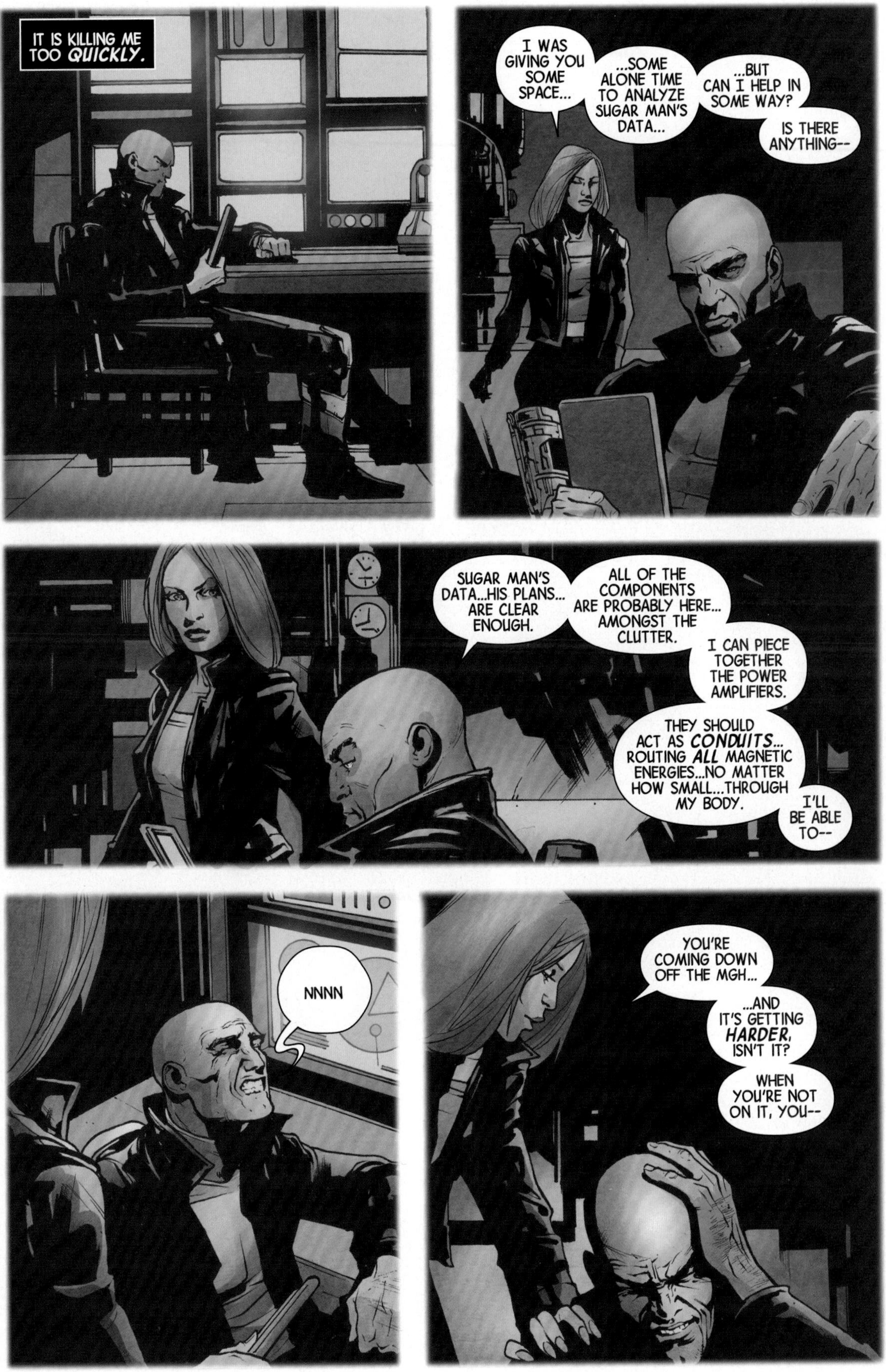
IT IS KILLING ME TOO *QUICKLY.*
I WAS GIVING YOU SOME SPACE...
...SOME ALONE TIME TO ANALYZE SUGAR MAN'S DATA...
...BUT CAN I HELP IN SOME WAY?
IS THERE ANYTHING--
SUGAR MAN'S DATA...HIS PLANS... ARE CLEAR ENOUGH.
ALL OF THE COMPONENTS ARE PROBABLY HERE... AMONGST THE CLUTTER.
I CAN PIECE TOGETHER THE POWER AMPLIFIERS.
THEY SHOULD ACT AS *CONDUITS*... ROUTING *ALL* MAGNETIC ENERGIES...NO MATTER HOW SMALL...THROUGH MY BODY.
I'LL BE ABLE TO--
NNNN
YOU'RE COMING DOWN OFF THE MGH...
...AND IT'S GETTING *HARDER,* ISN'T IT?
WHEN YOU'RE NOT ON IT, YOU--

ENOUGH.

I DON'T NEED A *NURSE*.

OKAY.

BRIAR...

...IT DAWNS ON ME THAT THERE IS LITTLE TIME LEFT.

WHENEVER THE NEXT INCURSION HAPPENS, IT WILL BE *TOO SOON*.

AND THEN...IT WILL BE *TOO LATE*.

ARE WE HAVING A MOMENT HERE?

BECAUSE I STILL HAVE BITS OF SUGAR MAN'S BLOOD IN MY HAIR AND--

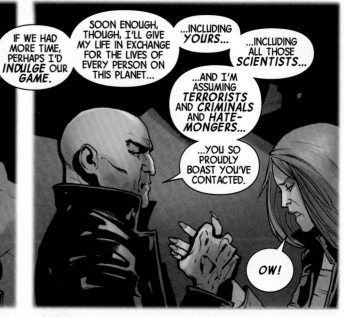

IF WE HAD MORE TIME, PERHAPS I'D *INDULGE* OUR *GAME*.

SOON ENOUGH, THOUGH, I'LL GIVE MY LIFE IN EXCHANGE FOR THE LIVES OF EVERY PERSON ON THIS PLANET...

...INCLUDING *YOURS*...

...INCLUDING ALL THOSE *SCIENTISTS*...

...AND I'M ASSUMING *TERRORISTS* AND *CRIMINALS* AND *HATE-MONGERS*...

...YOU SO PROUDLY BOAST YOU'VE CONTACTED.

OW!

YOU'VE FED ME INFORMATION AS IT SUITED YOU...

...AS IF YOU WERE GIVING A HOUND A SCENT TO TRACK.

...PROVIDING LEADS FOR ME TO FOLLOW...

HERE AT THE END, THOUGH, I ONLY NEED TO KNOW ONE THING.

I WANT TO KNOW WHO YOU REALLY ARE.

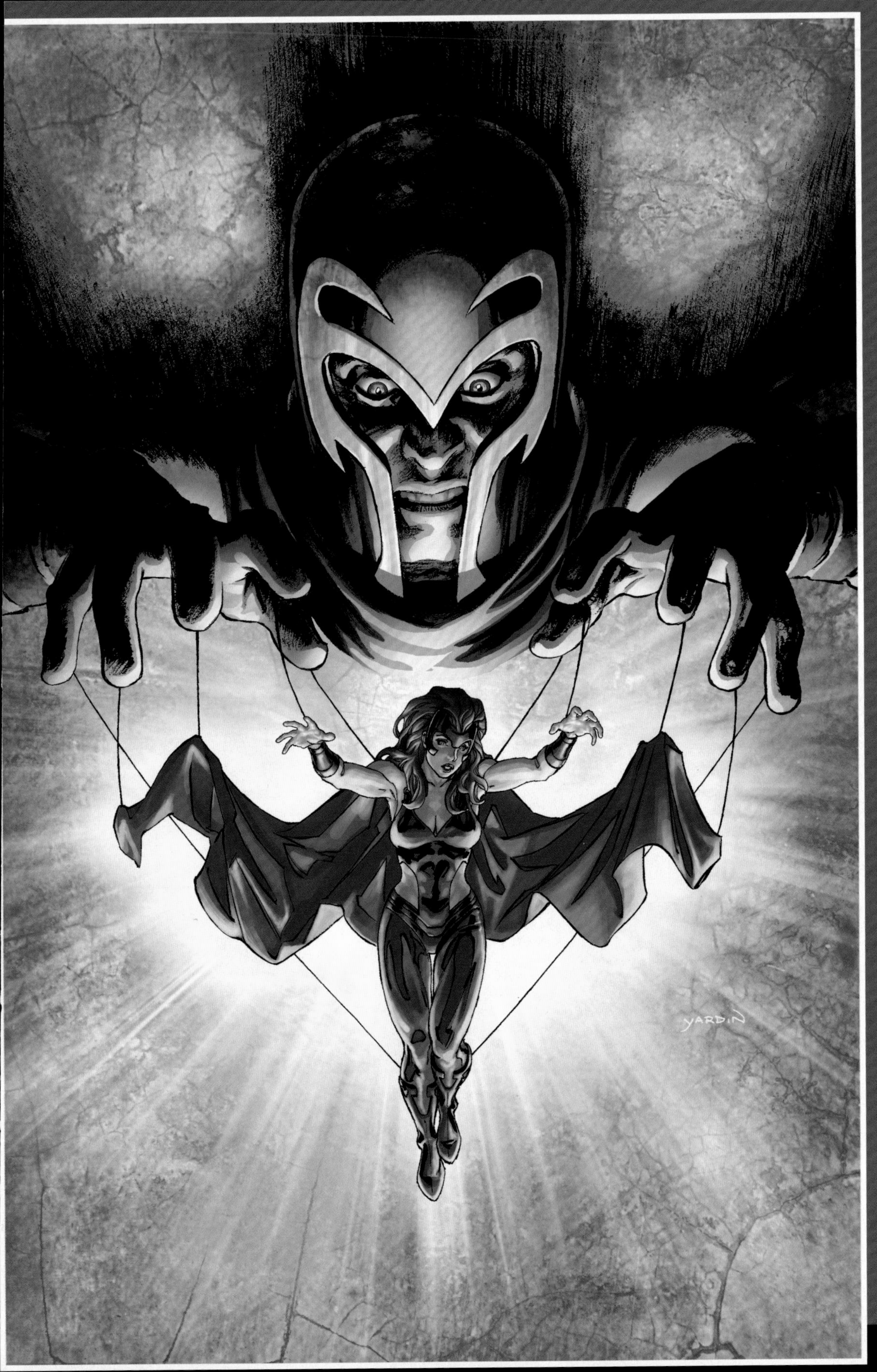
YARDIN

I WONDER...

...AS I STRIVE TO REPEL THIS OTHER VERSION OF EARTH...

...AS I TRY TO RIP A WORLD APART...

...IS MY OWN *DOPPELGANGER* SOMEWHERE OUT THERE...

...ON THE OPPOSITE SIDE OF THIS BREACH BETWEEN UNIVERSES...

...TRYING TO DO THE SAME?

AM I...

...EVEN NOW...

...WORKING AT *CROSS PURPOSES* WITH MYSELF?

AND IF I AM...

...HAVE I FOUND A WAY TO DEFEAT THIS REFLECTION OF MYSELF?

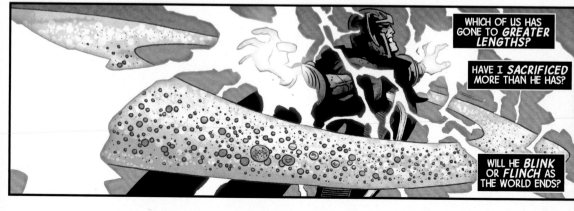

WHICH OF US HAS GONE TO *GREATER LENGTHS*?

HAVE I *SACRIFICED* MORE THAN HE HAS?

WILL HE *BLINK* OR *FLINCH* AS THE WORLD ENDS?

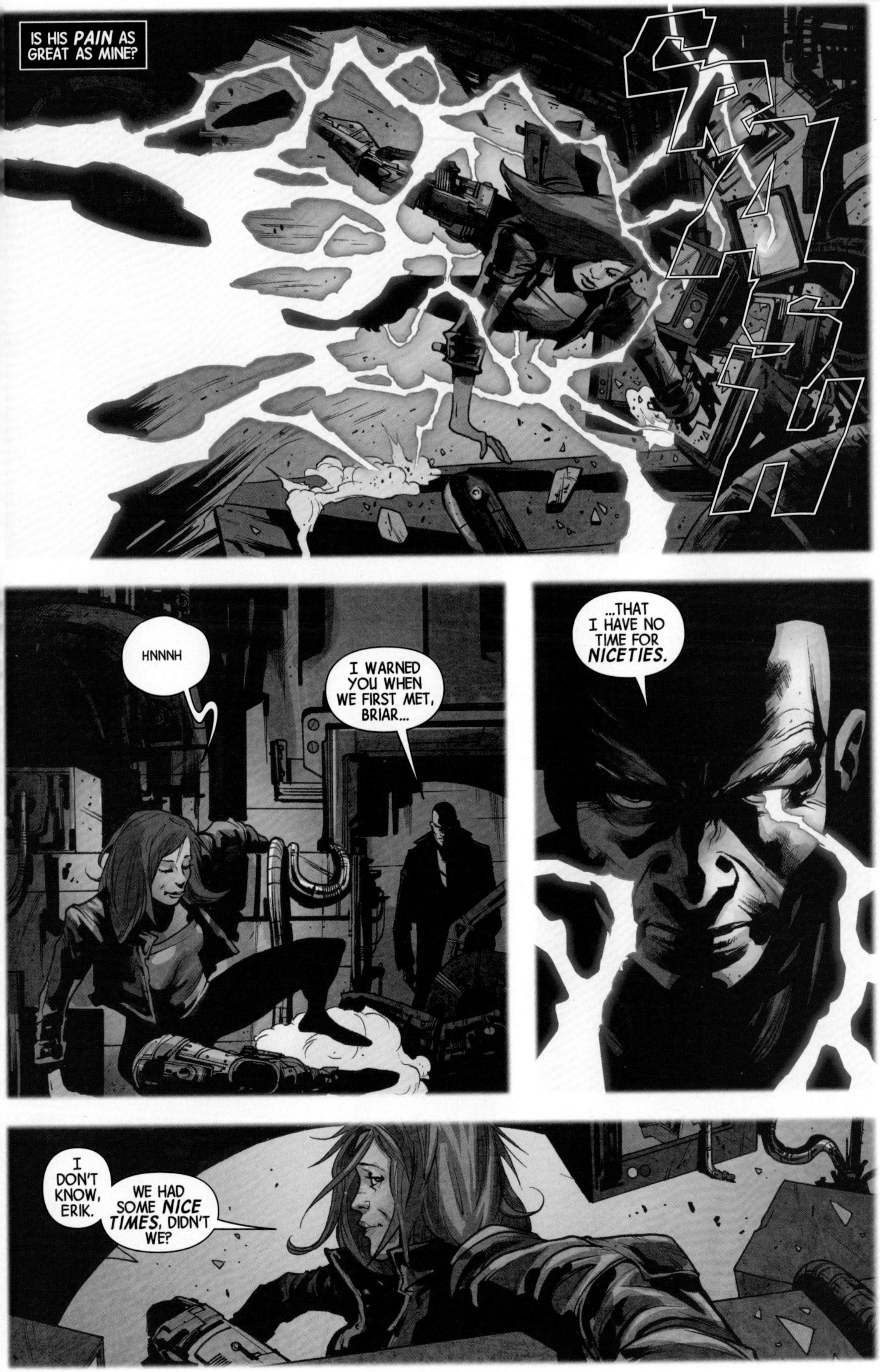
IS HIS PAIN AS GREAT AS MINE?
HNNNH
I WARNED YOU WHEN WE FIRST MET, BRIAR...
...THAT I HAVE NO TIME FOR NICETIES.
I DON'T KNOW, ERIK.
WE HAD SOME NICE TIMES, DIDN'T WE?

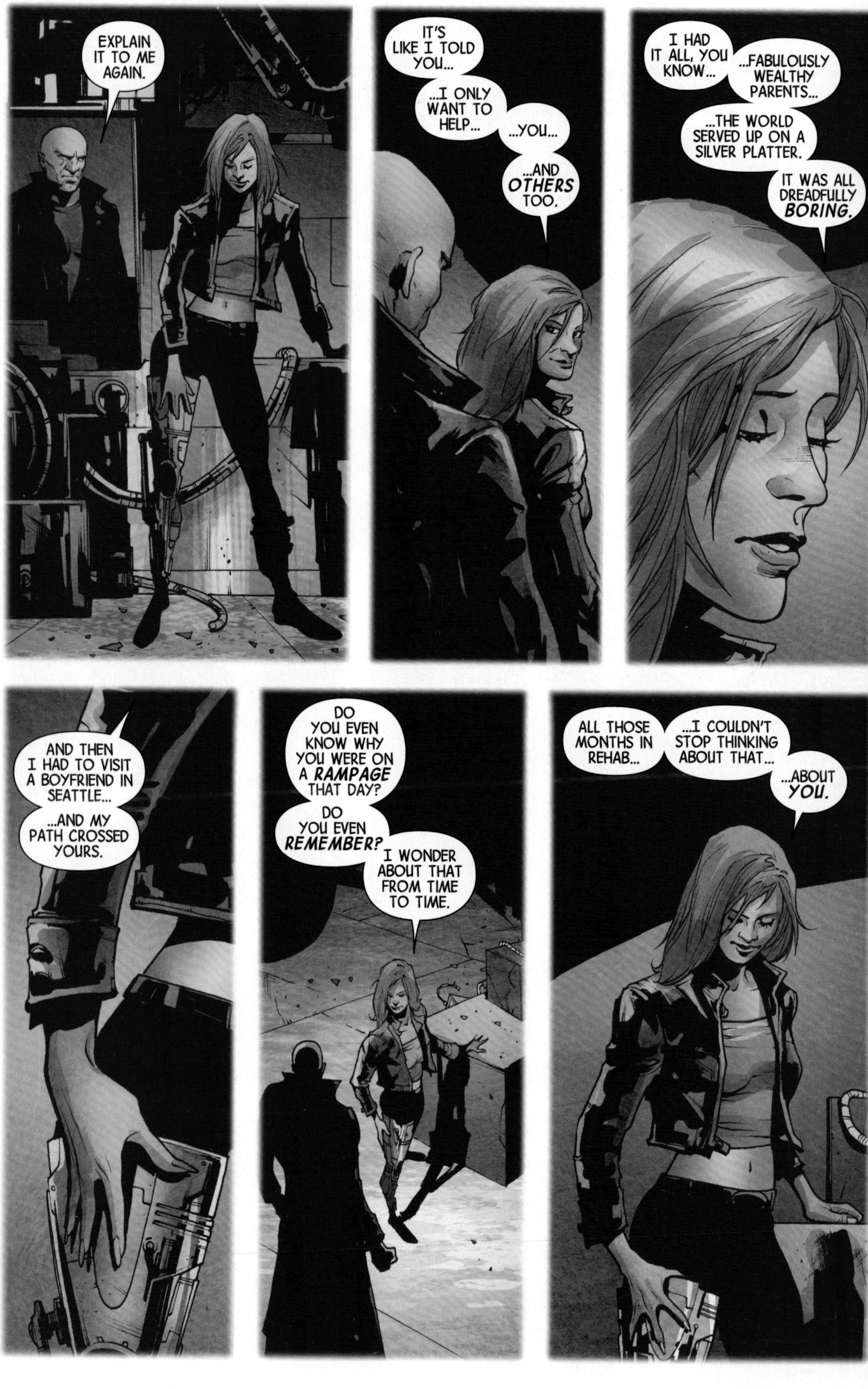
EXPLAIN IT TO ME AGAIN.
IT'S LIKE I TOLD YOU...
...I ONLY WANT TO HELP...
...YOU...
...AND OTHERS TOO.
I HAD IT ALL, YOU KNOW...
...FABULOUSLY WEALTHY PARENTS...
...THE WORLD SERVED UP ON A SILVER PLATTER.
IT WAS ALL DREADFULLY BORING.
AND THEN I HAD TO VISIT A BOYFRIEND IN SEATTLE...
...AND MY PATH CROSSED YOURS.
DO YOU EVEN KNOW WHY YOU WERE ON A RAMPAGE THAT DAY?
DO YOU EVEN REMEMBER?
I WONDER ABOUT THAT FROM TIME TO TIME.
ALL THOSE MONTHS IN REHAB...
...I COULDN'T STOP THINKING ABOUT THAT...
...ABOUT YOU.

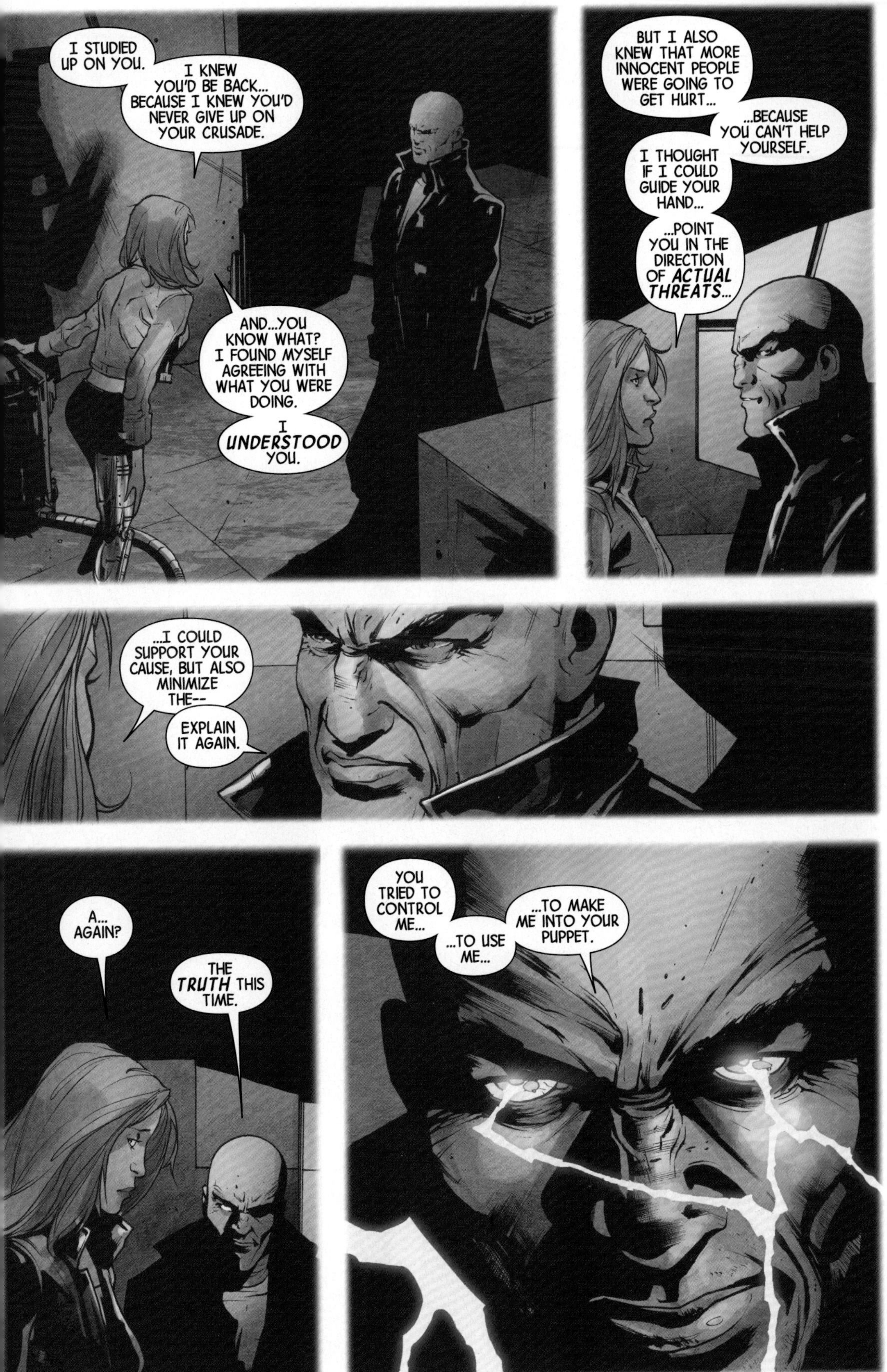
I STUDIED UP ON YOU.
I KNEW YOU'D BE BACK... BECAUSE I KNEW YOU'D NEVER GIVE UP ON YOUR CRUSADE.
AND...YOU KNOW WHAT? I FOUND MYSELF AGREEING WITH WHAT YOU WERE DOING.
I UNDERSTOOD YOU.
BUT I ALSO KNEW THAT MORE INNOCENT PEOPLE WERE GOING TO GET HURT...
...BECAUSE YOU CAN'T HELP YOURSELF.
I THOUGHT IF I COULD GUIDE YOUR HAND...
...POINT YOU IN THE DIRECTION OF ACTUAL THREATS...
...I COULD SUPPORT YOUR CAUSE, BUT ALSO MINIMIZE THE--
EXPLAIN IT AGAIN.
A... AGAIN?
THE TRUTH THIS TIME.
YOU TRIED TO CONTROL ME...
...TO USE ME...
...TO MAKE ME INTO YOUR PUPPET.

BUT DON'T DARE LIE TO ME ABOUT YOUR MOTIVES.

HRRRRN

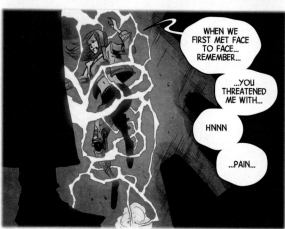

WHEN WE FIRST MET FACE TO FACE... REMEMBER...

...YOU THREATENED ME WITH...

HNNN

...PAIN...

...IT WAS YOU AT YOUR BEST...

...AND YOU DIDN'T EVEN REALIZE IT...

...BECAUSE IT CAME SO NATURALLY...

I LIKE THIS SIDE OF YOU.

YOU DISGUST ME, BRIAR.

OH... PLEASE.

LIKE YOU CAN'T UNDERSTAND WHERE I'M COMING FROM.

YOU KNOW AS WELL AS I DO...

...IT'S THE PAIN THAT MAKES YOU FEEL ALIVE.

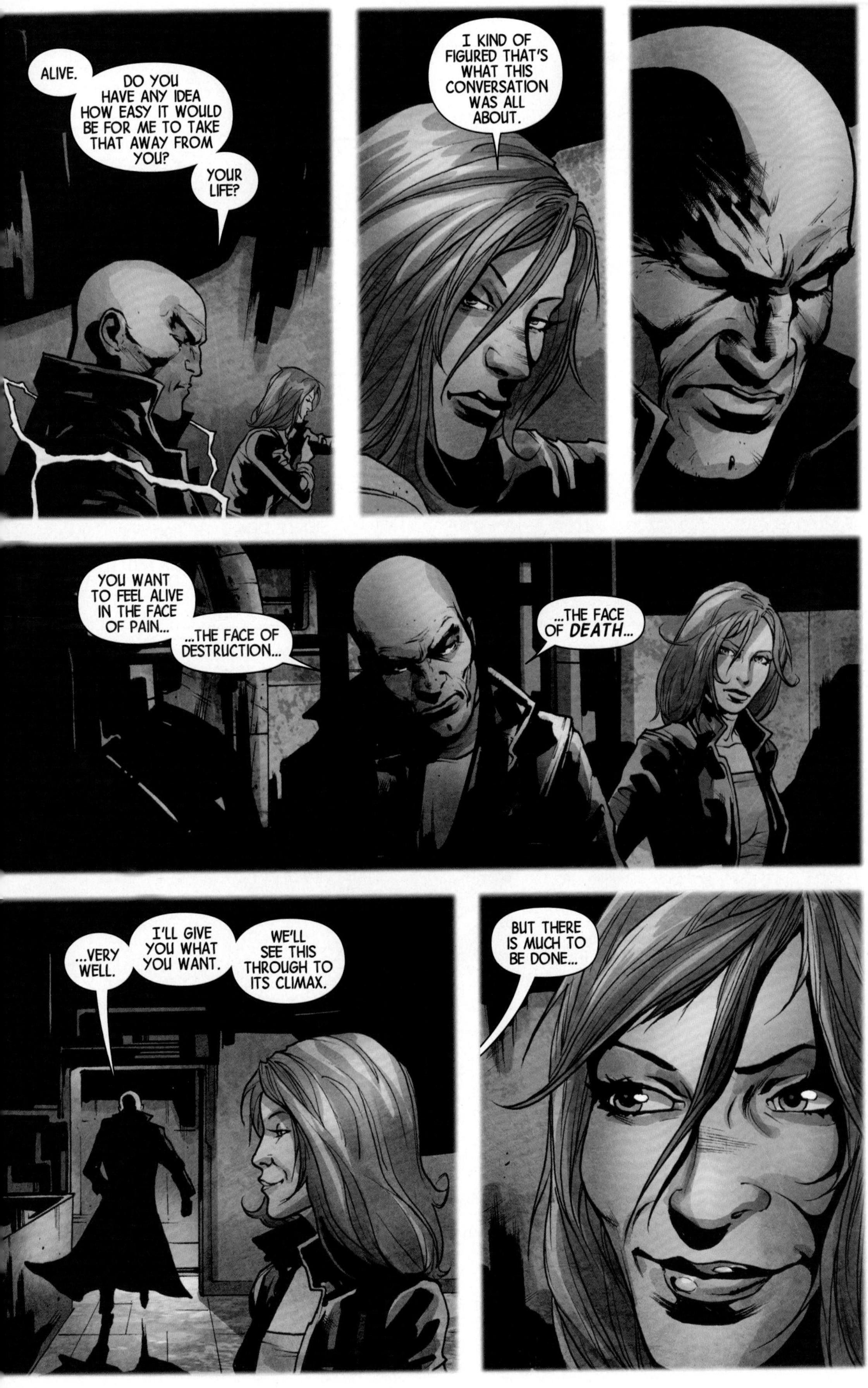
ALIVE.
DO YOU HAVE ANY IDEA HOW EASY IT WOULD BE FOR ME TO TAKE THAT AWAY FROM YOU?
YOUR LIFE?
I KIND OF FIGURED THAT'S WHAT THIS CONVERSATION WAS ALL ABOUT.
YOU WANT TO FEEL ALIVE IN THE FACE OF PAIN...
...THE FACE OF DESTRUCTION...
...THE FACE OF DEATH...
...VERY WELL.
I'LL GIVE YOU WHAT YOU WANT.
WE'LL SEE THIS THROUGH TO ITS CLIMAX.
BUT THERE IS MUCH TO BE DONE...

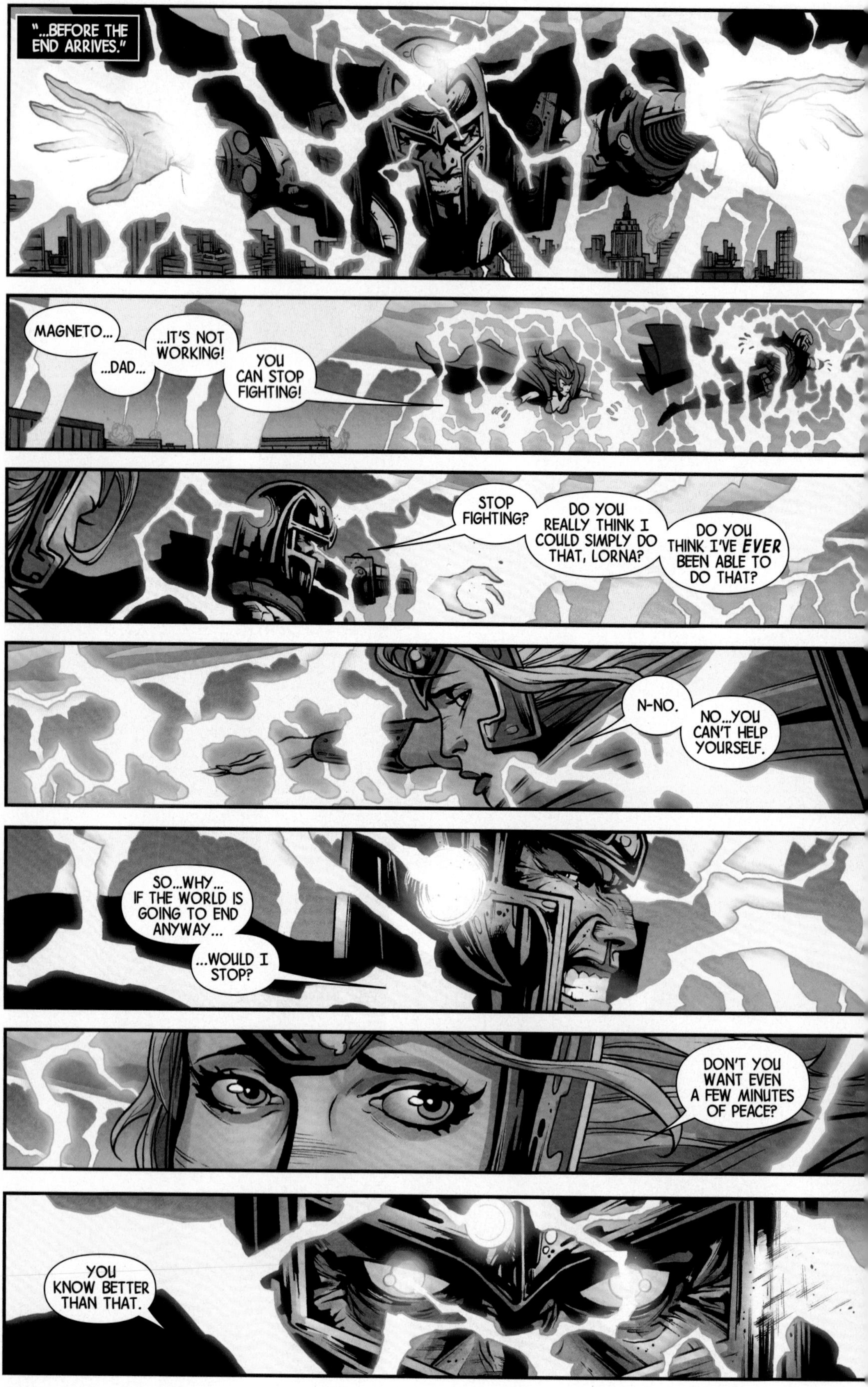
"...BEFORE THE END ARRIVES."
MAGNETO...
...DAD...
...IT'S NOT WORKING!
YOU CAN STOP FIGHTING!
STOP FIGHTING?
DO YOU REALLY THINK I COULD SIMPLY DO THAT, LORNA?
DO YOU THINK I'VE *EVER* BEEN ABLE TO DO THAT?
N-NO.
NO...YOU CAN'T HELP YOURSELF.
SO...WHY... IF THE WORLD IS GOING TO END ANYWAY...
...WOULD I STOP?
DON'T YOU WANT EVEN A FEW MINUTES OF PEACE?
YOU KNOW BETTER THAN THAT.

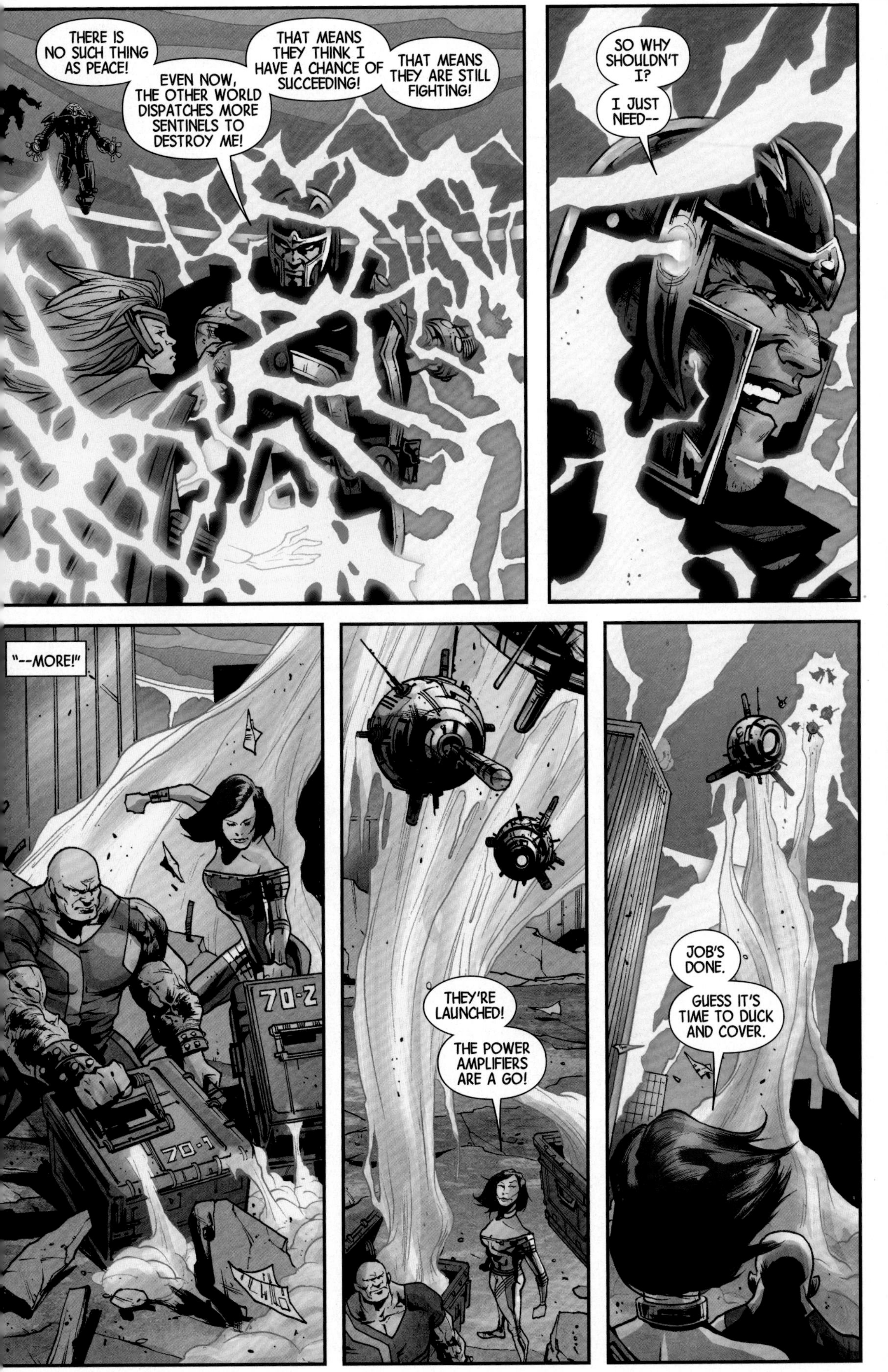
THERE IS NO SUCH THING AS PEACE!
EVEN NOW, THE OTHER WORLD DISPATCHES MORE SENTINELS TO DESTROY ME!
THAT MEANS THEY THINK I HAVE A CHANCE OF SUCCEEDING!
THAT MEANS THEY ARE STILL FIGHTING!
SO WHY SHOULDN'T I?
I JUST NEED--
"--MORE!"
70-2
70-1
THEY'RE LAUNCHED!
THE POWER AMPLIFIERS ARE A GO!
JOB'S DONE.
GUESS IT'S TIME TO DUCK AND COVER.

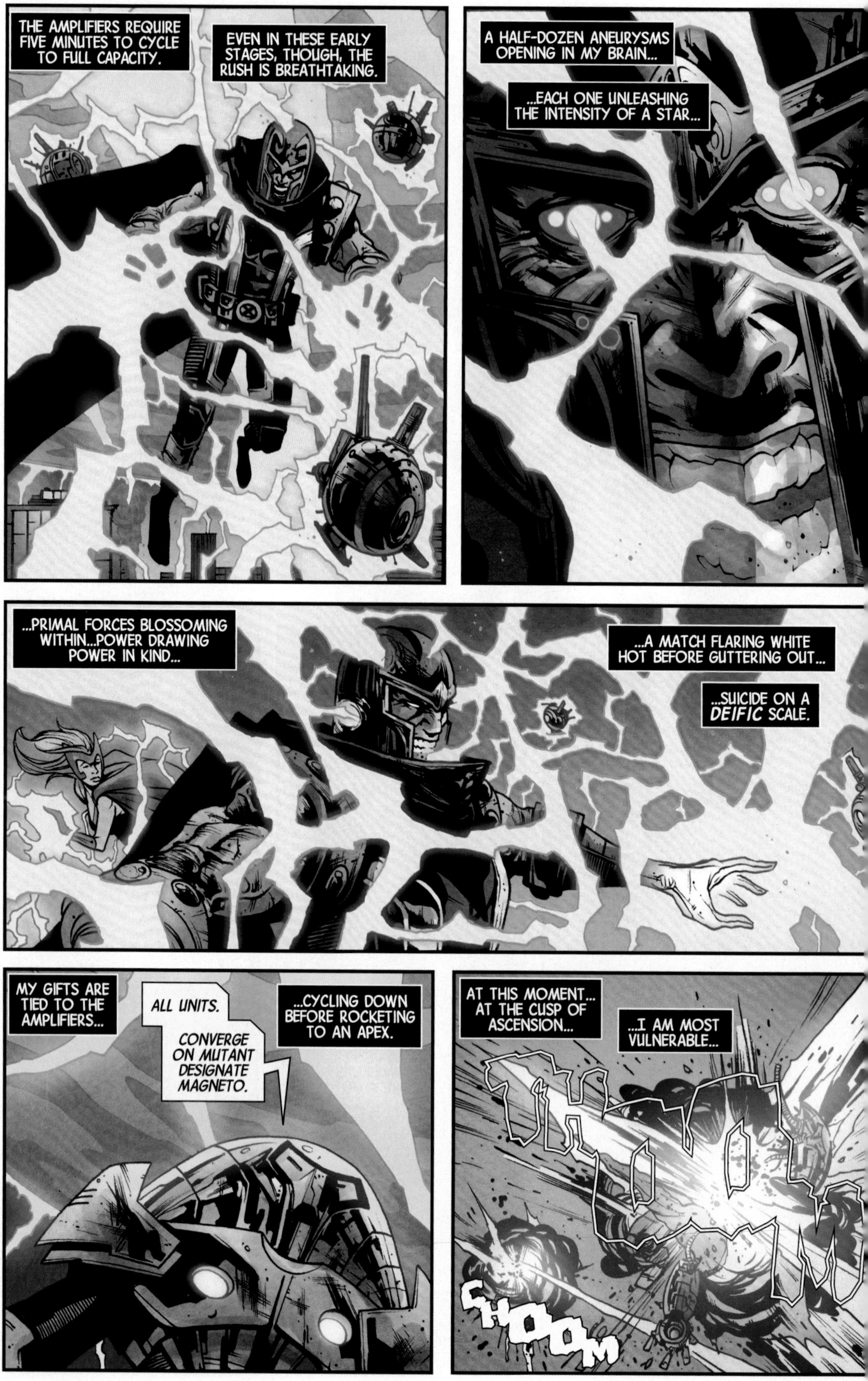
THE AMPLIFIERS REQUIRE FIVE MINUTES TO CYCLE TO FULL CAPACITY.
EVEN IN THESE EARLY STAGES, THOUGH, THE RUSH IS BREATHTAKING.
A HALF-DOZEN ANEURYSMS OPENING IN MY BRAIN...
...EACH ONE UNLEASHING THE INTENSITY OF A STAR...
...PRIMAL FORCES BLOSSOMING WITHIN...POWER DRAWING POWER IN KIND...
...A MATCH FLARING WHITE HOT BEFORE GUTTERING OUT...
...SUICIDE ON A DEIFIC SCALE.
MY GIFTS ARE TIED TO THE AMPLIFIERS...
ALL UNITS.
CONVERGE ON MUTANT DESIGNATE MAGNETO.
...CYCLING DOWN BEFORE ROCKETING TO AN APEX.
AT THIS MOMENT... AT THE CUSP OF ASCENSION...
...I AM MOST VULNERABLE...
CHOOOM

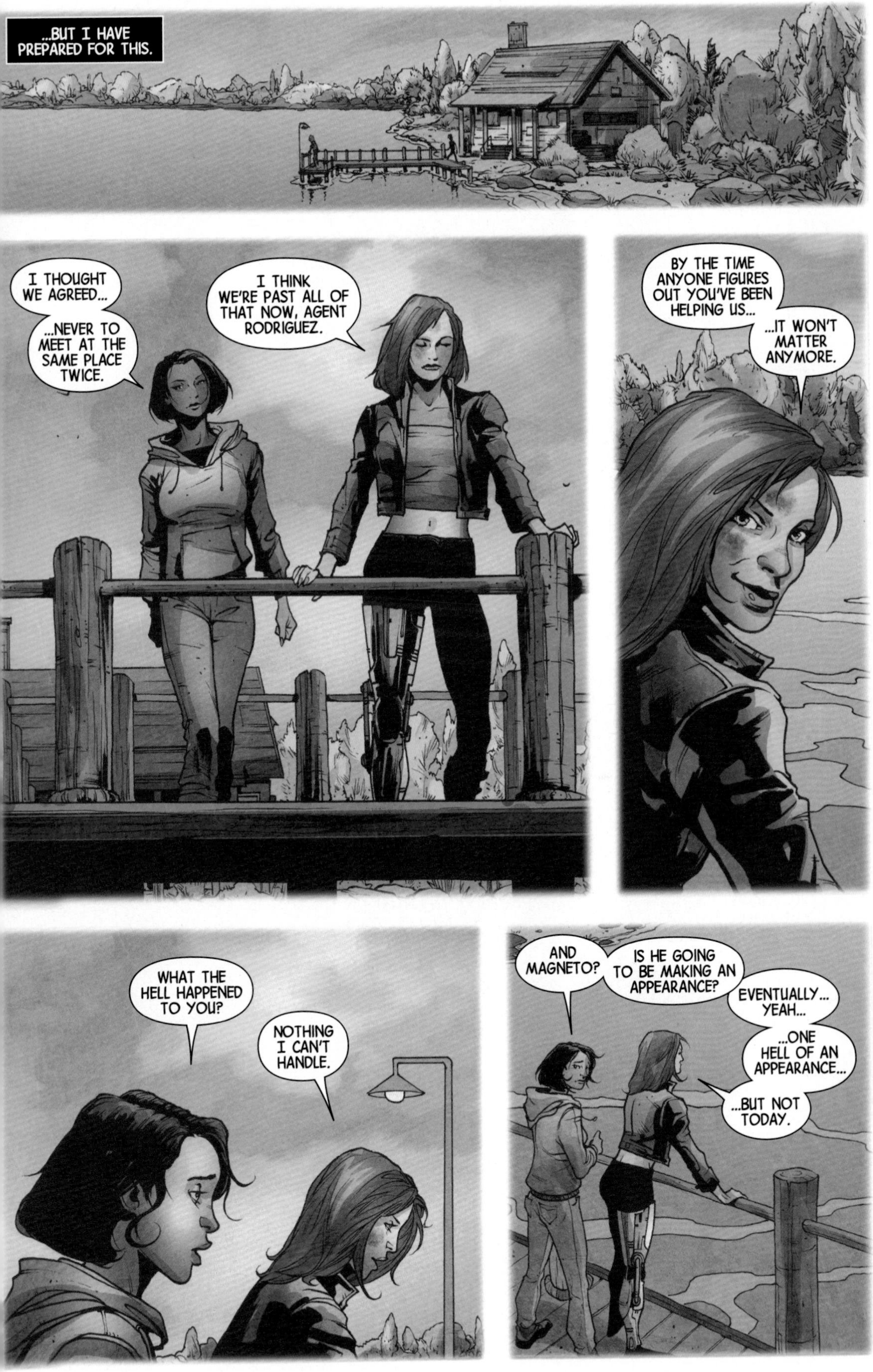
...BUT I HAVE PREPARED FOR THIS.
I THOUGHT WE AGREED...
...NEVER TO MEET AT THE SAME PLACE TWICE.
I THINK WE'RE PAST ALL OF THAT NOW, AGENT RODRIGUEZ.
BY THE TIME ANYONE FIGURES OUT YOU'VE BEEN HELPING US...
...IT WON'T MATTER ANYMORE.
WHAT THE HELL HAPPENED TO YOU?
NOTHING I CAN'T HANDLE.
AND MAGNETO?
IS HE GOING TO BE MAKING AN APPEARANCE?
EVENTUALLY... YEAH...
...ONE HELL OF AN APPEARANCE...
...BUT NOT TODAY.

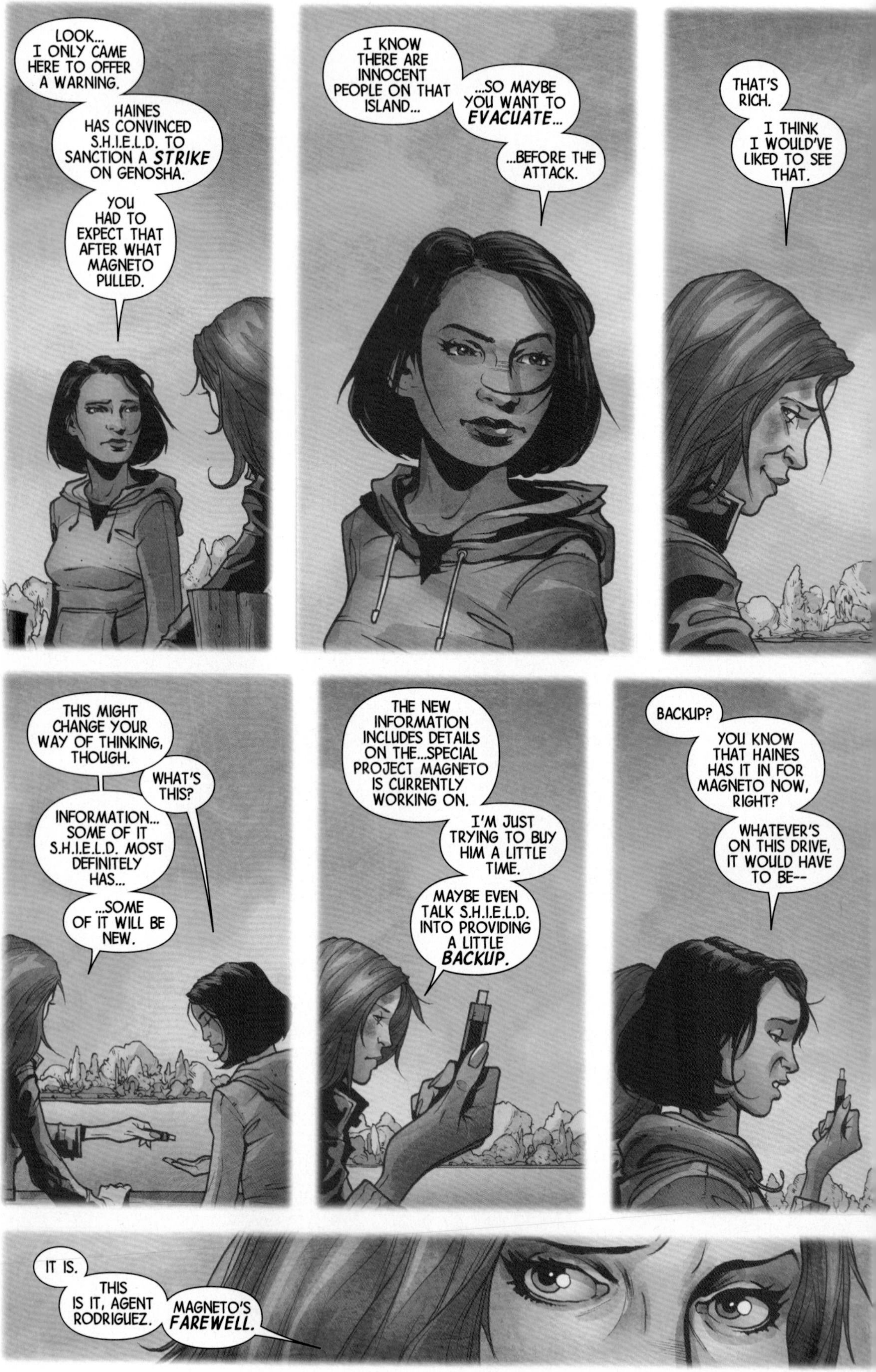

LOOK... I ONLY CAME HERE TO OFFER A WARNING.
HAINES HAS CONVINCED S.H.I.E.L.D. TO SANCTION A STRIKE ON GENOSHA.
YOU HAD TO EXPECT THAT AFTER WHAT MAGNETO PULLED.
I KNOW THERE ARE INNOCENT PEOPLE ON THAT ISLAND...
...SO MAYBE YOU WANT TO EVACUATE...
...BEFORE THE ATTACK.
THAT'S RICH.
I THINK I WOULD'VE LIKED TO SEE THAT.
THIS MIGHT CHANGE YOUR WAY OF THINKING, THOUGH.
WHAT'S THIS?
INFORMATION... SOME OF IT S.H.I.E.L.D. MOST DEFINITELY HAS...
...SOME OF IT WILL BE NEW.
THE NEW INFORMATION INCLUDES DETAILS ON THE...SPECIAL PROJECT MAGNETO IS CURRENTLY WORKING ON.
I'M JUST TRYING TO BUY HIM A LITTLE TIME.
MAYBE EVEN TALK S.H.I.E.L.D. INTO PROVIDING A LITTLE BACKUP.
BACKUP?
YOU KNOW THAT HAINES HAS IT IN FOR MAGNETO NOW, RIGHT?
WHATEVER'S ON THIS DRIVE, IT WOULD HAVE TO BE--
IT IS.
THIS IS IT, AGENT RODRIGUEZ.
MAGNETO'S FAREWELL.

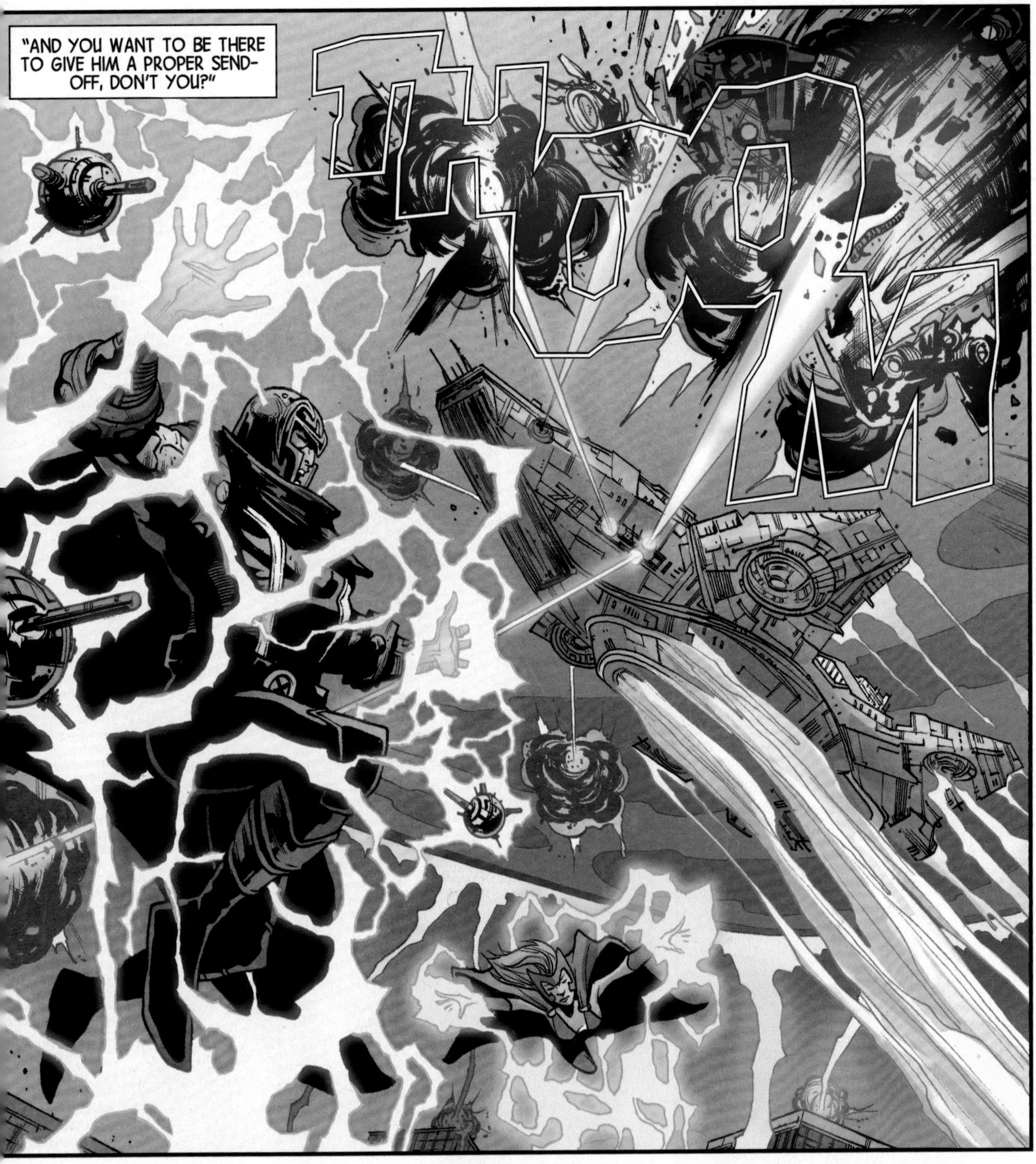
"AND YOU WANT TO BE THERE TO GIVE HIM A PROPER SEND-OFF, DON'T YOU?"
THOOOM

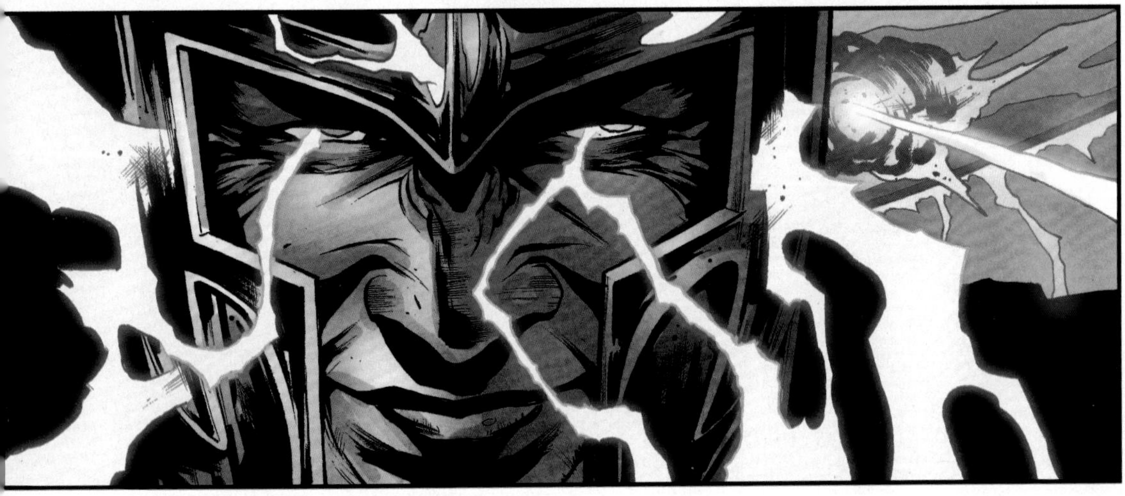

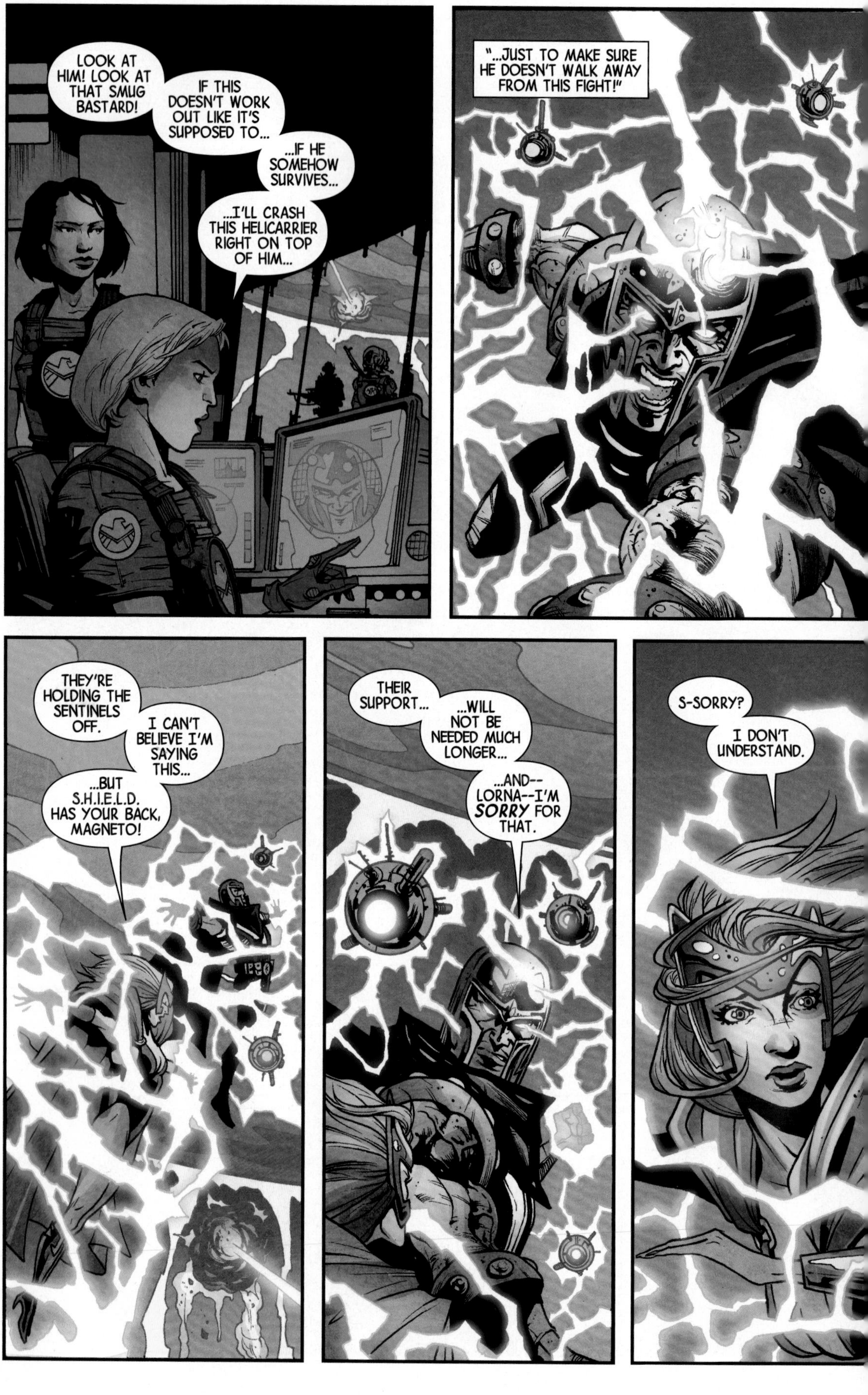
LOOK AT HIM! LOOK AT THAT SMUG BASTARD!
IF THIS DOESN'T WORK OUT LIKE IT'S SUPPOSED TO...
...IF HE SOMEHOW SURVIVES...
...I'LL CRASH THIS HELICARRIER RIGHT ON TOP OF HIM...
"...JUST TO MAKE SURE HE DOESN'T WALK AWAY FROM THIS FIGHT!"
THEY'RE HOLDING THE SENTINELS OFF.
I CAN'T BELIEVE I'M SAYING THIS...
...BUT S.H.I.E.L.D. HAS YOUR BACK, MAGNETO!
THEIR SUPPORT...
...WILL NOT BE NEEDED MUCH LONGER...
...AND--LORNA--I'M SORRY FOR THAT.
S-SORRY?
I DON'T UNDERSTAND.

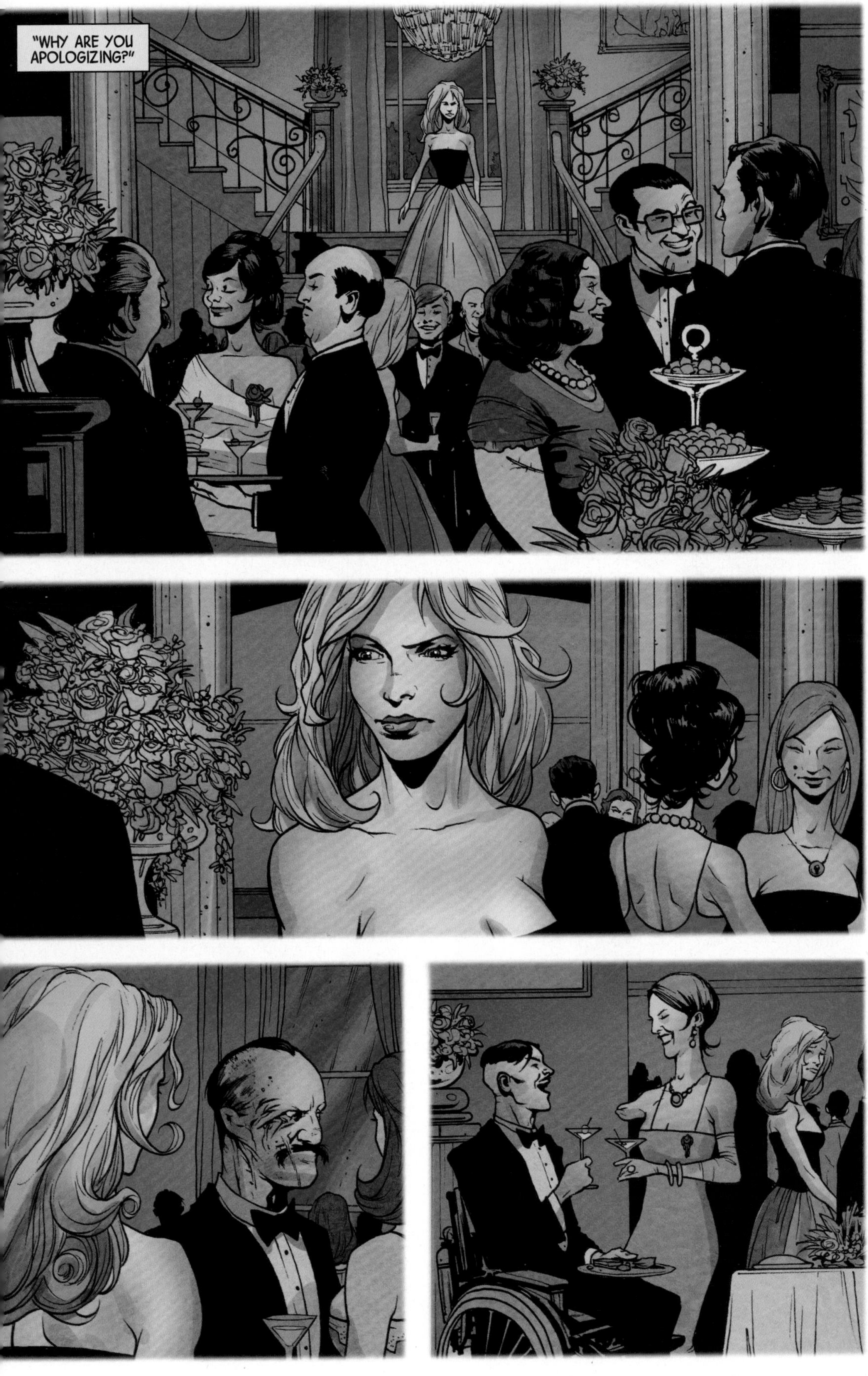
"WHY ARE YOU APOLOGIZING?"

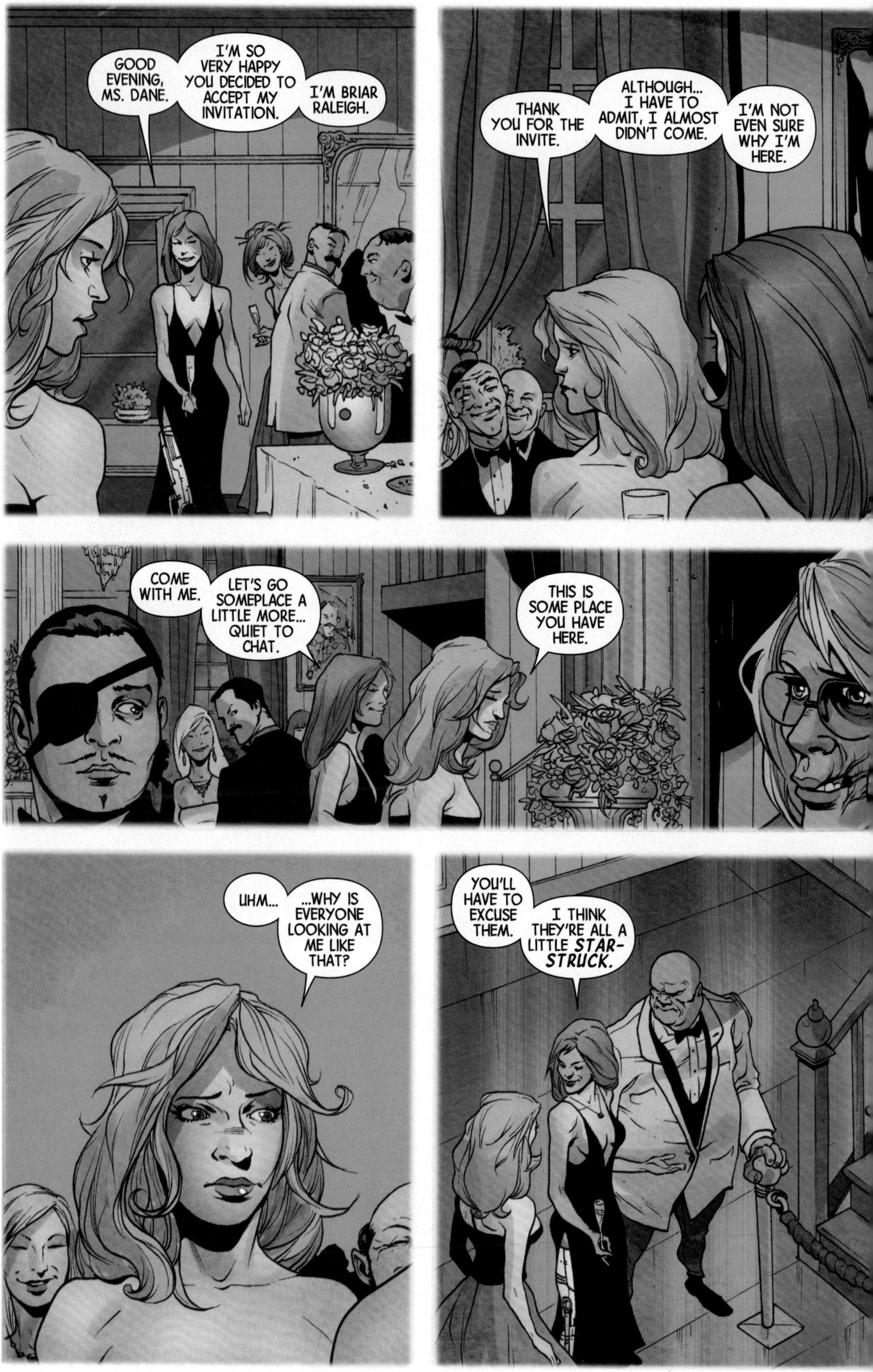
GOOD EVENING, MS. DANE.
I'M SO VERY HAPPY YOU DECIDED TO ACCEPT MY INVITATION.
I'M BRIAR RALEIGH.
THANK YOU FOR THE INVITE.
ALTHOUGH... I HAVE TO ADMIT, I ALMOST DIDN'T COME.
I'M NOT EVEN SURE WHY I'M HERE.
COME WITH ME.
LET'S GO SOMEPLACE A LITTLE MORE... QUIET TO CHAT.
THIS IS SOME PLACE YOU HAVE HERE.
UHM...
...WHY IS EVERYONE LOOKING AT ME LIKE THAT?
YOU'LL HAVE TO EXCUSE THEM.
I THINK THEY'RE ALL A LITTLE STAR-STRUCK.

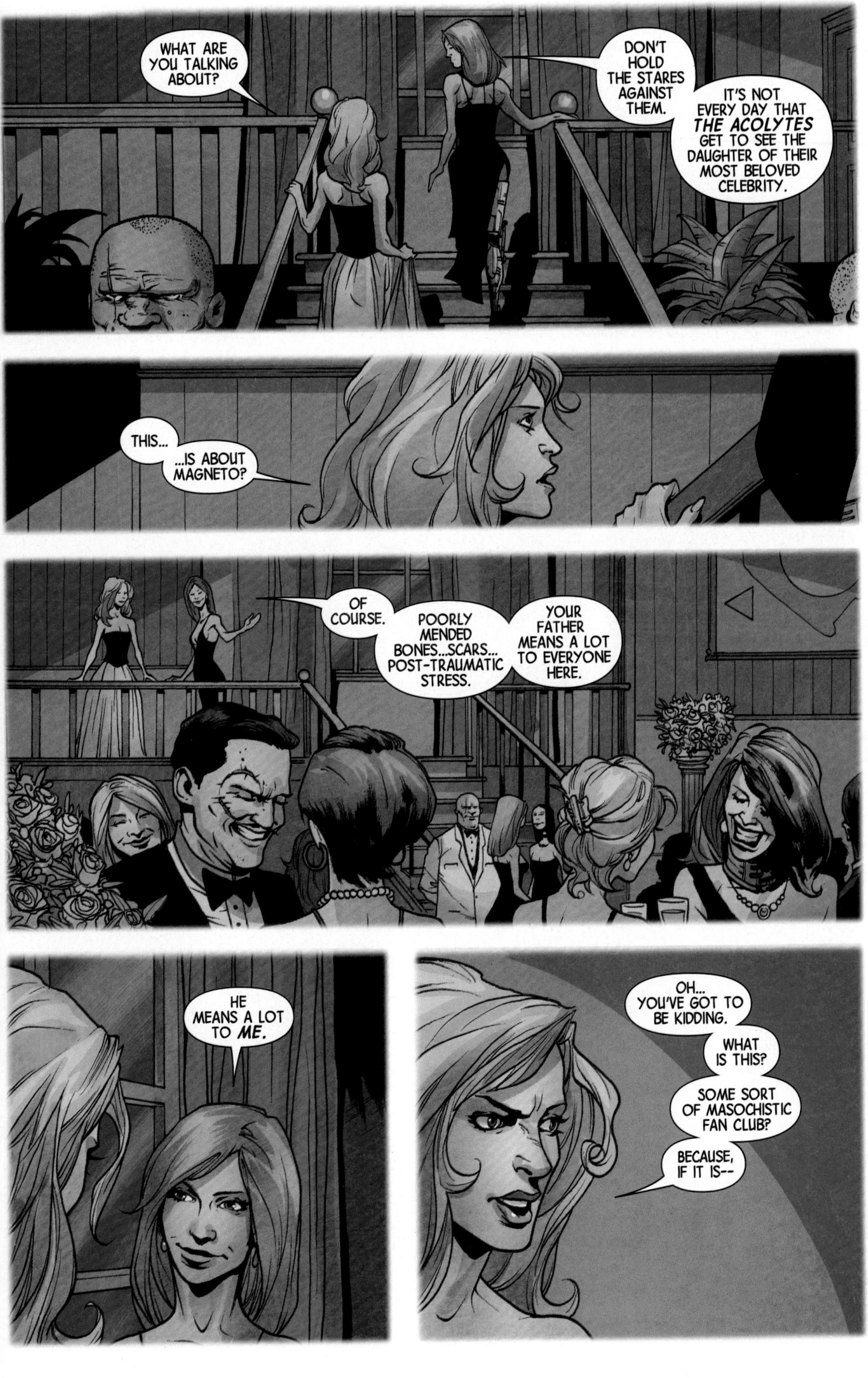
WHAT ARE YOU TALKING ABOUT?
DON'T HOLD THE STARES AGAINST THEM.
IT'S NOT EVERY DAY THAT THE ACOLYTES GET TO SEE THE DAUGHTER OF THEIR MOST BELOVED CELEBRITY.
THIS...
...IS ABOUT MAGNETO?
OF COURSE.
POORLY MENDED BONES...SCARS... POST-TRAUMATIC STRESS.
YOUR FATHER MEANS A LOT TO EVERYONE HERE.
HE MEANS A LOT TO ME.
OH... YOU'VE GOT TO BE KIDDING.
WHAT IS THIS?
SOME SORT OF MASOCHISTIC FAN CLUB?
BECAUSE, IF IT IS--

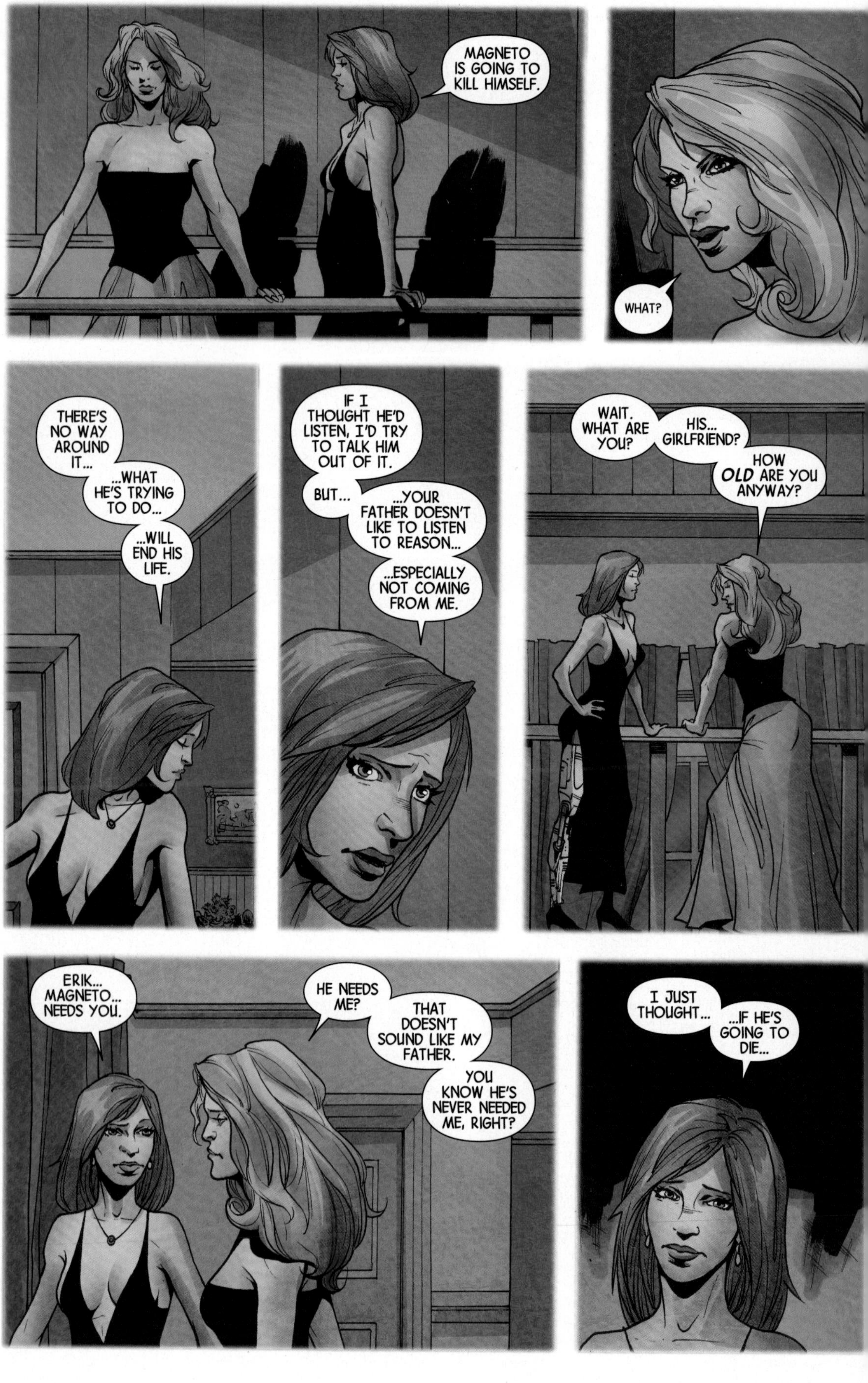

MAGNETO IS GOING TO KILL HIMSELF.
WHAT?
THERE'S NO WAY AROUND IT...
...WHAT HE'S TRYING TO DO...
...WILL END HIS LIFE.
IF I THOUGHT HE'D LISTEN, I'D TRY TO TALK HIM OUT OF IT.
BUT...
...YOUR FATHER DOESN'T LIKE TO LISTEN TO REASON...
...ESPECIALLY NOT COMING FROM ME.
WAIT. WHAT ARE YOU?
HIS... GIRLFRIEND?
HOW OLD ARE YOU ANYWAY?
ERIK... MAGNETO... NEEDS YOU.
HE NEEDS ME?
THAT DOESN'T SOUND LIKE MY FATHER.
YOU KNOW HE'S NEVER NEEDED ME, RIGHT?
I JUST THOUGHT...
...IF HE'S GOING TO DIE...

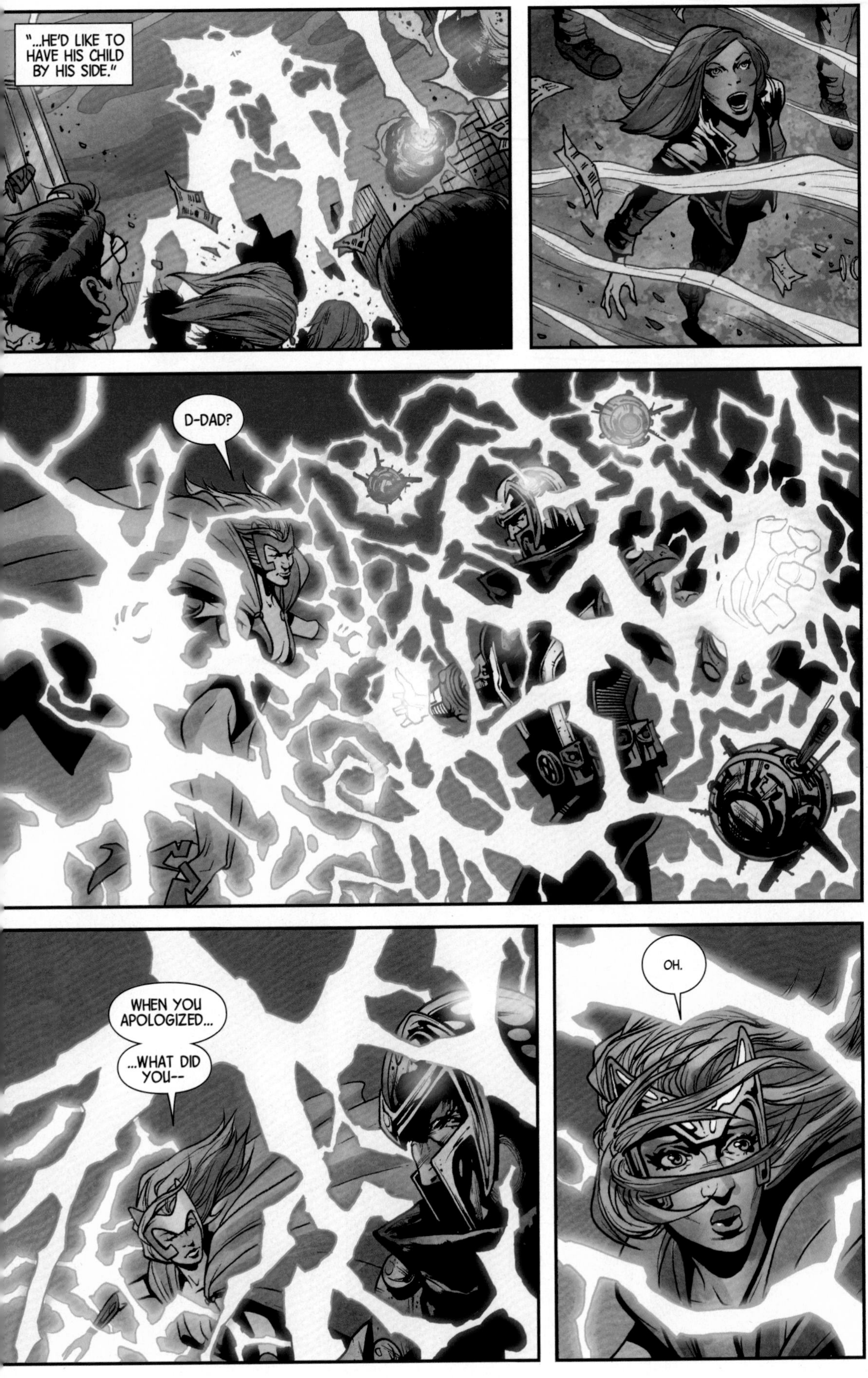
"...HE'D LIKE TO HAVE HIS CHILD BY HIS SIDE."
D-DAD?
WHEN YOU APOLOGIZED...
...WHAT DID YOU--
OH.

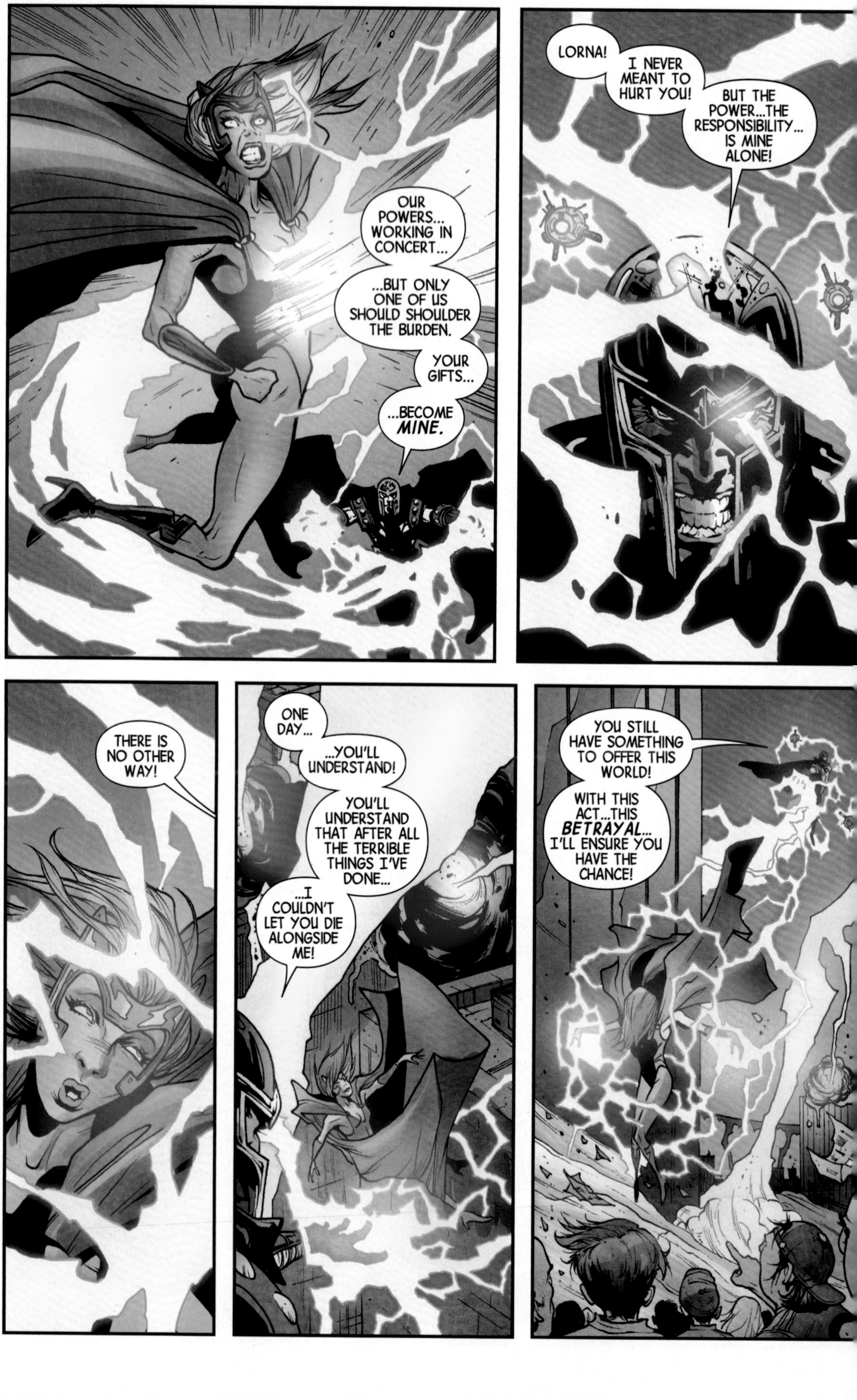

OUR POWERS... WORKING IN CONCERT...
...BUT ONLY ONE OF US SHOULD SHOULDER THE BURDEN.
YOUR GIFTS...
...BECOME *MINE.*
LORNA!
I NEVER MEANT TO HURT YOU!
BUT THE POWER...THE RESPONSIBILITY... IS MINE ALONE!
THERE IS NO OTHER WAY!
ONE DAY...
...YOU'LL UNDERSTAND!
YOU'LL UNDERSTAND THAT AFTER ALL THE TERRIBLE THINGS I'VE DONE...
...I COULDN'T LET YOU DIE ALONGSIDE ME!
YOU STILL HAVE SOMETHING TO OFFER THIS WORLD!
WITH THIS ACT...THIS *BETRAYAL*... I'LL ENSURE YOU HAVE THE CHANCE!

WHAT ROLE IS LEFT FOR ME?
FATHER?
PUPPET?
REFLECTION OF ANOTHER LIFE?
NOT EVEN SAVIOR.
NOT DESTROYER.
ALL GUISES ARE CAST ASIDE... REPLACED BY RAW POWER...
...ALL MAGNETIC FORCES...
...ALL THE BIOELECTRIC ENERGIES OF THE EARTH...
...COURSING THROUGH THIS VESSEL.
THIS IS MY FINAL ACT.
THIS IS HOW THE WORLD ENDS.
I HAVE NO CHOICE BUT TO BEAR WITNESS.
I WILL NOT FLINCH.

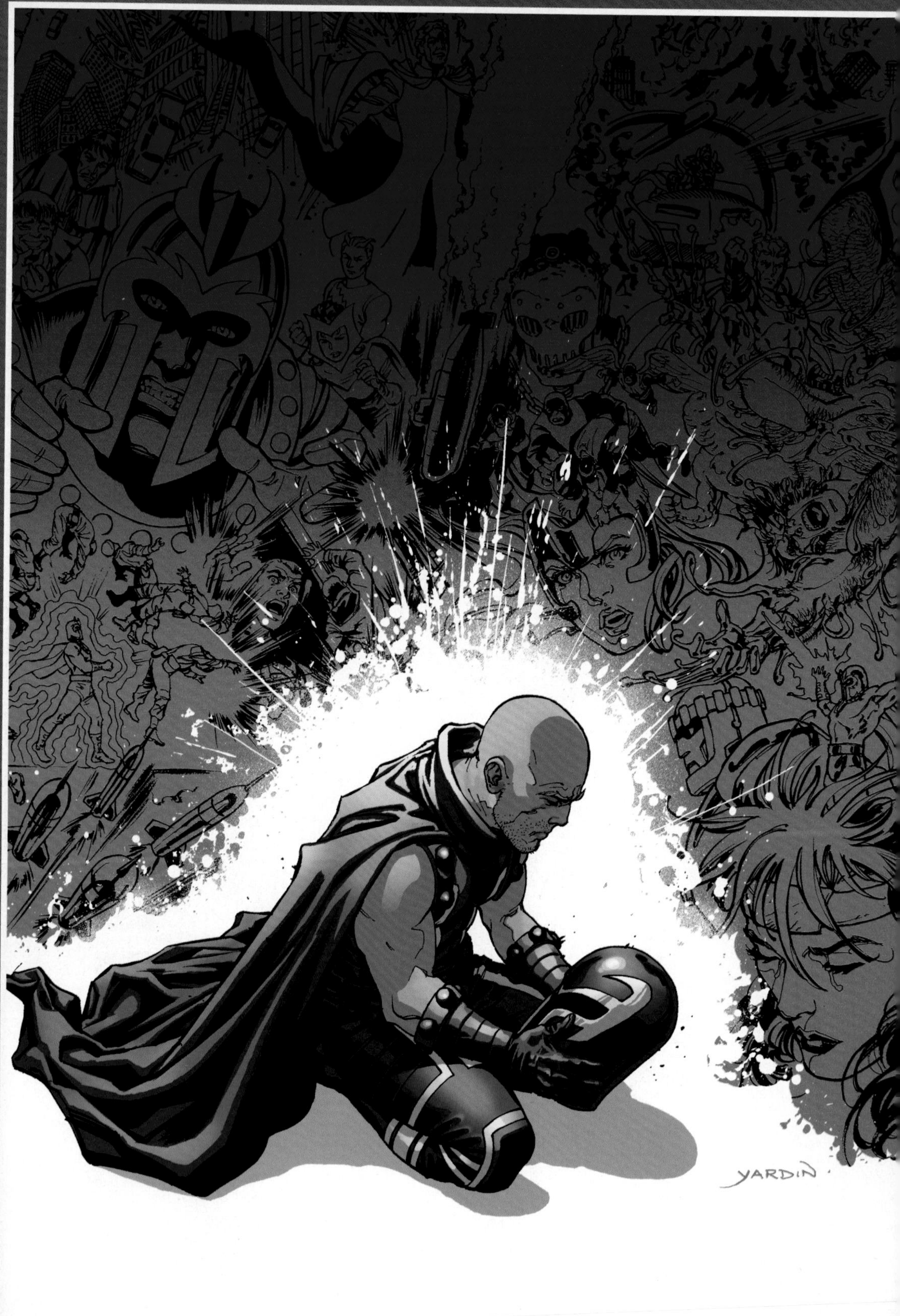
YARDIN

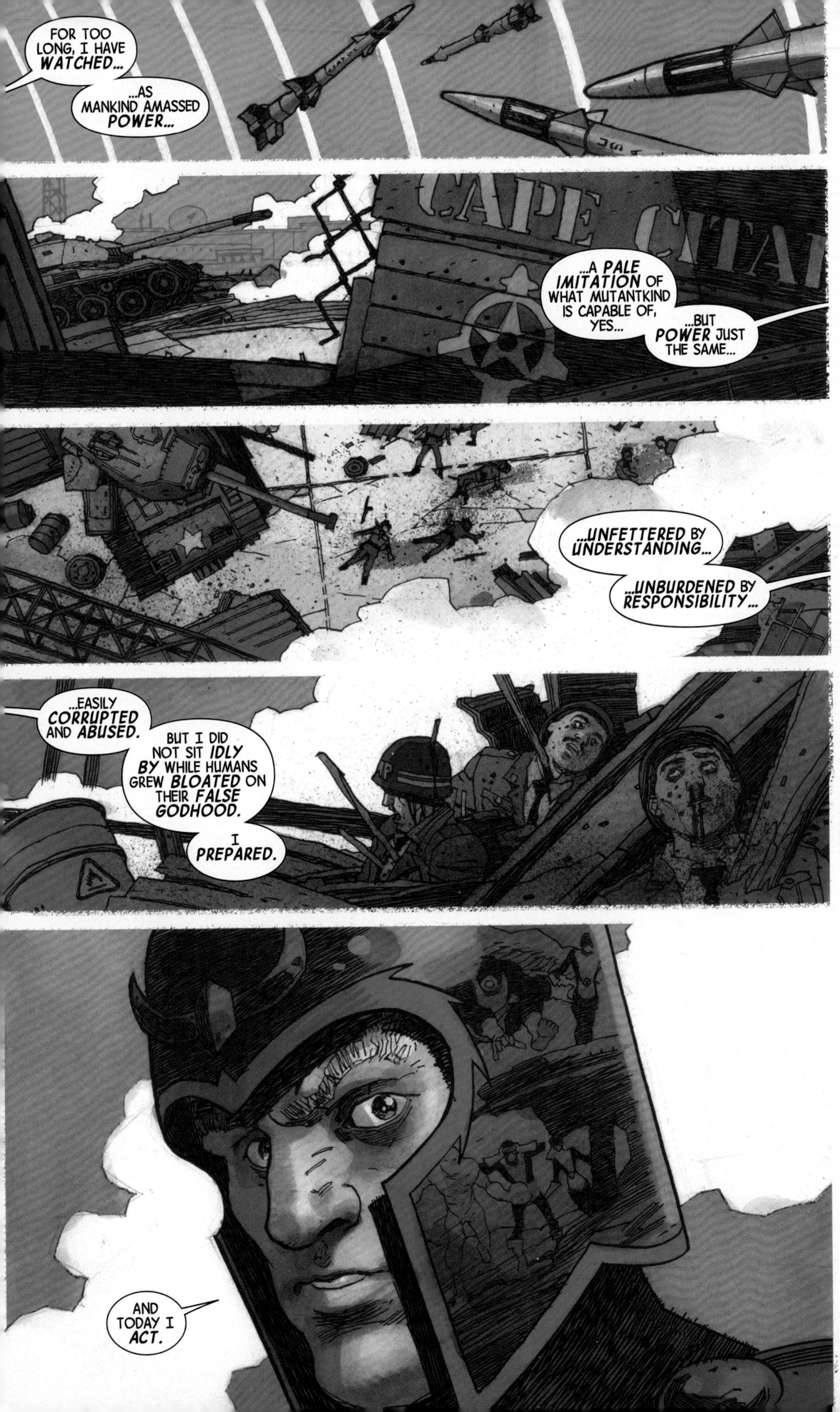
FOR TOO LONG, I HAVE WATCHED...
...AS MANKIND AMASSED POWER...
CAPE
...A PALE IMITATION OF WHAT MUTANTKIND IS CAPABLE OF, YES...
...BUT POWER JUST THE SAME...
...UNFETTERED BY UNDERSTANDING...
...UNBURDENED BY RESPONSIBILITY...
...EASILY CORRUPTED AND ABUSED.
BUT I DID NOT SIT IDLY BY WHILE HUMANS GREW BLOATED ON THEIR FALSE GODHOOD.
I PREPARED.
AND TODAY I ACT.

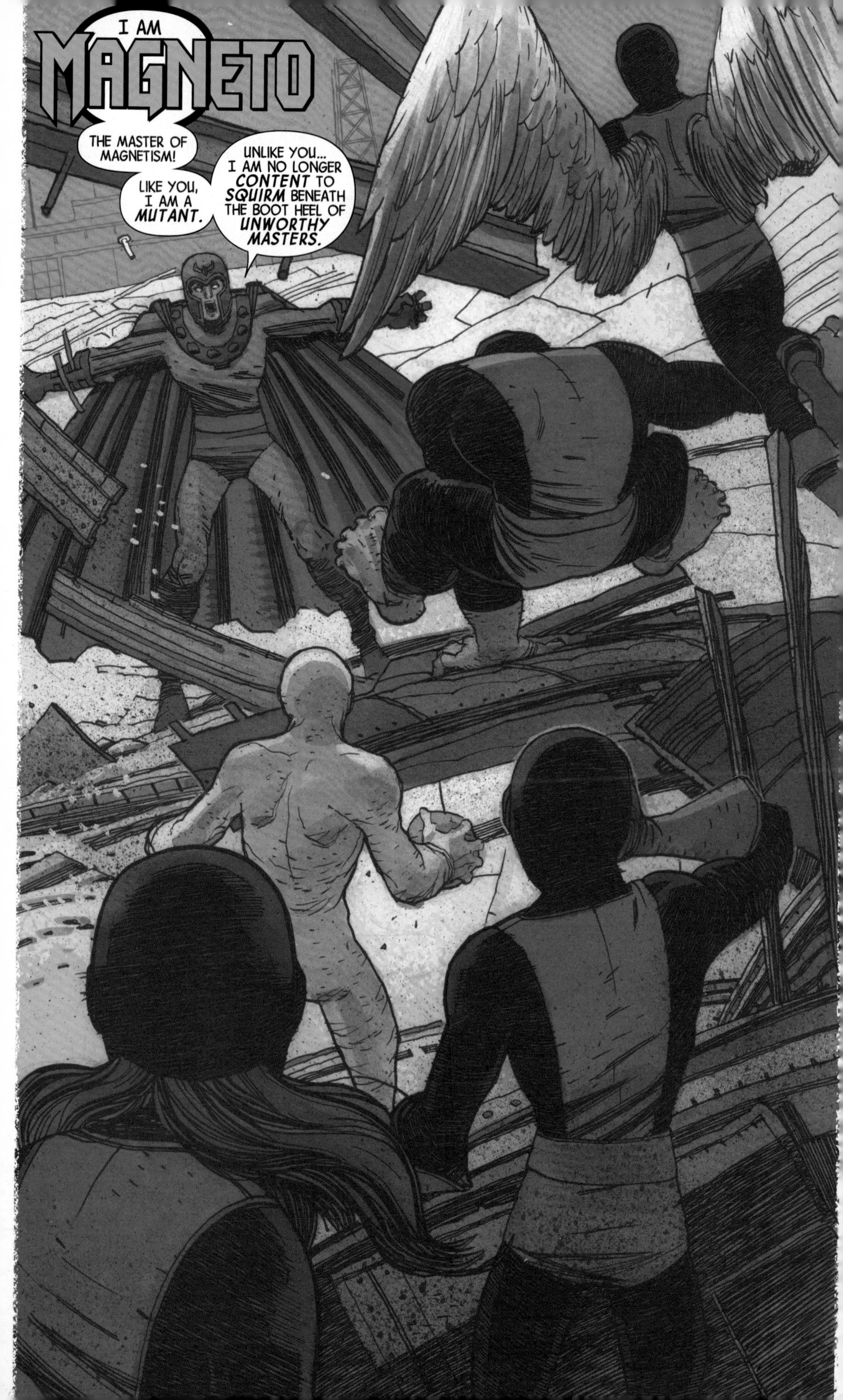
I AM MAGNETO
THE MASTER OF MAGNETISM!
LIKE YOU, I AM A MUTANT.
UNLIKE YOU... I AM NO LONGER CONTENT TO SQUIRM BENEATH THE BOOT HEEL OF UNWORTHY MASTERS.

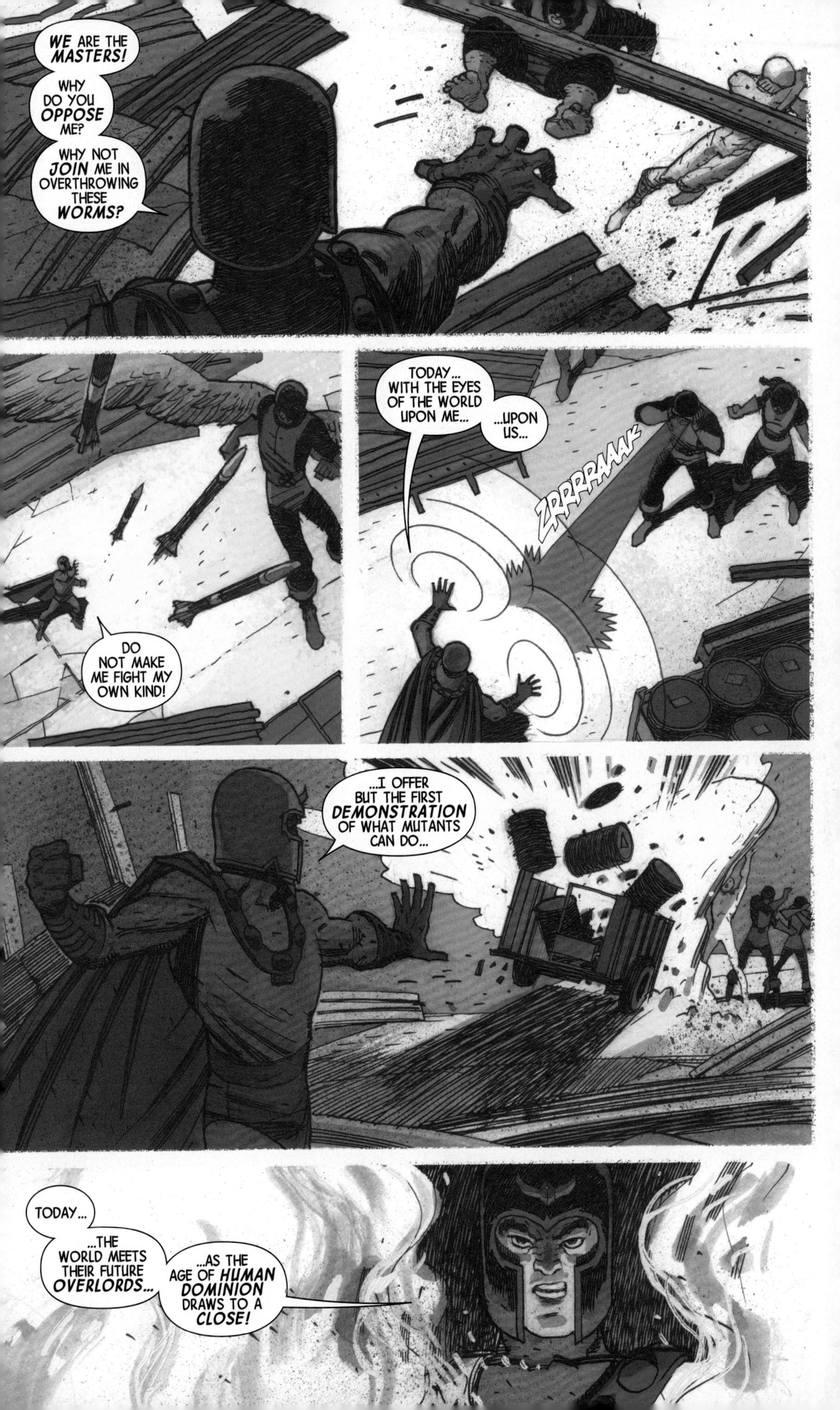

WE ARE THE MASTERS!
WHY DO YOU OPPOSE ME?
WHY NOT JOIN ME IN OVERTHROWING THESE WORMS?
DO NOT MAKE ME FIGHT MY OWN KIND!
TODAY... WITH THE EYES OF THE WORLD UPON ME...
...UPON US...
ZRRRRAAAK
...I OFFER BUT THE FIRST DEMONSTRATION OF WHAT MUTANTS CAN DO...
TODAY...
...THE WORLD MEETS THEIR FUTURE OVERLORDS...
...AS THE AGE OF HUMAN DOMINION DRAWS TO A CLOSE!

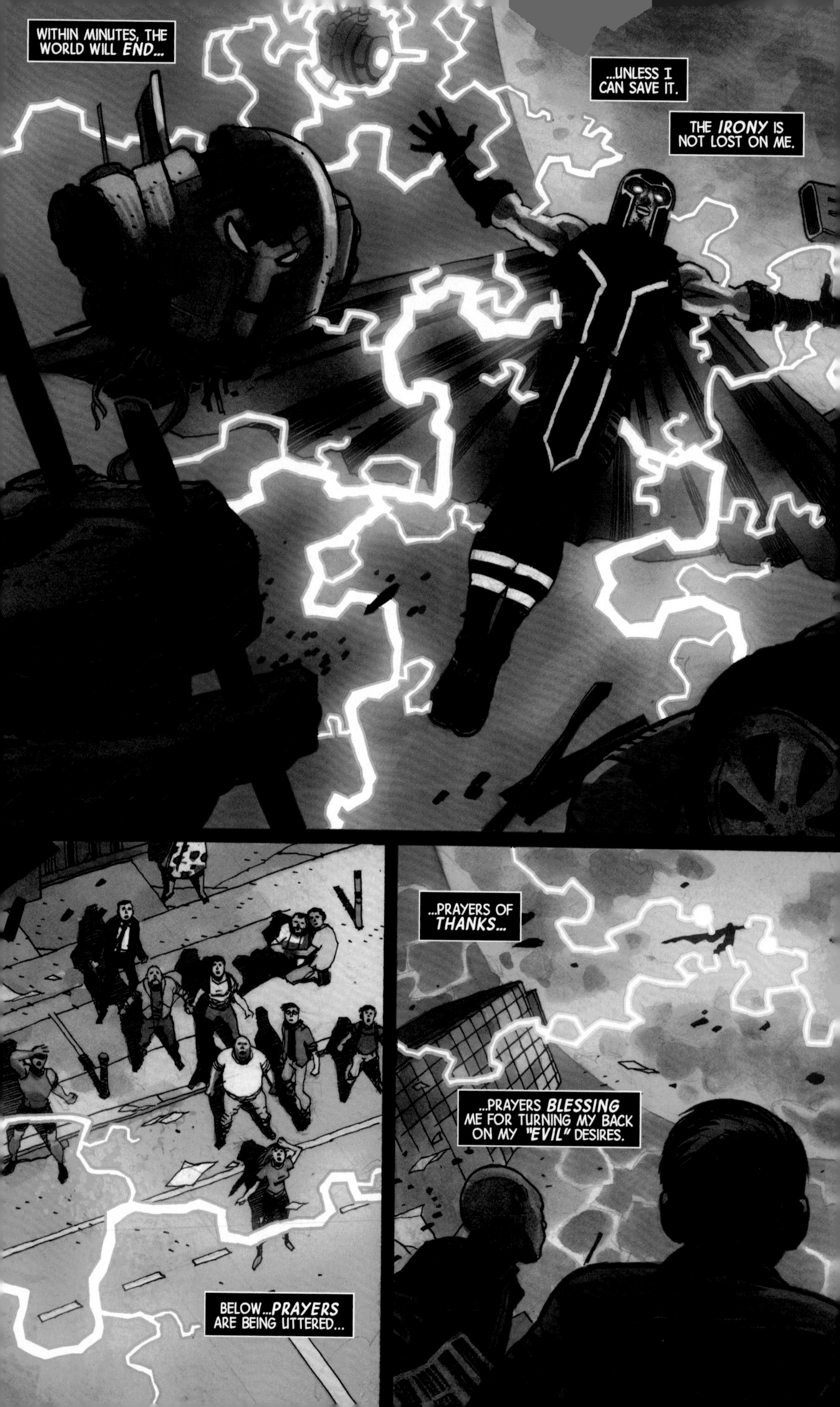
WITHIN MINUTES, THE WORLD WILL END...
...UNLESS I CAN SAVE IT.
THE IRONY IS NOT LOST ON ME.
BELOW...PRAYERS ARE BEING UTTERED...
...PRAYERS OF THANKS...
...PRAYERS BLESSING ME FOR TURNING MY BACK ON MY "EVIL" DESIRES.

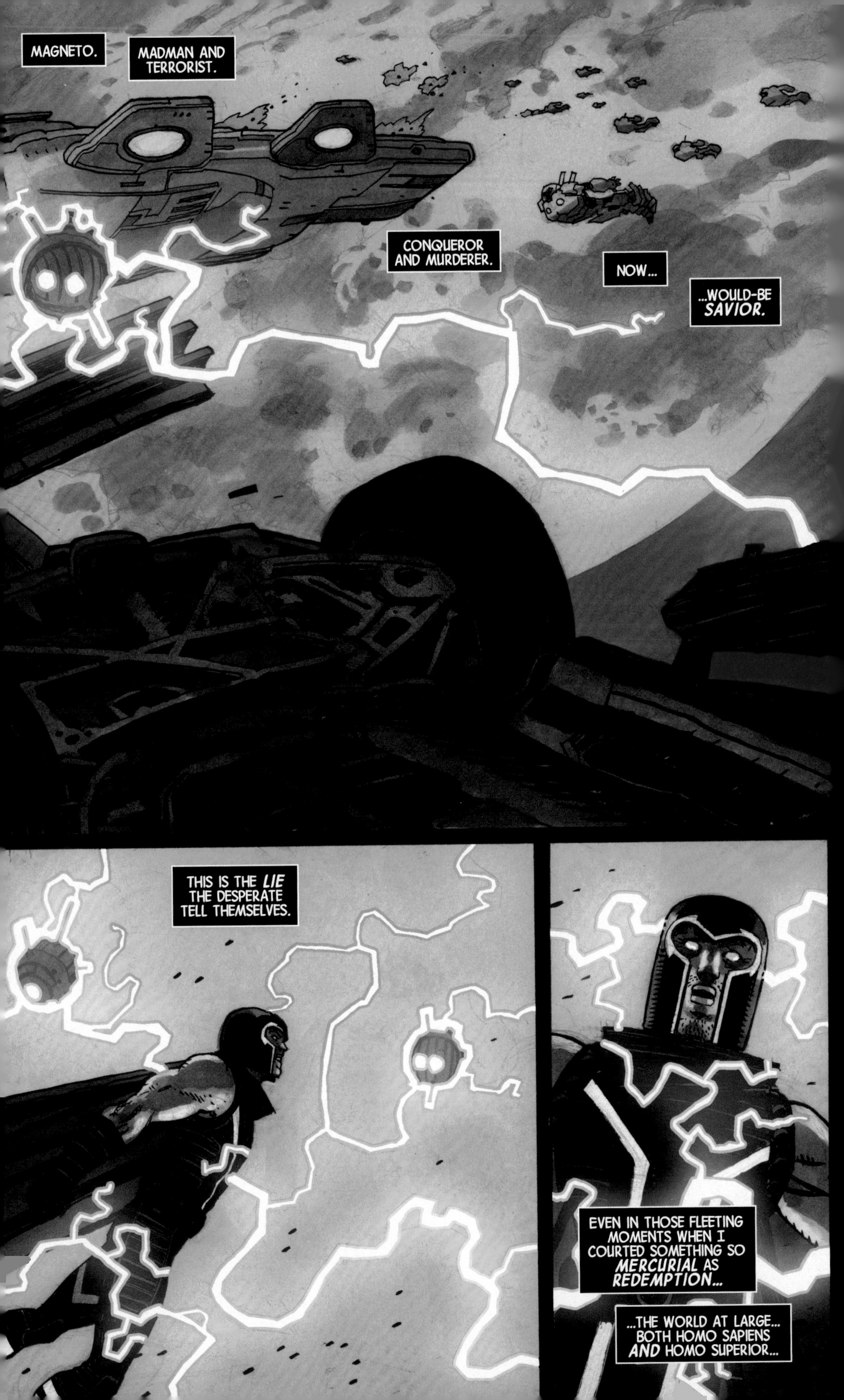
MAGNETO.
MADMAN AND TERRORIST.
CONQUEROR AND MURDERER.
NOW...
...WOULD-BE *SAVIOR.*
THIS IS THE *LIE* THE DESPERATE TELL THEMSELVES.
EVEN IN THOSE FLEETING MOMENTS WHEN I COURTED SOMETHING SO *MERCURIAL* AS *REDEMPTION...*
...THE WORLD AT LARGE... BOTH HOMO SAPIENS *AND* HOMO SUPERIOR...

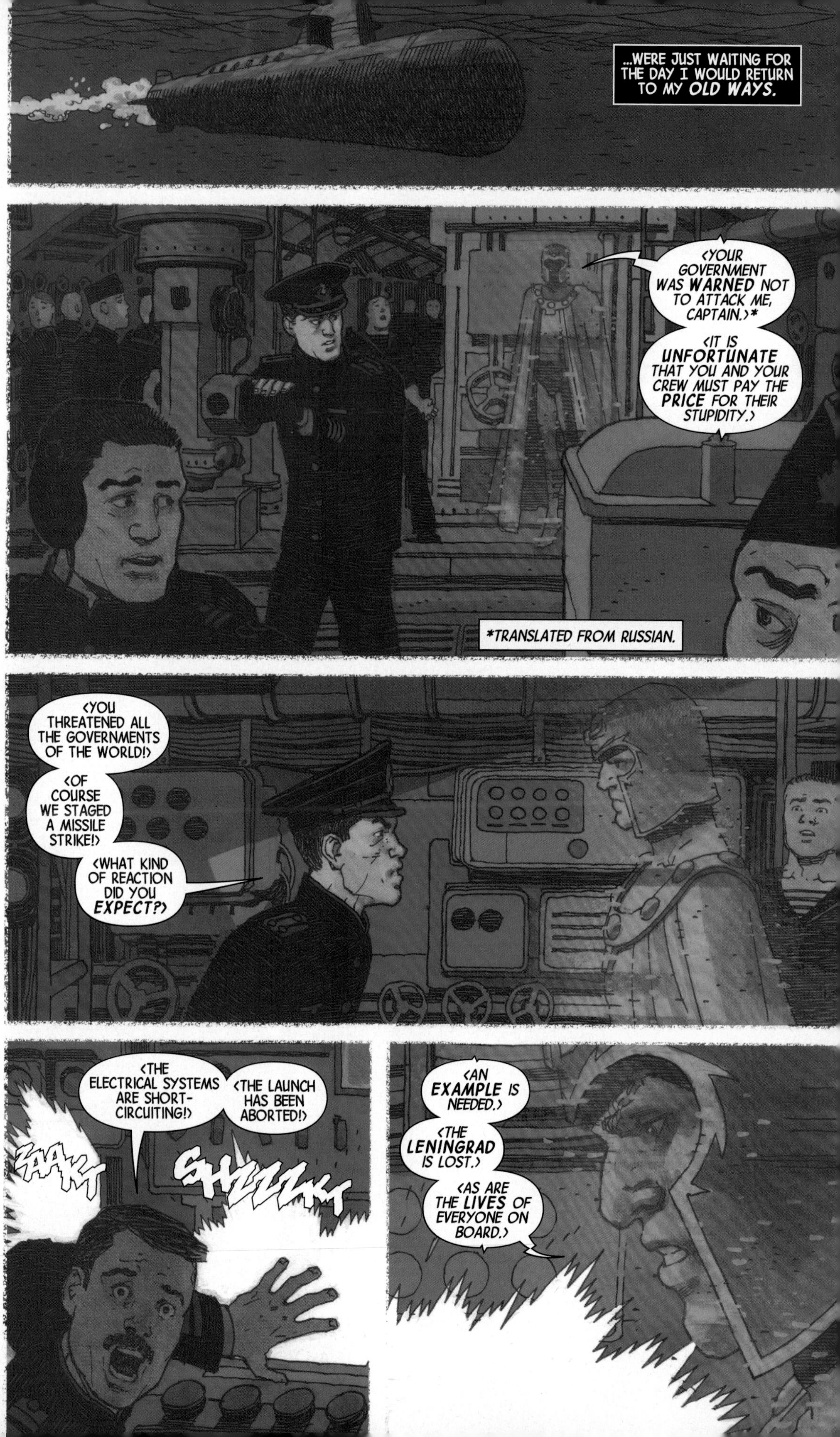

...WERE JUST WAITING FOR THE DAY I WOULD RETURN TO MY OLD WAYS.
<YOUR GOVERNMENT WAS WARNED NOT TO ATTACK ME, CAPTAIN.>*
<IT IS UNFORTUNATE THAT YOU AND YOUR CREW MUST PAY THE PRICE FOR THEIR STUPIDITY.>
*TRANSLATED FROM RUSSIAN.
<YOU THREATENED ALL THE GOVERNMENTS OF THE WORLD!>
<OF COURSE WE STAGED A MISSILE STRIKE!>
<WHAT KIND OF REACTION DID YOU EXPECT?>
<THE ELECTRICAL SYSTEMS ARE SHORT-CIRCUITING!>
<THE LAUNCH HAS BEEN ABORTED!>
ZAAKT
SHZZZKT
<AN EXAMPLE IS NEEDED.>
<THE LENINGRAD IS LOST.>
<AS ARE THE LIVES OF EVERYONE ON BOARD.>

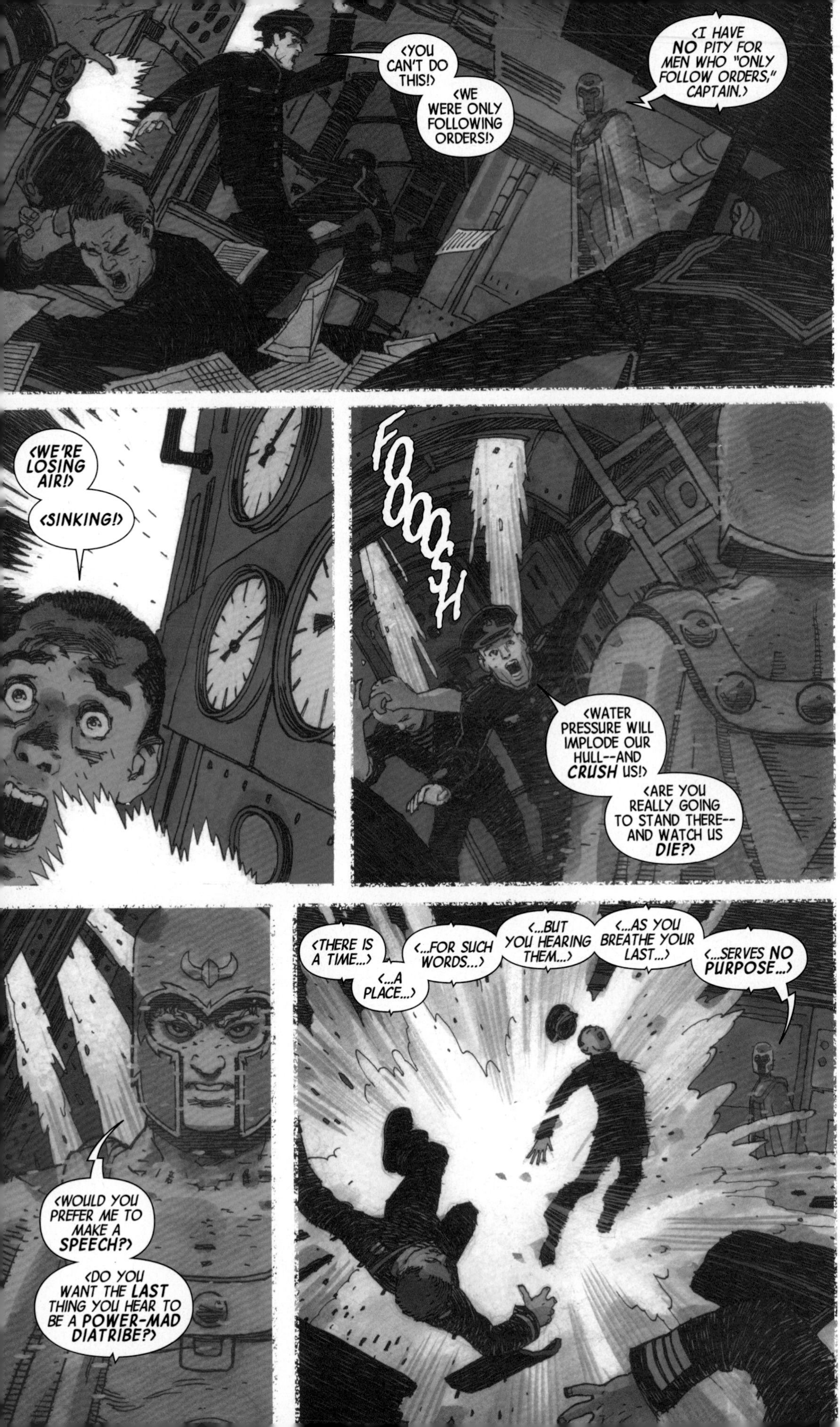
<YOU CAN'T DO THIS!>
<WE WERE ONLY FOLLOWING ORDERS!>
<I HAVE NO PITY FOR MEN WHO "ONLY FOLLOW ORDERS," CAPTAIN.>
<WE'RE LOSING AIR!>
<SINKING!>
FOOOSH
<WATER PRESSURE WILL IMPLODE OUR HULL--AND CRUSH US!>
<ARE YOU REALLY GOING TO STAND THERE--AND WATCH US DIE?>
<WOULD YOU PREFER ME TO MAKE A SPEECH?>
<DO YOU WANT THE LAST THING YOU HEAR TO BE A POWER-MAD DIATRIBE?>
<THERE IS A TIME...>
<...A PLACE...>
<...FOR SUCH WORDS...>
<...BUT YOU HEARING THEM...>
<...AS YOU BREATHE YOUR LAST...>
<...SERVES NO PURPOSE...>

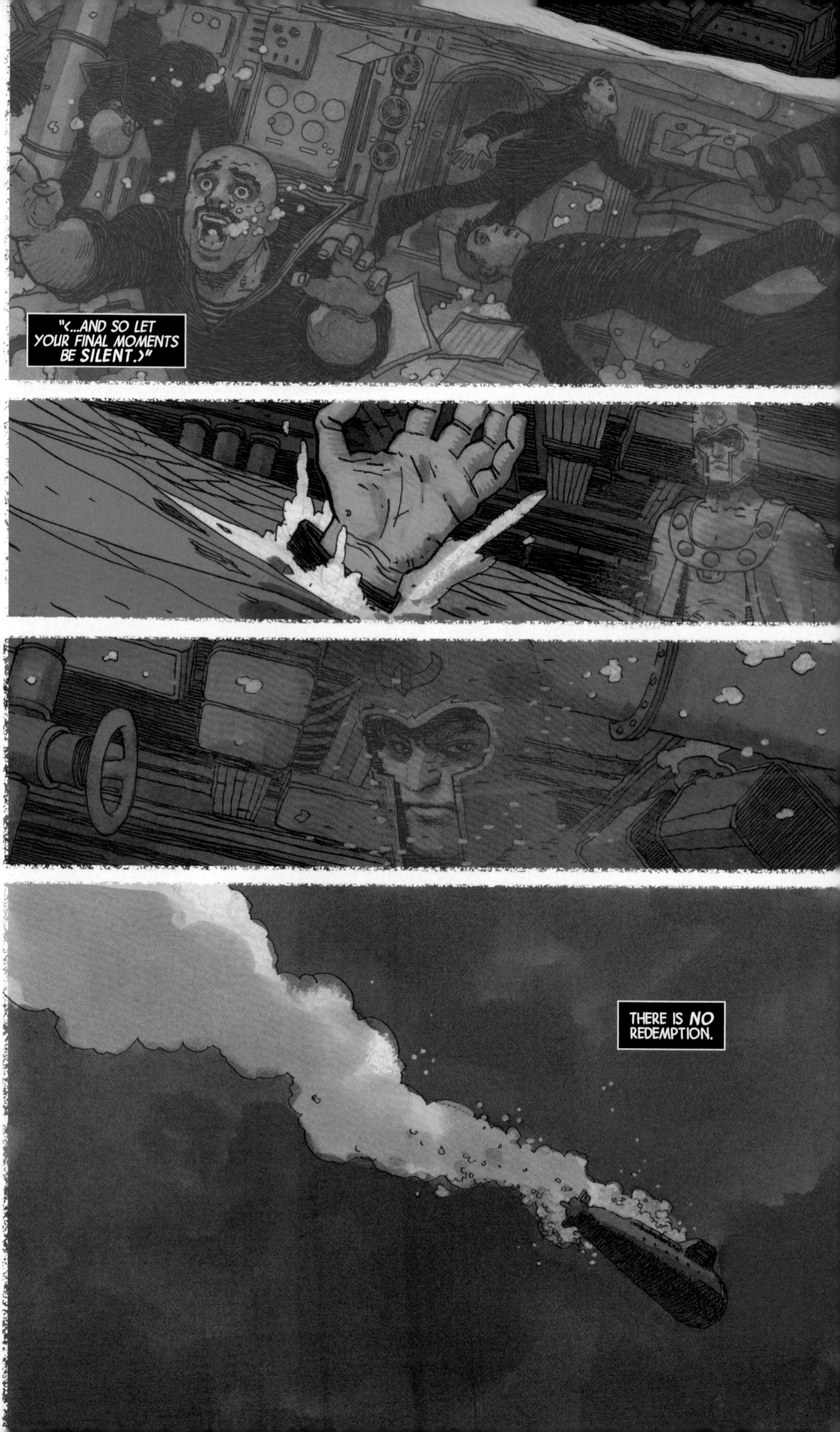
"‹...AND SO LET YOUR FINAL MOMENTS BE SILENT.›"
THERE IS NO REDEMPTION.

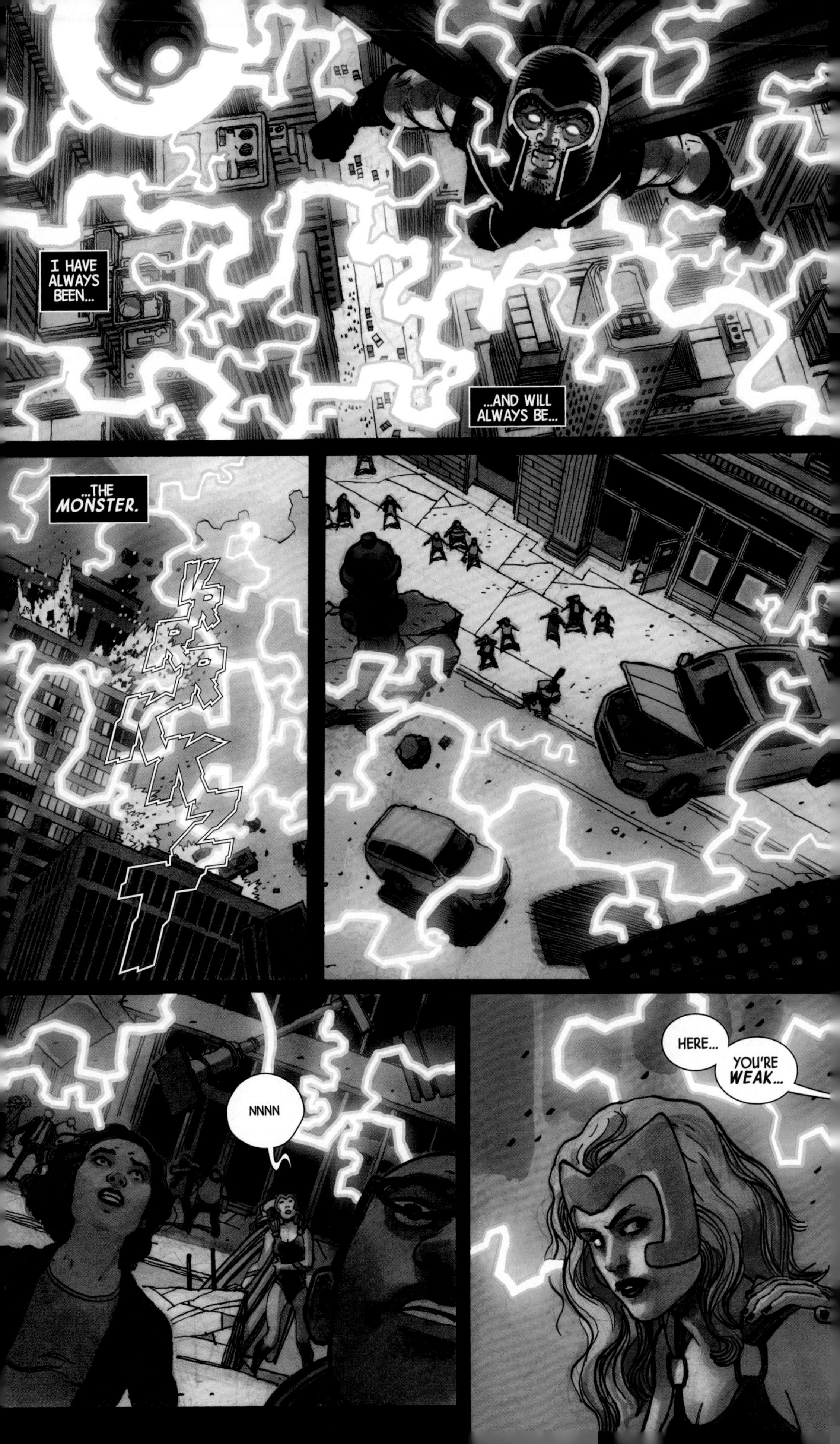
I HAVE ALWAYS BEEN...
...AND WILL ALWAYS BE...
...THE MONSTER.
KRRRKKZZT
NNNN
HERE...
YOU'RE WEAK...

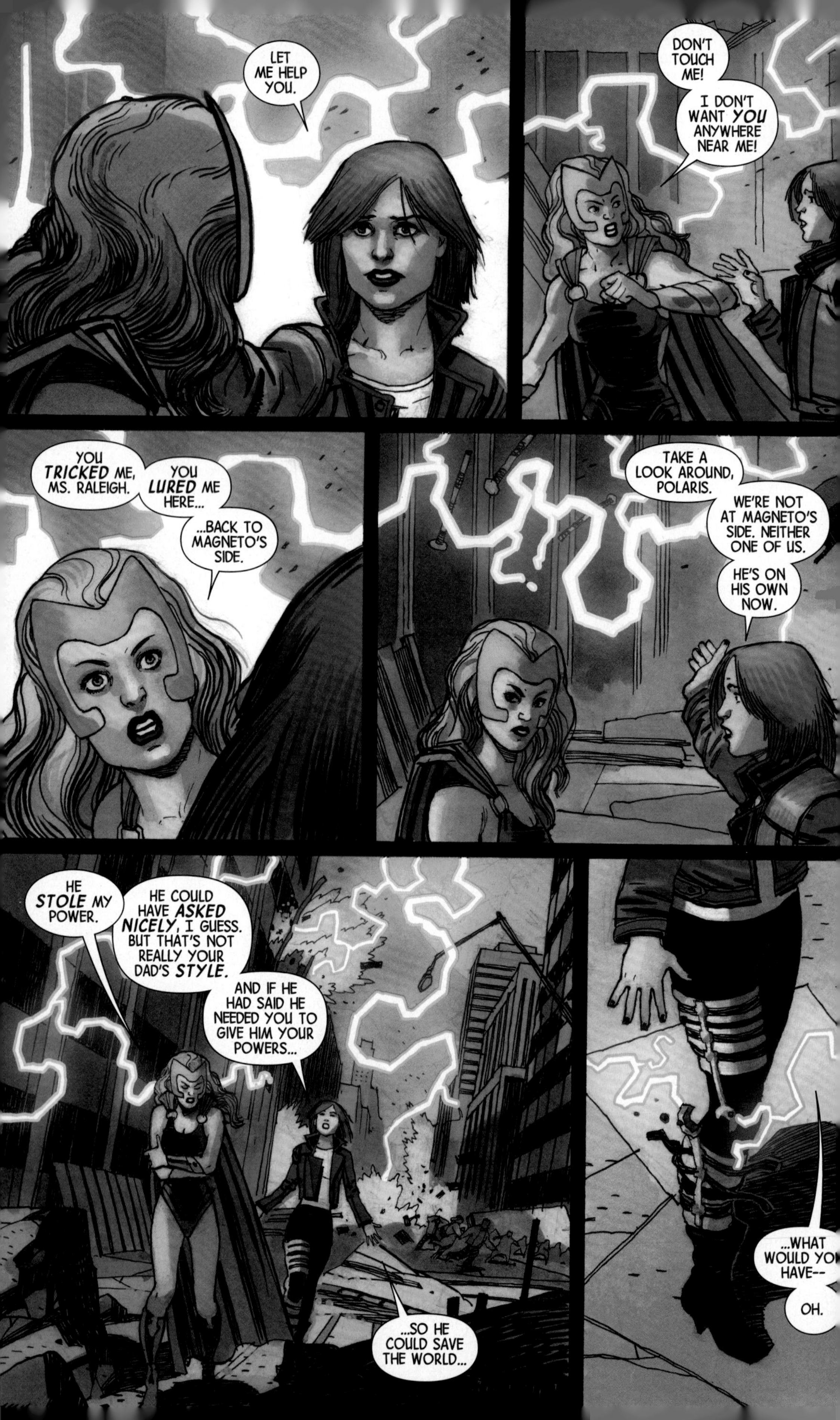
LET ME HELP YOU.
DON'T TOUCH ME!
I DON'T WANT YOU ANYWHERE NEAR ME!
YOU TRICKED ME, MS. RALEIGH.
YOU LURED ME HERE...
...BACK TO MAGNETO'S SIDE.
TAKE A LOOK AROUND, POLARIS.
WE'RE NOT AT MAGNETO'S SIDE. NEITHER ONE OF US.
HE'S ON HIS OWN NOW.
HE STOLE MY POWER.
HE COULD HAVE ASKED NICELY, I GUESS. BUT THAT'S NOT REALLY YOUR DAD'S STYLE.
AND IF HE HAD SAID HE NEEDED YOU TO GIVE HIM YOUR POWERS...
...SO HE COULD SAVE THE WORLD...
...WHAT WOULD YO HAVE--
OH.

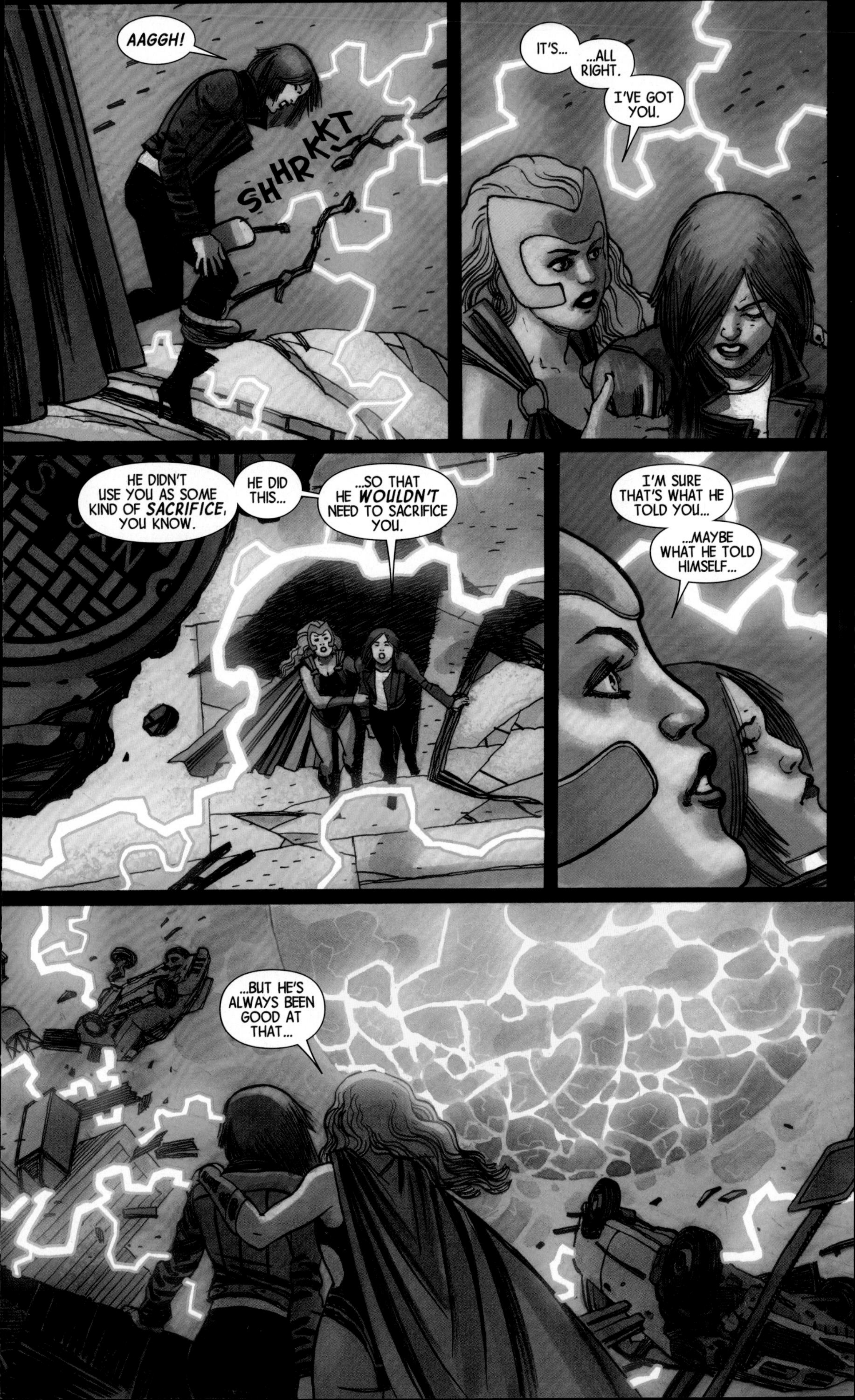
AAGGH!
SHHRKKT
IT'S...
...ALL RIGHT.
I'VE GOT YOU.
HE DIDN'T USE YOU AS SOME KIND OF SACRIFICE, YOU KNOW.
HE DID THIS...
...SO THAT HE WOULDN'T NEED TO SACRIFICE YOU.
I'M SURE THAT'S WHAT HE TOLD YOU...
...MAYBE WHAT HE TOLD HIMSELF...
...BUT HE'S ALWAYS BEEN GOOD AT THAT...

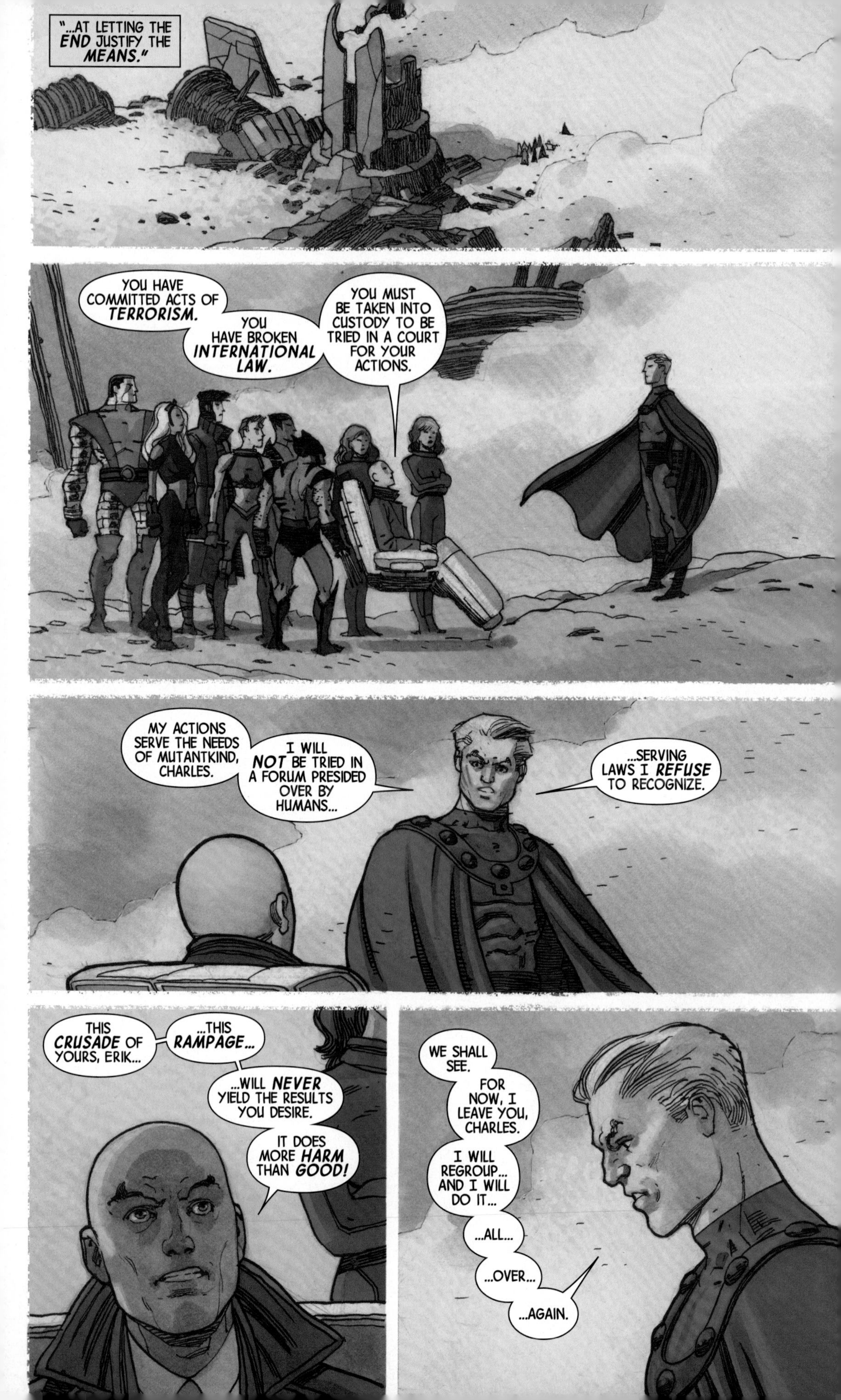
"...AT LETTING THE END JUSTIFY THE MEANS."
YOU HAVE COMMITTED ACTS OF TERRORISM.
YOU HAVE BROKEN INTERNATIONAL LAW.
YOU MUST BE TAKEN INTO CUSTODY TO BE TRIED IN A COURT FOR YOUR ACTIONS.
MY ACTIONS SERVE THE NEEDS OF MUTANTKIND, CHARLES.
I WILL NOT BE TRIED IN A FORUM PRESIDED OVER BY HUMANS...
...SERVING LAWS I REFUSE TO RECOGNIZE.
THIS CRUSADE OF YOURS, ERIK...
...THIS RAMPAGE...
...WILL NEVER YIELD THE RESULTS YOU DESIRE.
IT DOES MORE HARM THAN GOOD!
WE SHALL SEE.
FOR NOW, I LEAVE YOU, CHARLES.
I WILL REGROUP... AND I WILL DO IT...
...ALL...
...OVER...
...AGAIN.

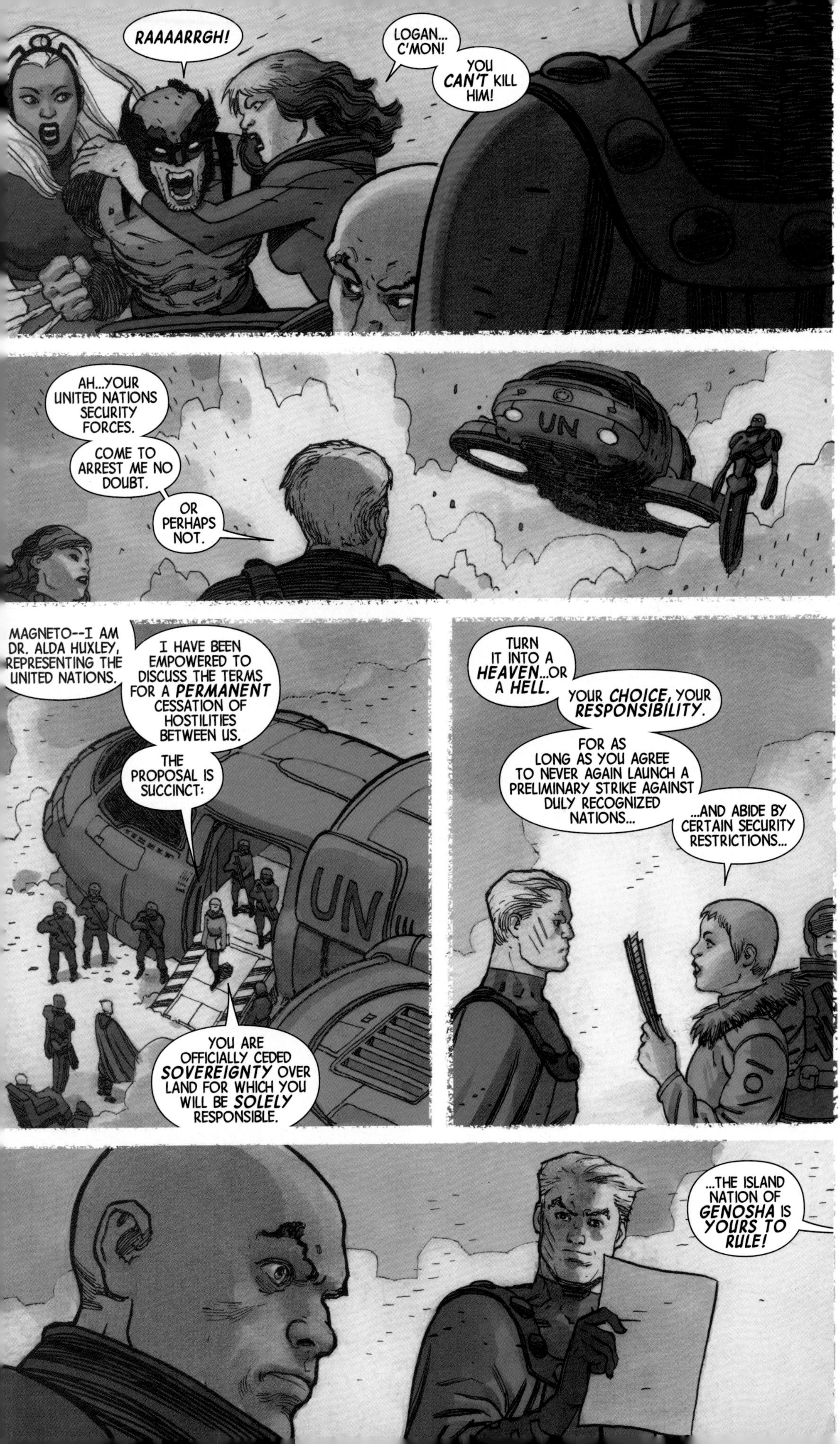

RAAAARRGH!
LOGAN... C'MON!
YOU CAN'T KILL HIM!
AH...YOUR UNITED NATIONS SECURITY FORCES.
COME TO ARREST ME NO DOUBT.
OR PERHAPS NOT.
MAGNETO--I AM DR. ALDA HUXLEY, REPRESENTING THE UNITED NATIONS.
I HAVE BEEN EMPOWERED TO DISCUSS THE TERMS FOR A PERMANENT CESSATION OF HOSTILITIES BETWEEN US.
THE PROPOSAL IS SUCCINCT:
YOU ARE OFFICIALLY CEDED SOVEREIGNTY OVER LAND FOR WHICH YOU WILL BE SOLELY RESPONSIBLE.
TURN IT INTO A HEAVEN...OR A HELL.
YOUR CHOICE, YOUR RESPONSIBILITY.
FOR AS LONG AS YOU AGREE TO NEVER AGAIN LAUNCH A PRELIMINARY STRIKE AGAINST DULY RECOGNIZED NATIONS...
...AND ABIDE BY CERTAIN SECURITY RESTRICTIONS...
...THE ISLAND NATION OF GENOSHA IS YOURS TO RULE!

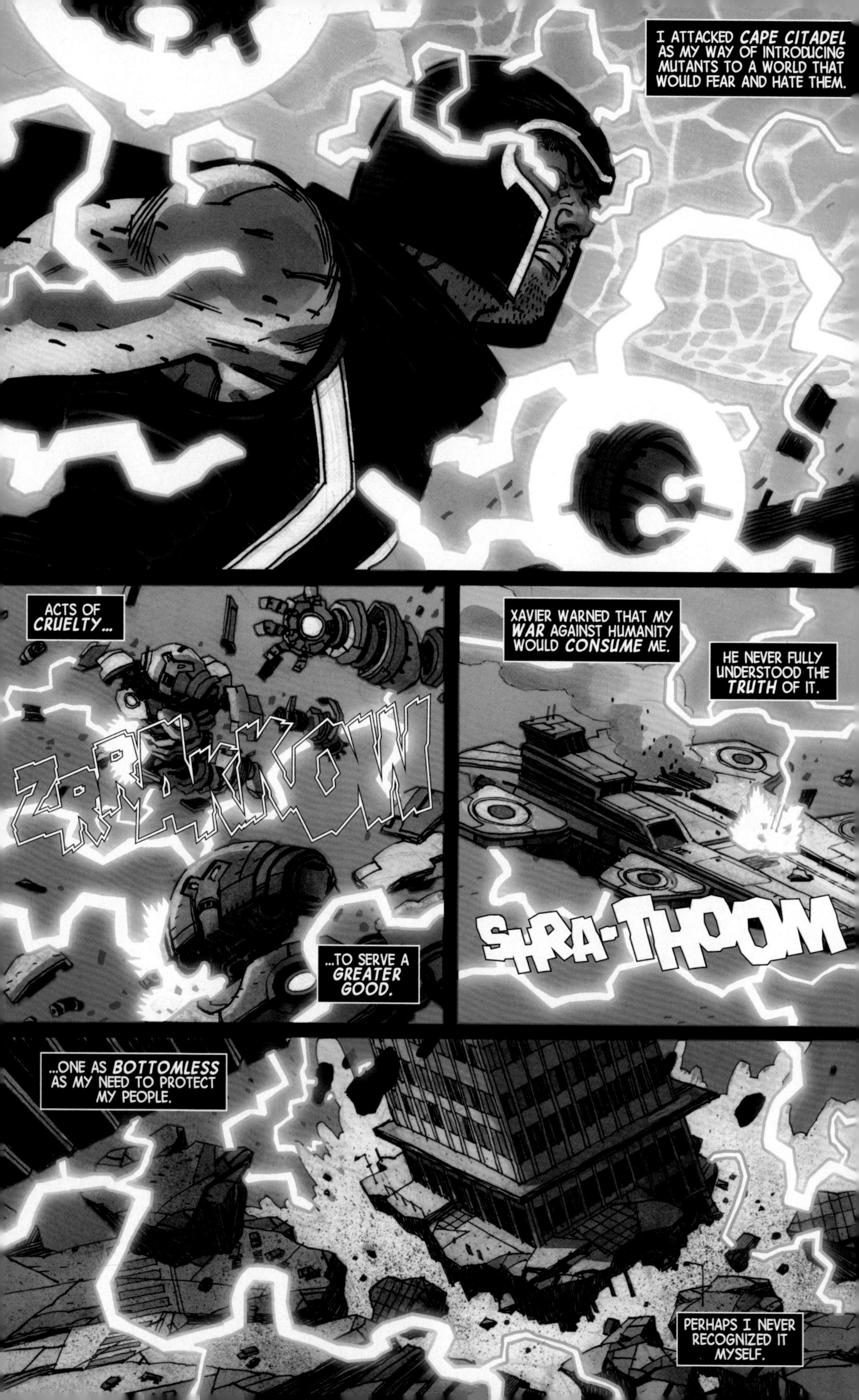
I ATTACKED CAPE CITADEL AS MY WAY OF INTRODUCING MUTANTS TO A WORLD THAT WOULD FEAR AND HATE THEM.
ACTS OF CRUELTY...
ZRAKKOW
...TO SERVE A GREATER GOOD.
XAVIER WARNED THAT MY WAR AGAINST HUMANITY WOULD CONSUME ME.
HE NEVER FULLY UNDERSTOOD THE TRUTH OF IT.
SHRA-THOOM
...ONE AS BOTTOMLESS AS MY NEED TO PROTECT MY PEOPLE.
PERHAPS I NEVER RECOGNIZED IT MYSELF.

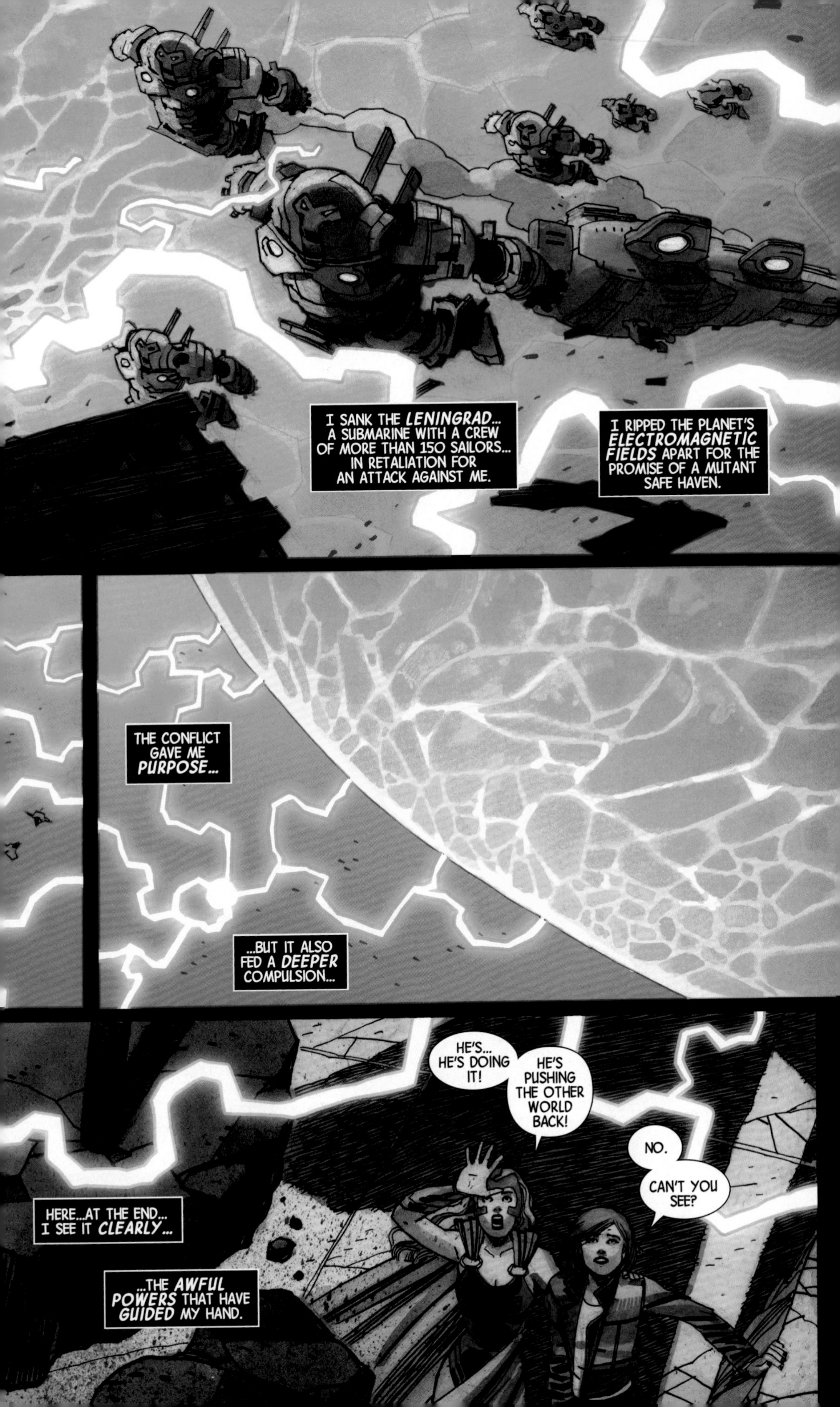

I SANK THE LENINGRAD... A SUBMARINE WITH A CREW OF MORE THAN 150 SAILORS... IN RETALIATION FOR AN ATTACK AGAINST ME.
I RIPPED THE PLANET'S ELECTROMAGNETIC FIELDS APART FOR THE PROMISE OF A MUTANT SAFE HAVEN.
THE CONFLICT GAVE ME PURPOSE...
...BUT IT ALSO FED A DEEPER COMPULSION...
HE'S... HE'S DOING IT!
HE'S PUSHING THE OTHER WORLD BACK!
NO.
CAN'T YOU SEE?
HERE...AT THE END... I SEE IT CLEARLY...
...THE AWFUL POWERS THAT HAVE GUIDED MY HAND.

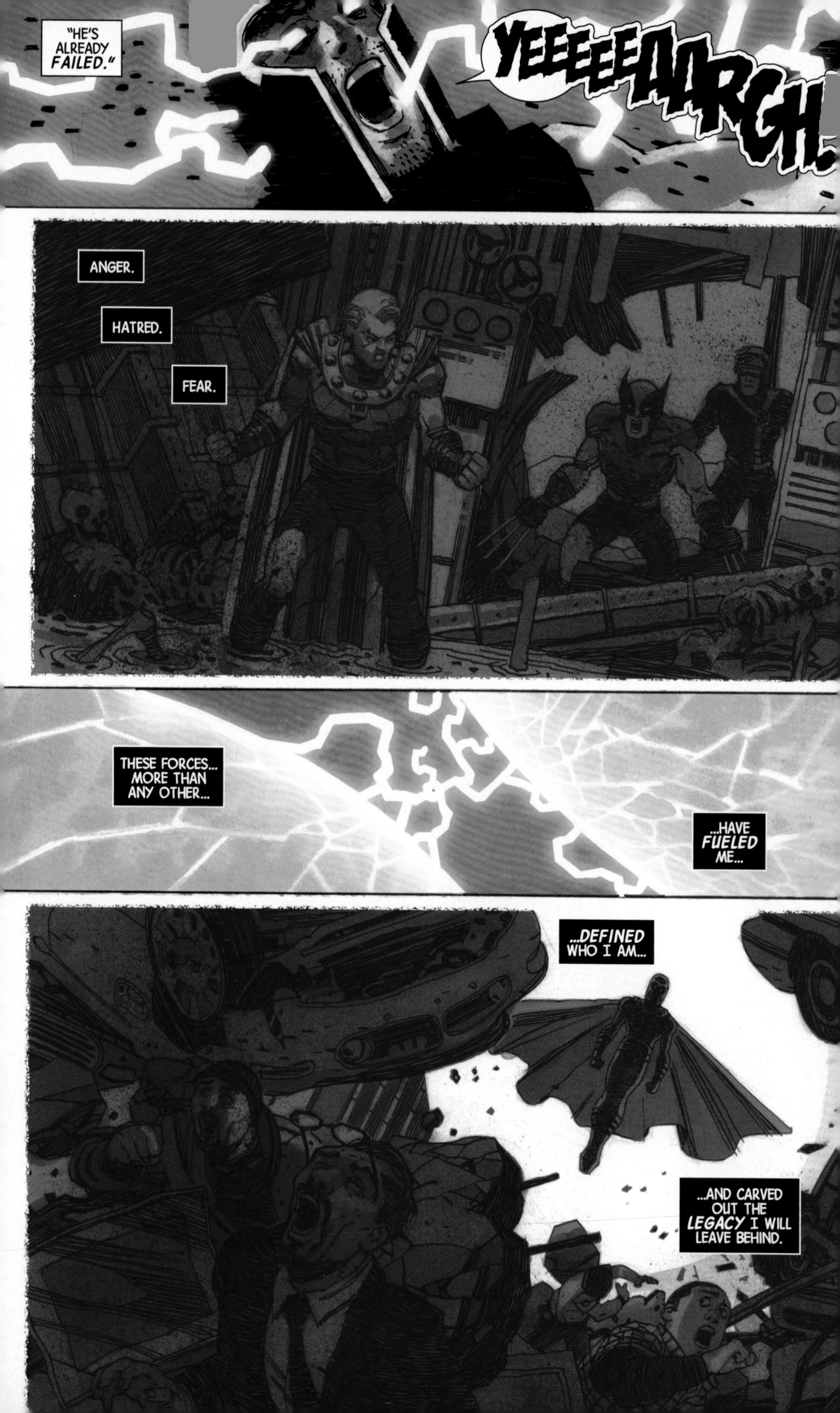
"HE'S ALREADY FAILED."
YEEEEEAARGH!
ANGER.
HATRED.
FEAR.
THESE FORCES... MORE THAN ANY OTHER...
...HAVE FUELED ME...
...DEFINED WHO I AM...
...AND CARVED OUT THE LEGACY I WILL LEAVE BEHIND.

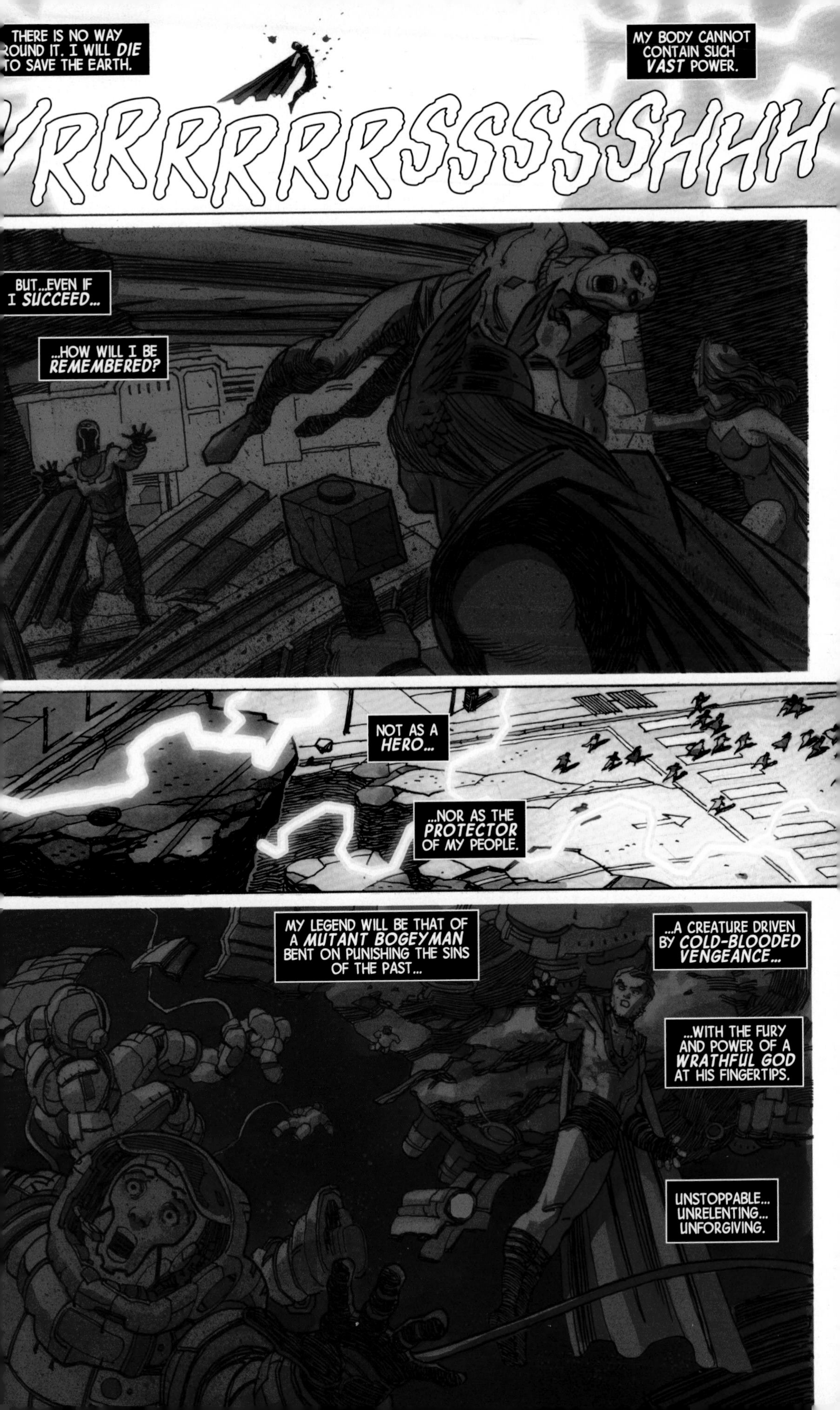

THERE IS NO WAY ROUND IT. I WILL *DIE* TO SAVE THE EARTH.
MY BODY CANNOT CONTAIN SUCH *VAST* POWER.
VRRRRRRRSSSSSSHHH
BUT...EVEN IF I *SUCCEED*...
...HOW WILL I BE *REMEMBERED?*
NOT AS A *HERO*...
...NOR AS THE *PROTECTOR* OF MY PEOPLE.
MY LEGEND WILL BE THAT OF A *MUTANT BOGEYMAN* BENT ON PUNISHING THE SINS OF THE PAST...
...A CREATURE DRIVEN BY *COLD-BLOODED VENGEANCE*...
...WITH THE FURY AND POWER OF A *WRATHFUL GOD* AT HIS FINGERTIPS.
UNSTOPPABLE... UNRELENTING... UNFORGIVING.

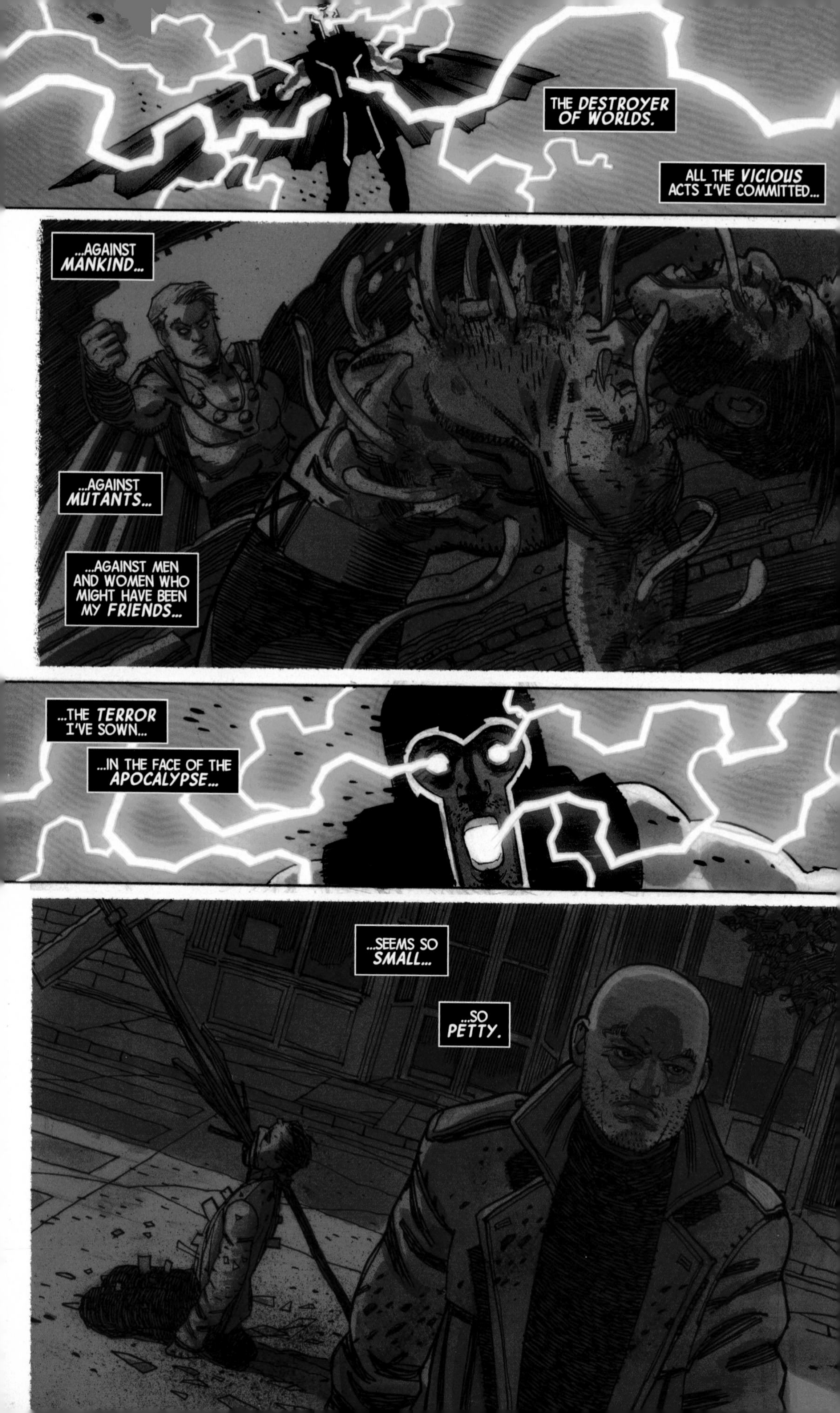

THE DESTROYER OF WORLDS.
ALL THE VICIOUS ACTS I'VE COMMITTED...
...AGAINST MANKIND...
...AGAINST MUTANTS...
...AGAINST MEN AND WOMEN WHO MIGHT HAVE BEEN MY FRIENDS...
...THE TERROR I'VE SOWN...
...IN THE FACE OF THE APOCALYPSE...
...SEEMS SO SMALL...
...SO PETTY.

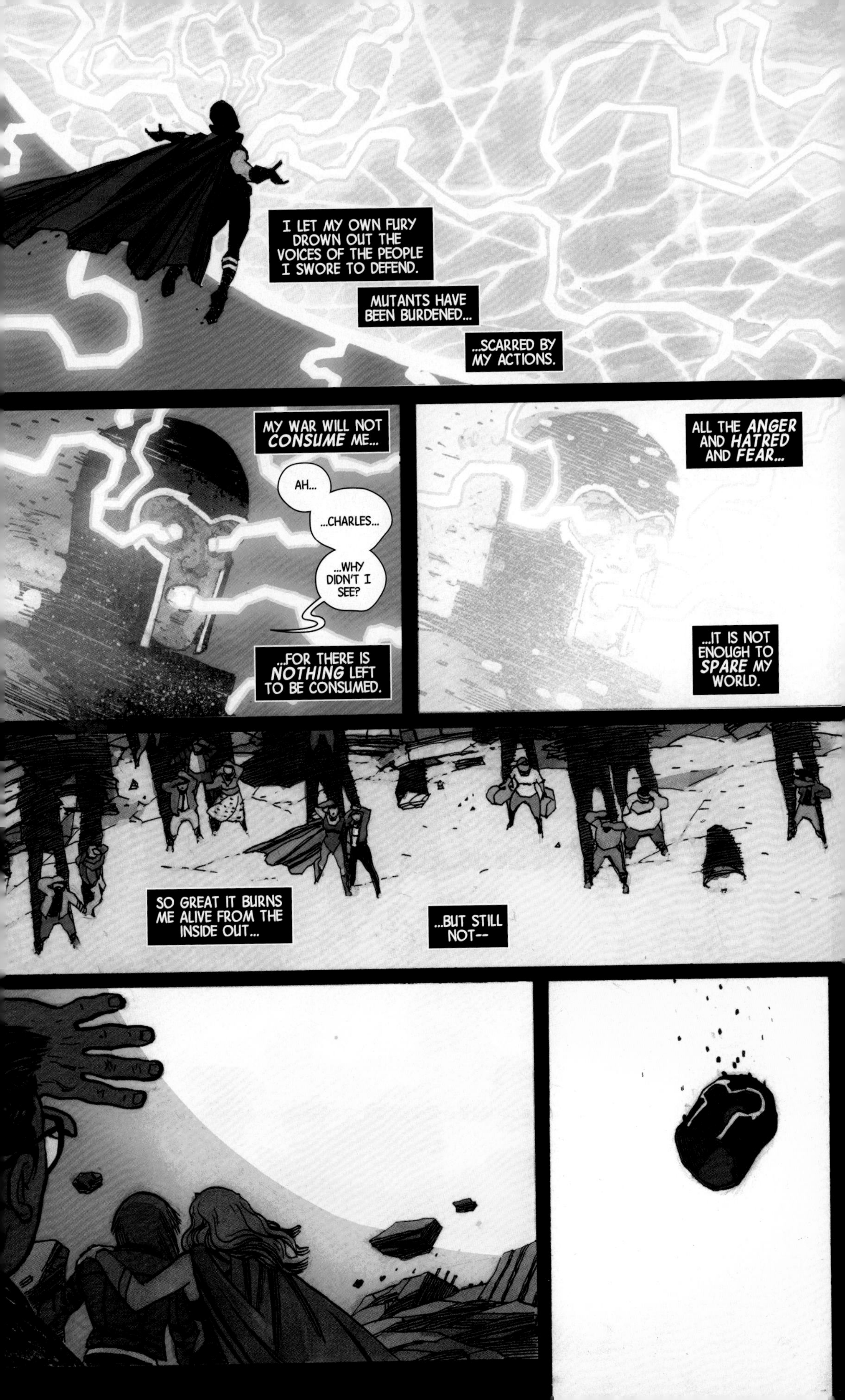
I LET MY OWN FURY DROWN OUT THE VOICES OF THE PEOPLE I SWORE TO DEFEND.
MUTANTS HAVE BEEN BURDENED...
...SCARRED BY MY ACTIONS.
MY WAR WILL NOT CONSUME ME...
AH...
...CHARLES...
...WHY DIDN'T I SEE?
...FOR THERE IS NOTHING LEFT TO BE CONSUMED.
ALL THE ANGER AND HATRED AND FEAR...
...IT IS NOT ENOUGH TO SPARE MY WORLD.
SO GREAT IT BURNS ME ALIVE FROM THE INSIDE OUT...
...BUT STILL NOT--

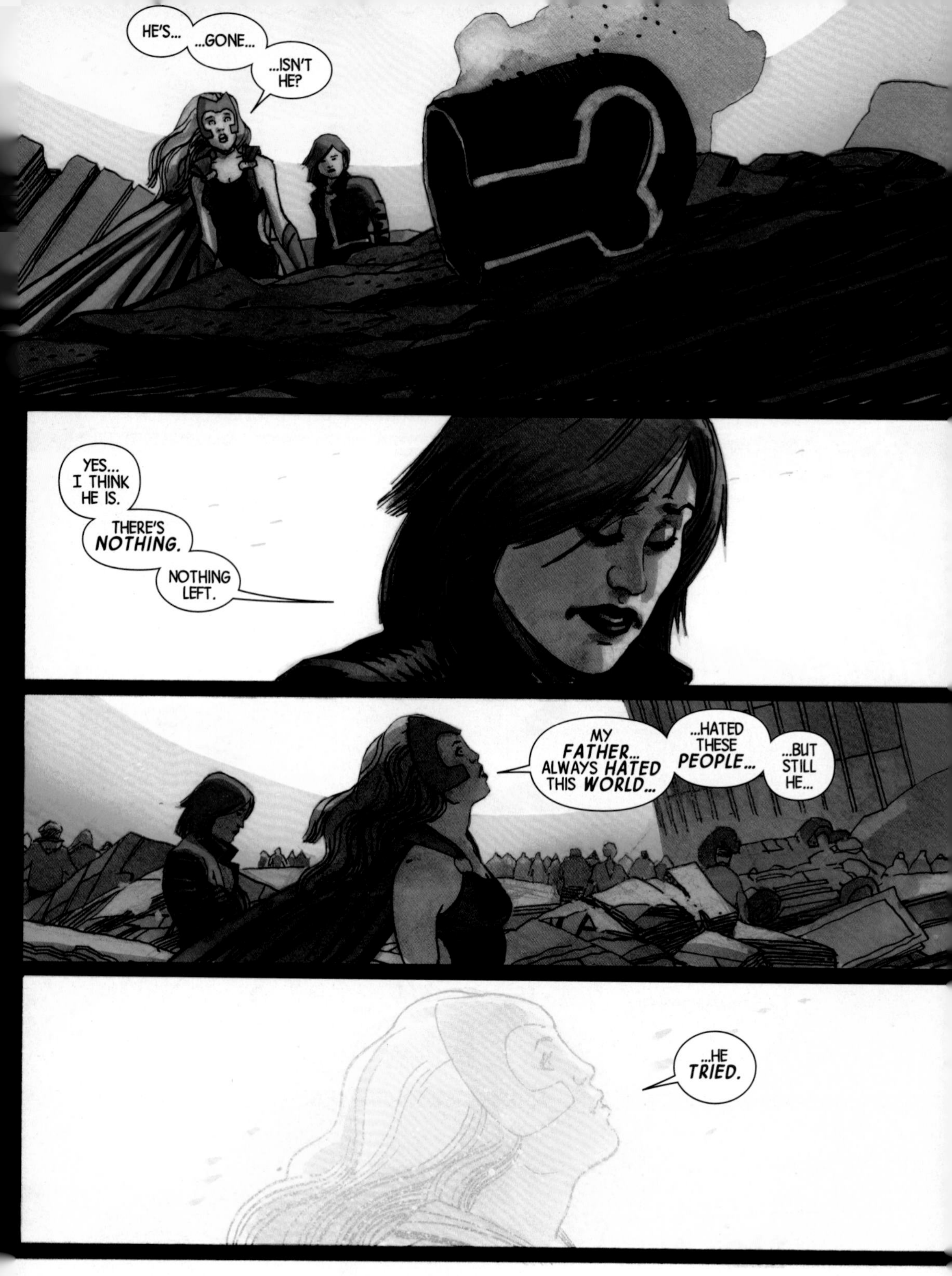
HE'S...
...GONE...
...ISN'T HE?
YES... I THINK HE IS.
THERE'S NOTHING.
NOTHING LEFT.
MY FATHER... ALWAYS HATED THIS WORLD...
...HATED THESE PEOPLE...
...BUT STILL HE...
...HE TRIED.

END.

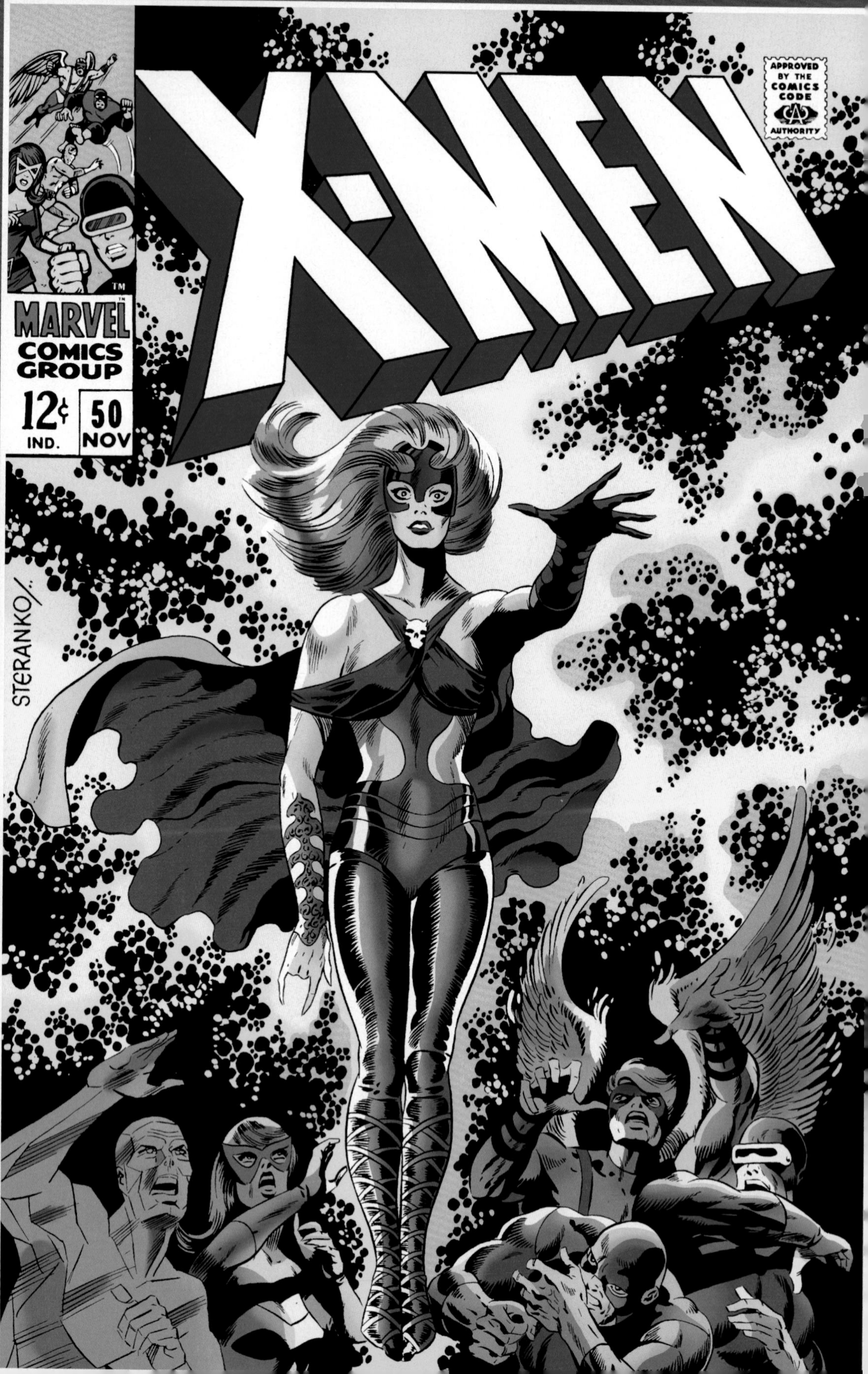
X-MEN
TM
MARVEL
COMICS GROUP
12¢
IND.
50
NOV
APPROVED BY THE COMICS CODE AUTHORITY
STERANKO/.

HAIL, QUEEN OF MUTANTS! ASK **NO** QUESTIONS YET-- BUT GAZE **DEEP** INTO MY EYES FOR ONE BRIEF SECOND! THERE, **ALL** ANSWERS ARE WRITTEN!

EDITOR _____ **STAN LEE**
WRITER _____ **ARNOLD DRAKE**
ARTIST _____ **JIM STERANKO**
INKER _____ **JOHN TARTAGLIONE**
LETTERER _____ **HERB COOPER**

THE X-MEN

ARE TOGETHER AGAIN-- AND THAT'S **ALL** THE GOOD NEWS! FOR THEY FACE AN ENEMY THAT **STAGGERS** THE IMAGINATION-- AND THREAT-ENS **SANITY** ITSELF! FROM A NEST, OF PUREST, BASEST **EVIL**, STRANGE PSYCHO-KINETIC COMMANDS FLY-- **CLARIONS** CALL TO THE UN-CONSCIOUS MUTANTS OF THE WORLD! AND... LIKE SOME STRANGE **ARMY** OF THE HALF-LIVING... **THEY MARCH!**

THEIR PERVERSE PIED-PIPER IS-- **MESMERO!** FOR IT IS **HE** WHO GUARDS THE VILE HERITAGE OF **MAGNETO**-- MASTER OF EVIL MUTANTS-- ! WHILE THE OTHER X-MEN SEARCH OUT MESMERO, **ICEMAN** REMAINS BEHIND TO PROTECT **LORNA DANE,** HERSELF A TARGET OF THE GREAT MUTANT **CONSPIRACY!**

SUDDENLY, MESMERO AND HIS ELITE GUARD BURST UPON THE SCENE, OVERWHELMING ICEMAN'S HEROIC DEFENSES AND PARALYZING HIS BODY! LORNA LISTENS IN **FEAR** AS MESMERO SPEAKS HIS STRANGELY SICKENING SALUTE

--HAIL, QUEEN OF MUTANTS!

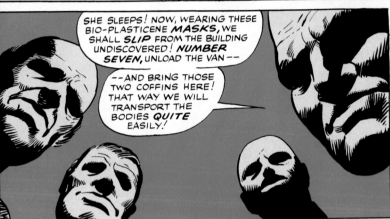

SHE SLEEPS! NOW, WEARING THESE BIO-PLASTICENE **MASKS,** WE SHALL **SLIP** FROM THE BUILDING UNDISCOVERED! **NUMBER SEVEN,** UNLOAD THE VAN--

--AND BRING THOSE TWO COFFINS HERE! THAT WAY WE WILL TRANSPORT THE BODIES **QUITE** EASILY!

TO **COMPLETE** THE DISGUISE, WEAR A SLIGHT FUNEREAL **SMILE** AS WE LEAVE, MY FRIENDS! THERE ARE **NO** UNSMILING UNDERTAKERS!

THOUGH HYPNOTIZED, LORNA DANE FELT A SENSE OF TRAVELING AND EVEN MADE ONE FUTILE EFFORT TO RAISE THE LID OF HER ENCLOSURE-- BUT **ONLY** ONE!

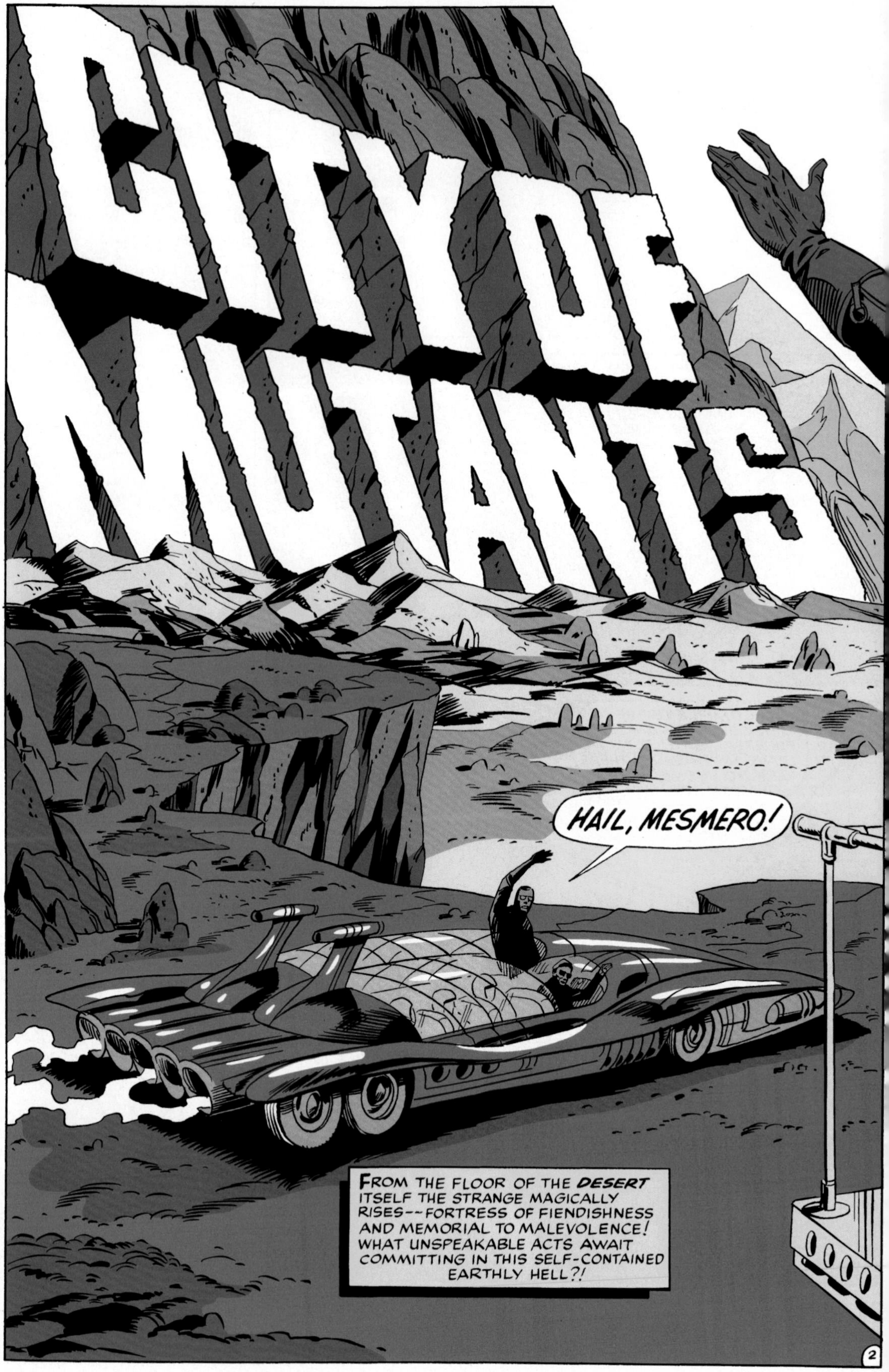
CITY OF MUTANTS
HAIL, MESMERO!
FROM THE FLOOR OF THE DESERT ITSELF THE STRANGE MAGICALLY RISES--FORTRESS OF FIENDISHNESS AND MEMORIAL TO MALEVOLENCE! WHAT UNSPEAKABLE ACTS AWAIT COMMITTING IN THIS SELF-CONTAINED EARTHLY HELL?!

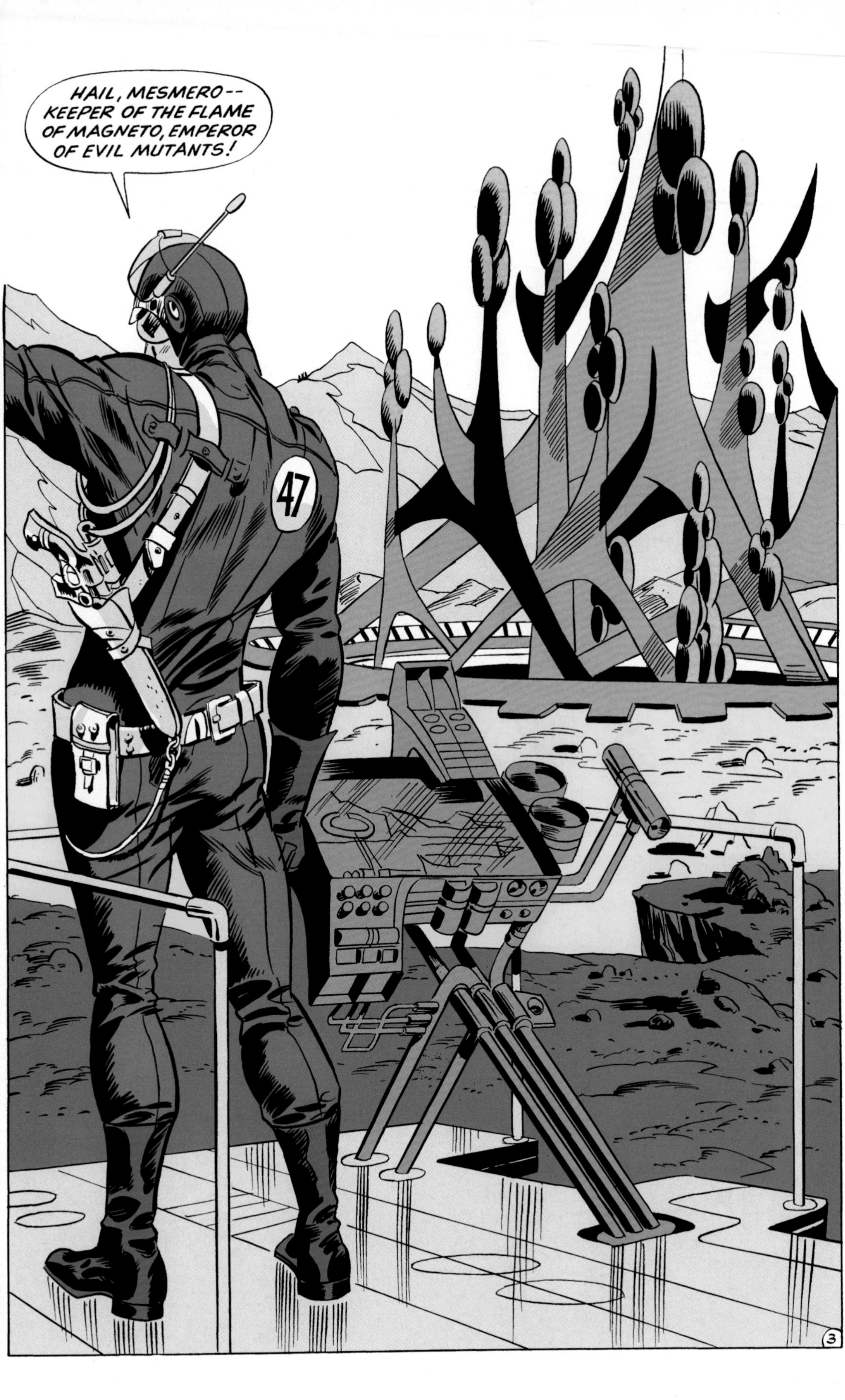
HAIL, MESMERO-- KEEPER OF THE FLAME OF MAGNETO, EMPEROR OF EVIL MUTANTS!
47
3

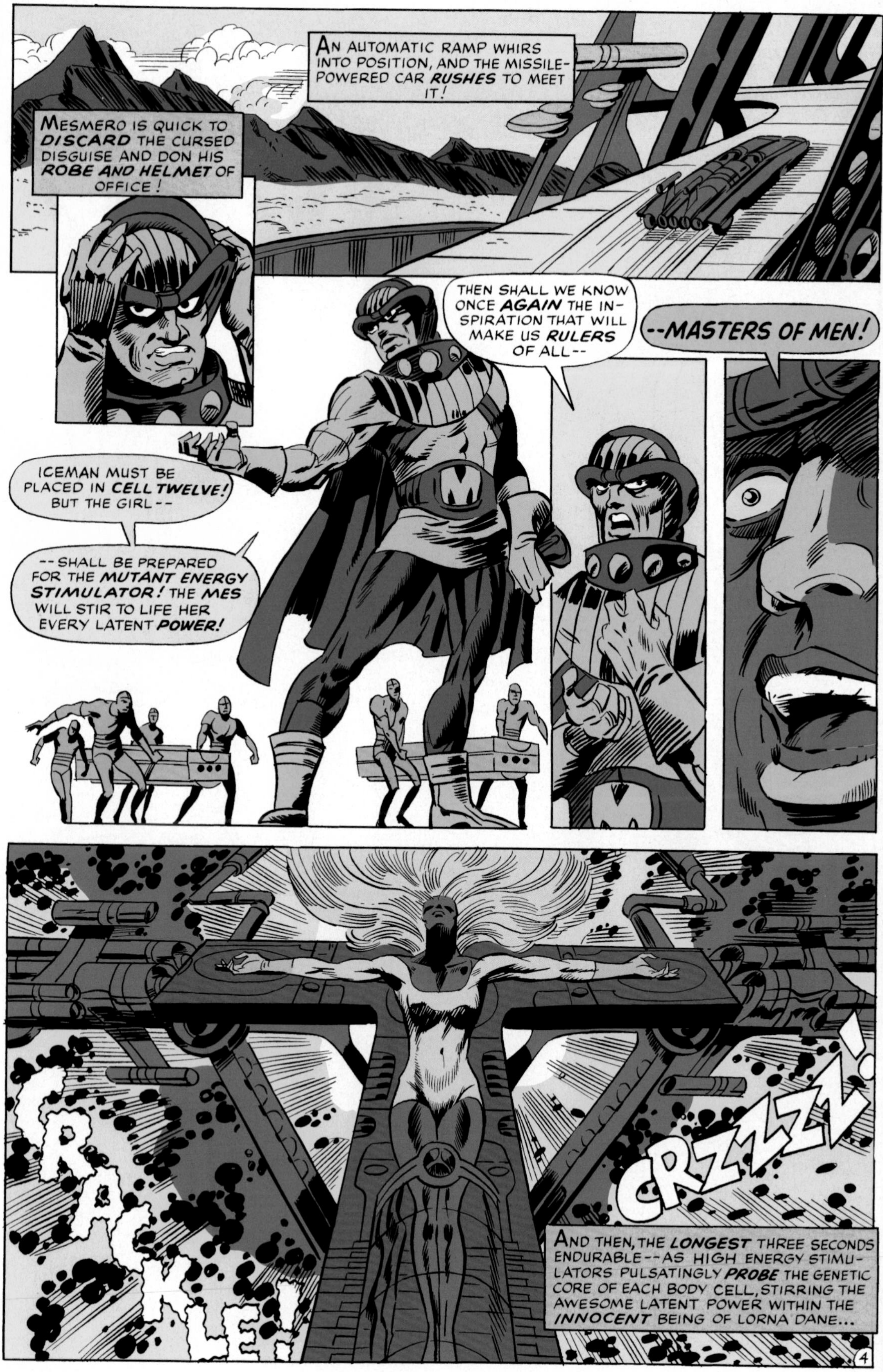

AN AUTOMATIC RAMP WHIRS INTO POSITION, AND THE MISSILE-POWERED CAR RUSHES TO MEET IT!
MESMERO IS QUICK TO DISCARD THE CURSED DISGUISE AND DON HIS ROBE AND HELMET OF OFFICE!
THEN SHALL WE KNOW ONCE AGAIN THE INSPIRATION THAT WILL MAKE US RULERS OF ALL--
--MASTERS OF MEN!
ICEMAN MUST BE PLACED IN CELL TWELVE! BUT THE GIRL--
--SHALL BE PREPARED FOR THE MUTANT ENERGY STIMULATOR! THE MES WILL STIR TO LIFE HER EVERY LATENT POWER!
CRACKLE!
CRZZZZN!
AND THEN, THE LONGEST THREE SECONDS ENDURABLE--AS HIGH ENERGY STIMULATORS PULSATINGLY PROBE THE GENETIC CORE OF EACH BODY CELL, STIRRING THE AWESOME LATENT POWER WITHIN THE INNOCENT BEING OF LORNA DANE...

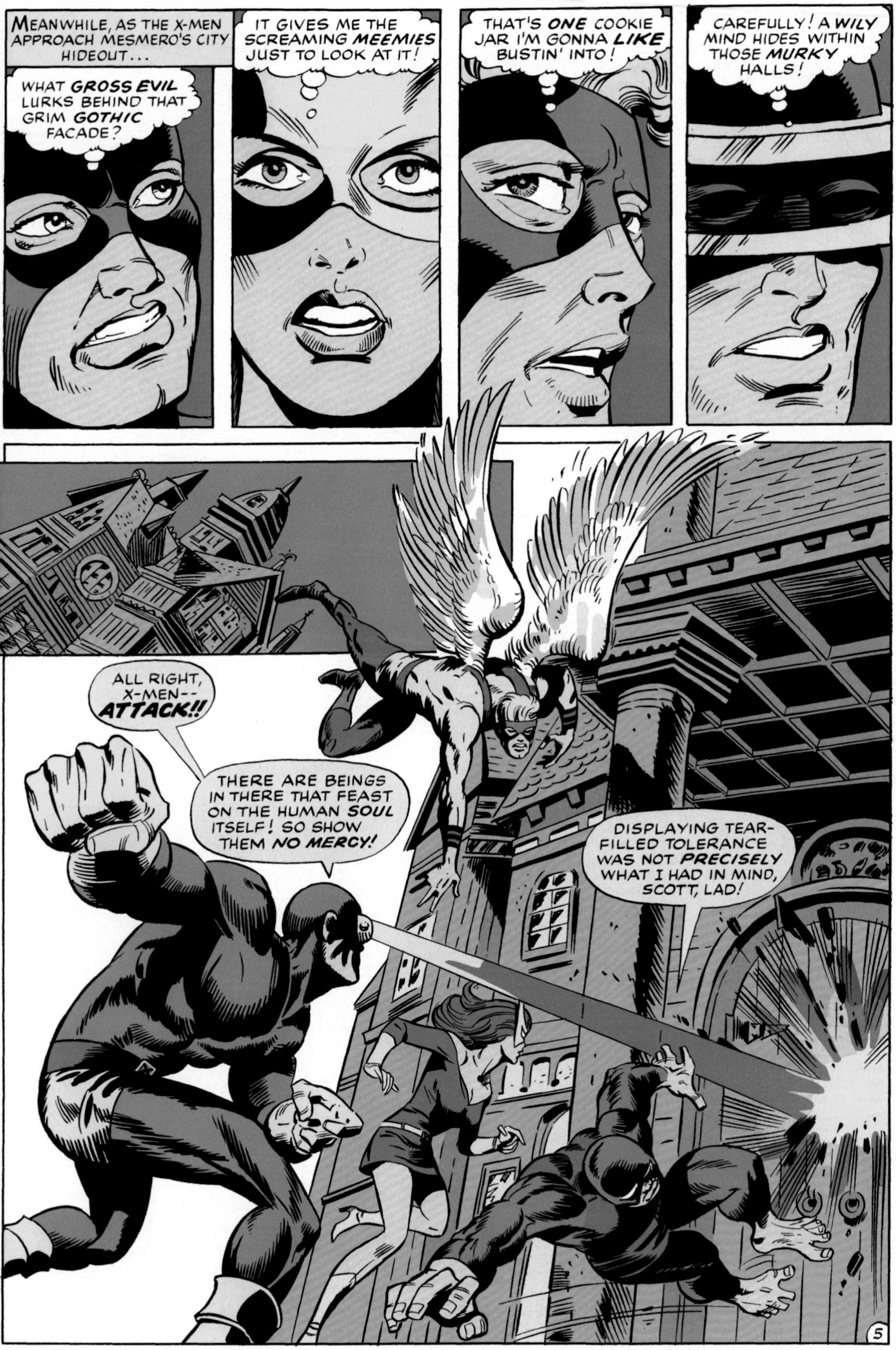

MEANWHILE, AS THE X-MEN APPROACH MESMERO'S CITY HIDEOUT...
WHAT GROSS EVIL LURKS BEHIND THAT GRIM GOTHIC FACADE?
IT GIVES ME THE SCREAMING MEEMIES JUST TO LOOK AT IT!
THAT'S ONE COOKIE JAR I'M GONNA LIKE BUSTIN' INTO!
CAREFULLY! A WILY MIND HIDES WITHIN THOSE MURKY HALLS!
ALL RIGHT, X-MEN-- ATTACK!!
THERE ARE BEINGS IN THERE THAT FEAST ON THE HUMAN SOUL ITSELF! SO SHOW THEM NO MERCY!
DISPLAYING TEAR-FILLED TOLERANCE WAS NOT PRECISELY WHAT I HAD IN MIND, SCOTT, LAD!
5

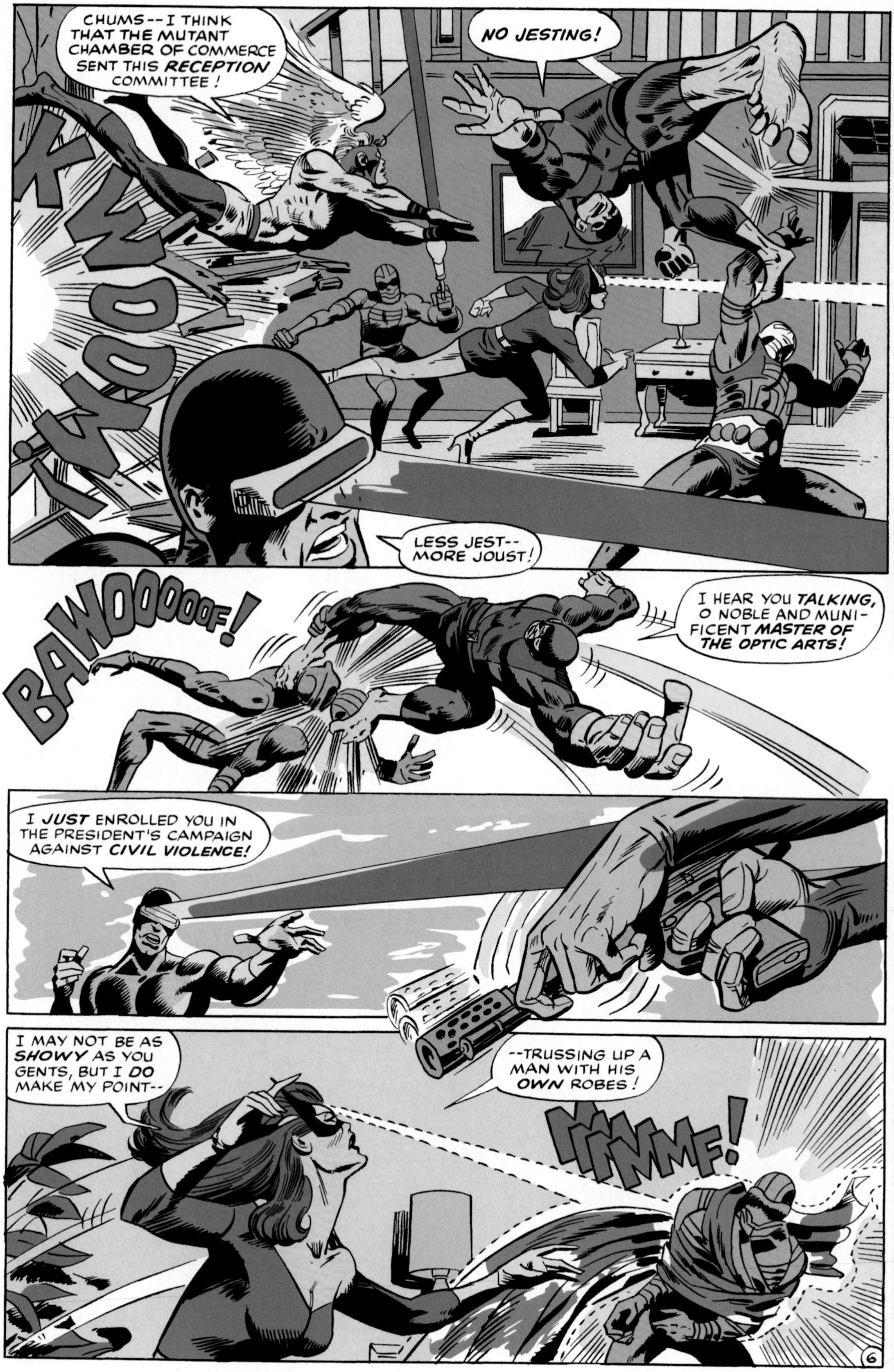

CHUMS--I THINK THAT THE MUTANT CHAMBER OF COMMERCE SENT THIS RECEPTION COMMITTEE!
NO JESTING!
KWOOOM!
LESS JEST--MORE JOUST!
BAWOOOOOOF!
I HEAR YOU TALKING, O NOBLE AND MUNIFICENT MASTER OF THE OPTIC ARTS!
I JUST ENROLLED YOU IN THE PRESIDENT'S CAMPAIGN AGAINST CIVIL VIOLENCE!
I MAY NOT BE AS SHOWY AS YOU GENTS, BUT I DO MAKE MY POINT--
--TRUSSING UP A MAN WITH HIS OWN ROBES!
MMMMF!

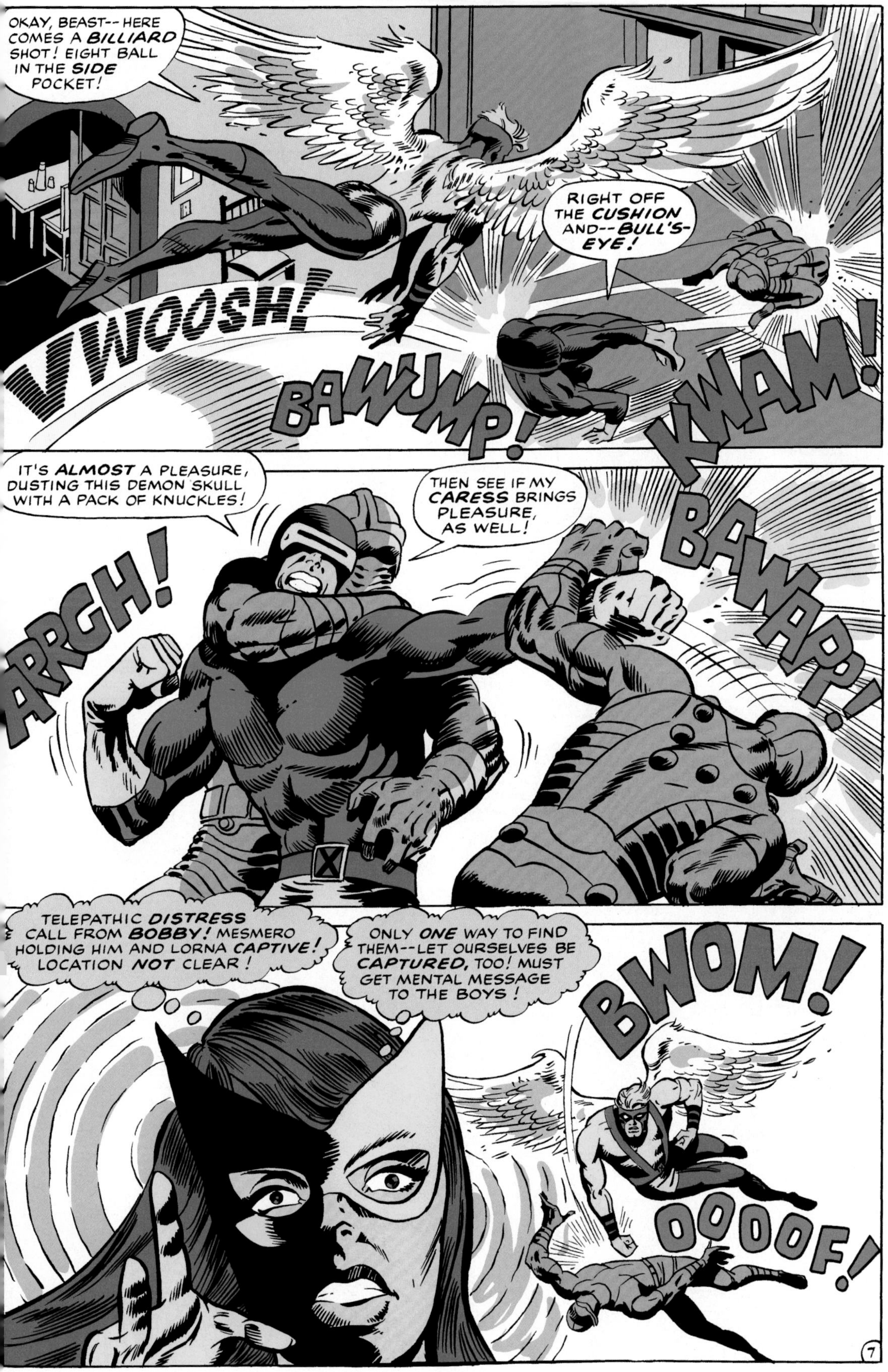
OKAY, BEAST--HERE COMES A BILLIARD SHOT! EIGHT BALL IN THE SIDE POCKET!
VWOOSH!
RIGHT OFF THE CUSHION AND--BULL'S-EYE!
BAWUMP!
KWAM!
IT'S ALMOST A PLEASURE, DUSTING THIS DEMON SKULL WITH A PACK OF KNUCKLES!
THEN SEE IF MY CARESS BRINGS PLEASURE, AS WELL!
ARRGH!
BAWAPP!
TELEPATHIC DISTRESS CALL FROM BOBBY! MESMERO HOLDING HIM AND LORNA CAPTIVE! LOCATION NOT CLEAR!
ONLY ONE WAY TO FIND THEM--LET OURSELVES BE CAPTURED, TOO! MUST GET MENTAL MESSAGE TO THE BOYS!
BWOM!
OOOOF!

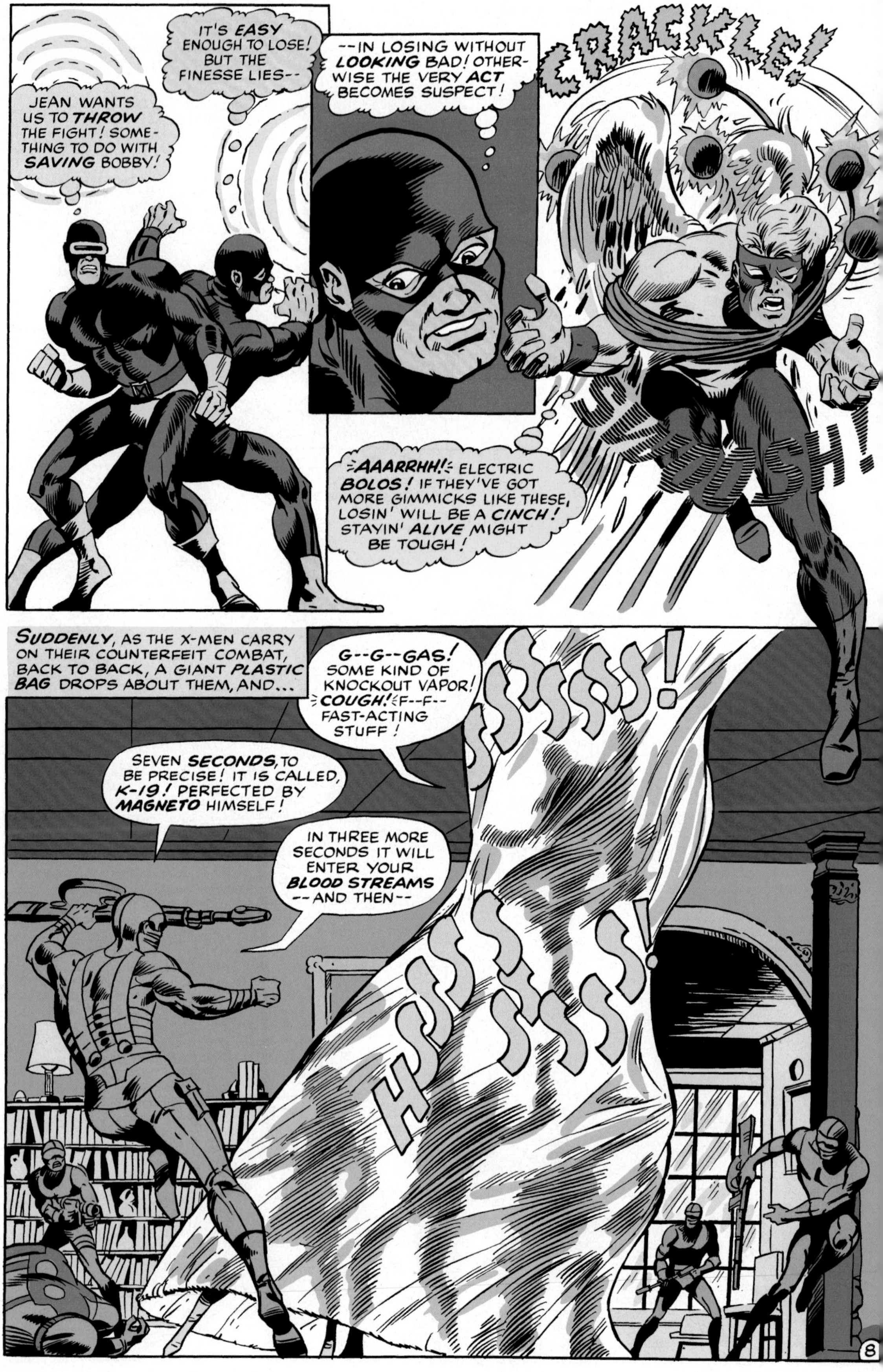

JEAN WANTS US TO THROW THE FIGHT! SOMETHING TO DO WITH SAVING BOBBY!
IT'S EASY ENOUGH TO LOSE! BUT THE FINESSE LIES--
--IN LOSING WITHOUT LOOKING BAD! OTHERWISE THE VERY ACT BECOMES SUSPECT!
CRACKLE!
AAARRHH! ELECTRIC BOLOS! IF THEY'VE GOT MORE GIMMICKS LIKE THESE, LOSIN' WILL BE A CINCH! STAYIN' ALIVE MIGHT BE TOUGH!
SUDDENLY, AS THE X-MEN CARRY ON THEIR COUNTERFEIT COMBAT, BACK TO BACK, A GIANT PLASTIC BAG DROPS ABOUT THEM, AND...
G--G--GAS! SOME KIND OF KNOCKOUT VAPOR! COUGH! F--F--FAST-ACTING STUFF!
SEVEN SECONDS, TO BE PRECISE! IT IS CALLED, K-19! PERFECTED BY MAGNETO HIMSELF!
IN THREE MORE SECONDS IT WILL ENTER YOUR BLOOD STREAMS --AND THEN--

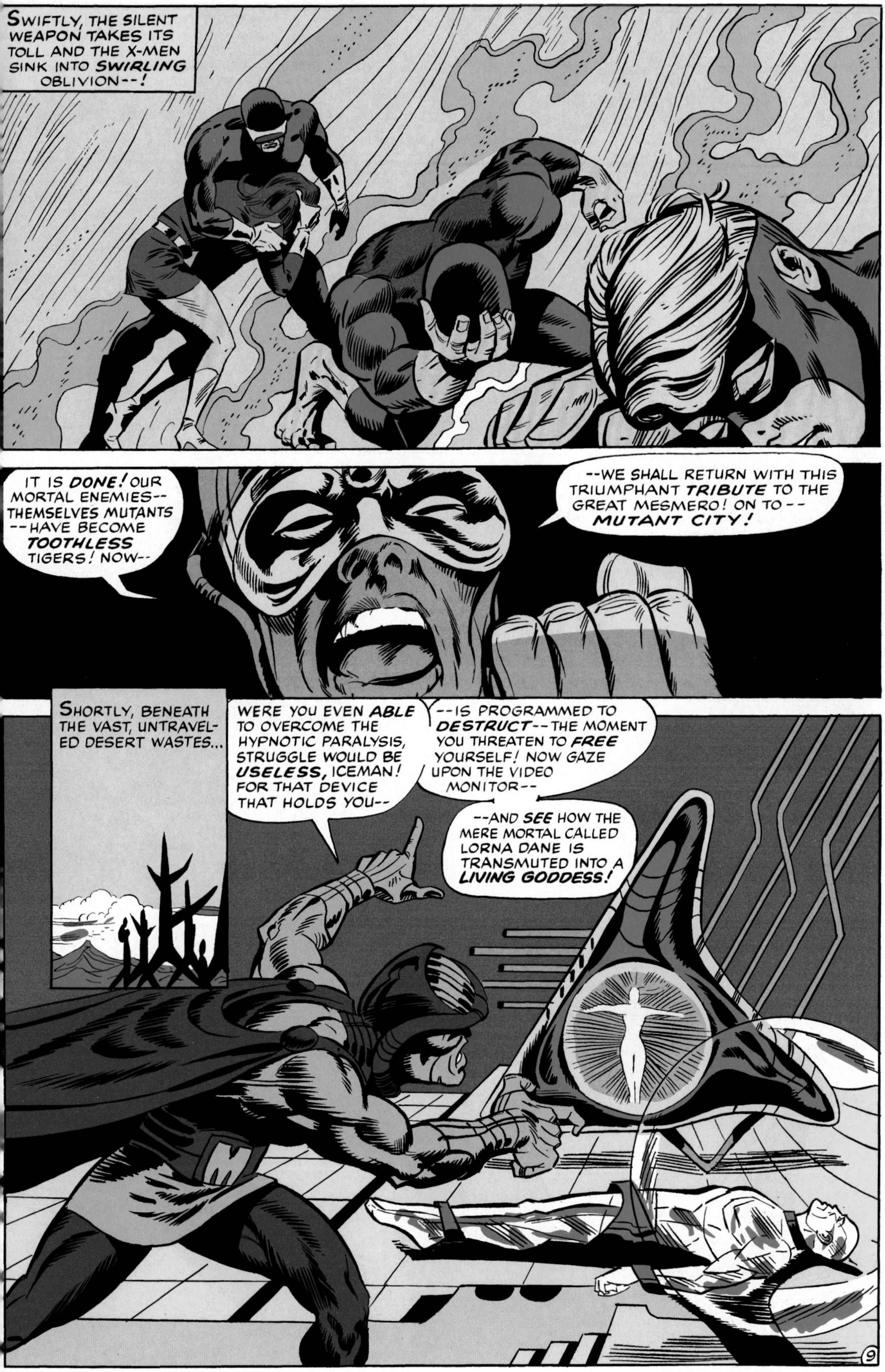
SWIFTLY, THE SILENT WEAPON TAKES ITS TOLL AND THE X-MEN SINK INTO SWIRLING OBLIVION--!
IT IS DONE! OUR MORTAL ENEMIES-- THEMSELVES MUTANTS --HAVE BECOME TOOTHLESS TIGERS! NOW--
--WE SHALL RETURN WITH THIS TRIUMPHANT TRIBUTE TO THE GREAT MESMERO! ON TO -- MUTANT CITY!
SHORTLY, BENEATH THE VAST, UNTRAVEL-ED DESERT WASTES...
WERE YOU EVEN ABLE TO OVERCOME THE HYPNOTIC PARALYSIS, STRUGGLE WOULD BE USELESS, ICEMAN! FOR THAT DEVICE THAT HOLDS YOU--
--IS PROGRAMMED TO DESTRUCT--THE MOMENT YOU THREATEN TO FREE YOURSELF! NOW GAZE UPON THE VIDEO MONITOR--
--AND SEE HOW THE MERE MORTAL CALLED LORNA DANE IS TRANSMUTED INTO A LIVING GODDESS!
9

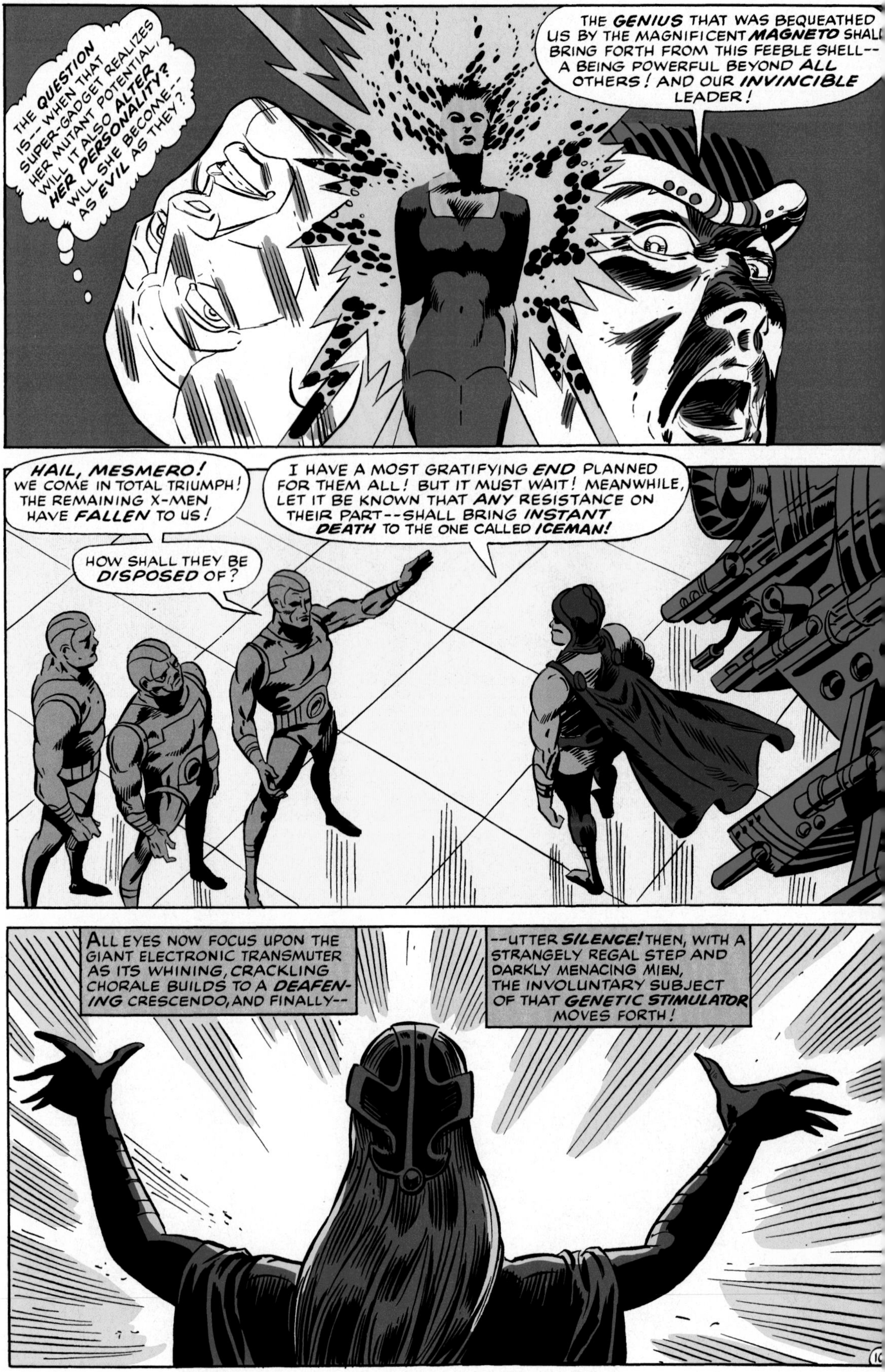

THE QUESTION IS--WHEN THAT SUPER-GADGET REALIZES HER MUTANT POTENTIAL, WILL IT ALSO ALTER HER PERSONALITY? WILL SHE BECOME--AS EVIL AS THEY?
THE GENIUS THAT WAS BEQUEATHED US BY THE MAGNIFICENT MAGNETO SHAL BRING FORTH FROM THIS FEEBLE SHELL--A BEING POWERFUL BEYOND ALL OTHERS! AND OUR INVINCIBLE LEADER!
HAIL, MESMERO! WE COME IN TOTAL TRIUMPH! THE REMAINING X-MEN HAVE FALLEN TO US!
HOW SHALL THEY BE DISPOSED OF?
I HAVE A MOST GRATIFYING END PLANNED FOR THEM ALL! BUT IT MUST WAIT! MEANWHILE, LET IT BE KNOWN THAT ANY RESISTANCE ON THEIR PART--SHALL BRING INSTANT DEATH TO THE ONE CALLED ICEMAN!
ALL EYES NOW FOCUS UPON THE GIANT ELECTRONIC TRANSMUTER AS ITS WHINING, CRACKLING CHORALE BUILDS TO A DEAFENING CRESCENDO, AND FINALLY--
--UTTER SILENCE! THEN, WITH A STRANGELY REGAL STEP AND DARKLY MENACING MIEN, THE INVOLUNTARY SUBJECT OF THAT GENETIC STIMULATOR MOVES FORTH!

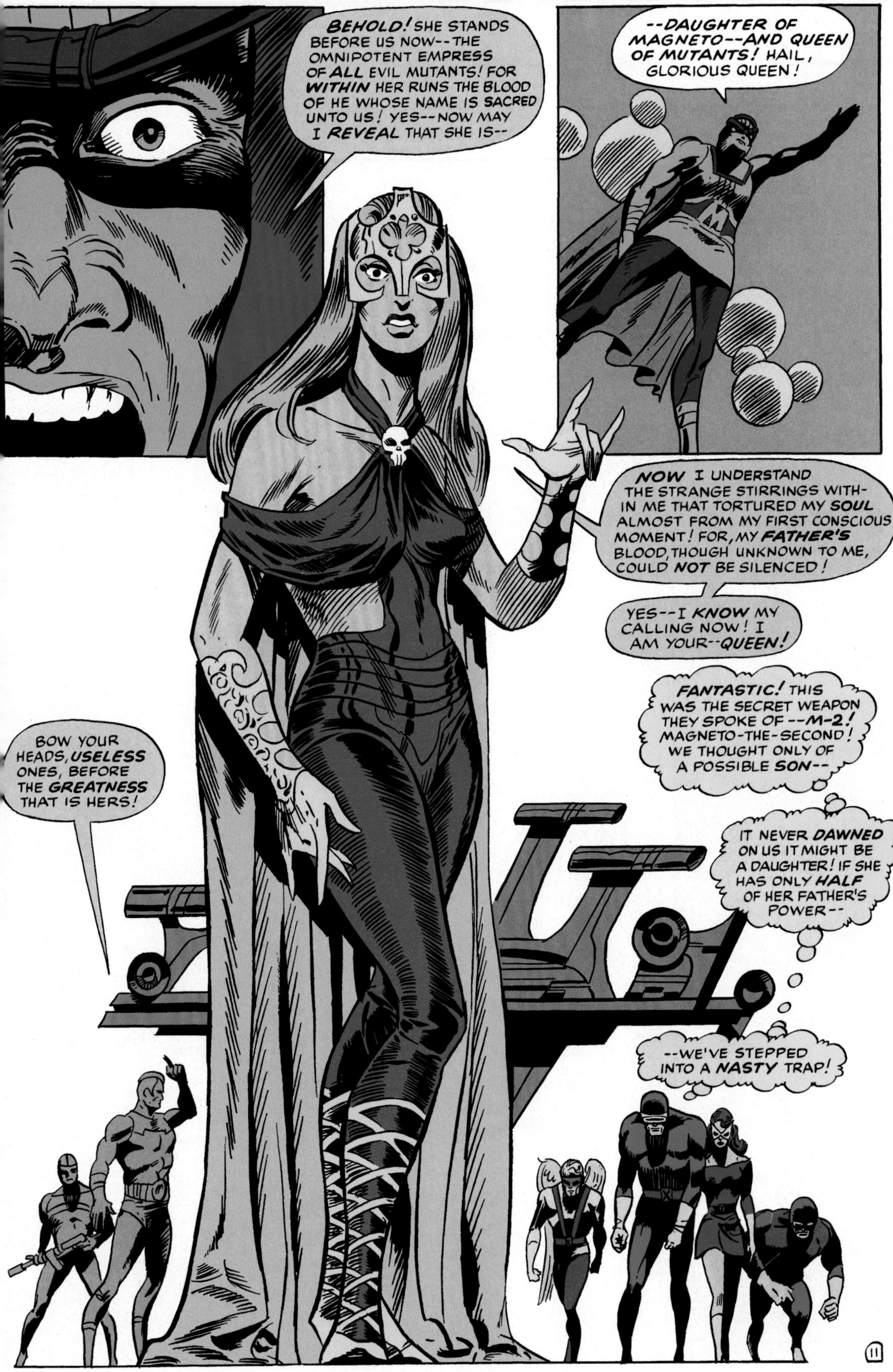
BEHOLD! SHE STANDS BEFORE US NOW--THE OMNIPOTENT EMPRESS OF ALL EVIL MUTANTS! FOR WITHIN HER RUNS THE BLOOD OF HE WHOSE NAME IS SACRED UNTO US! YES--NOW MAY I REVEAL THAT SHE IS--
--DAUGHTER OF MAGNETO--AND QUEEN OF MUTANTS! HAIL, GLORIOUS QUEEN!
NOW I UNDERSTAND THE STRANGE STIRRINGS WITHIN ME THAT TORTURED MY SOUL ALMOST FROM MY FIRST CONSCIOUS MOMENT! FOR, MY FATHER'S BLOOD, THOUGH UNKNOWN TO ME, COULD NOT BE SILENCED!
YES--I KNOW MY CALLING NOW! I AM YOUR--QUEEN!
BOW YOUR HEADS, USELESS ONES, BEFORE THE GREATNESS THAT IS HERS!
FANTASTIC! THIS WAS THE SECRET WEAPON THEY SPOKE OF--M-2! MAGNETO-THE-SECOND! WE THOUGHT ONLY OF A POSSIBLE SON--
IT NEVER DAWNED ON US IT MIGHT BE A DAUGHTER! IF SHE HAS ONLY HALF OF HER FATHER'S POWER--
--WE'VE STEPPED INTO A NASTY TRAP!

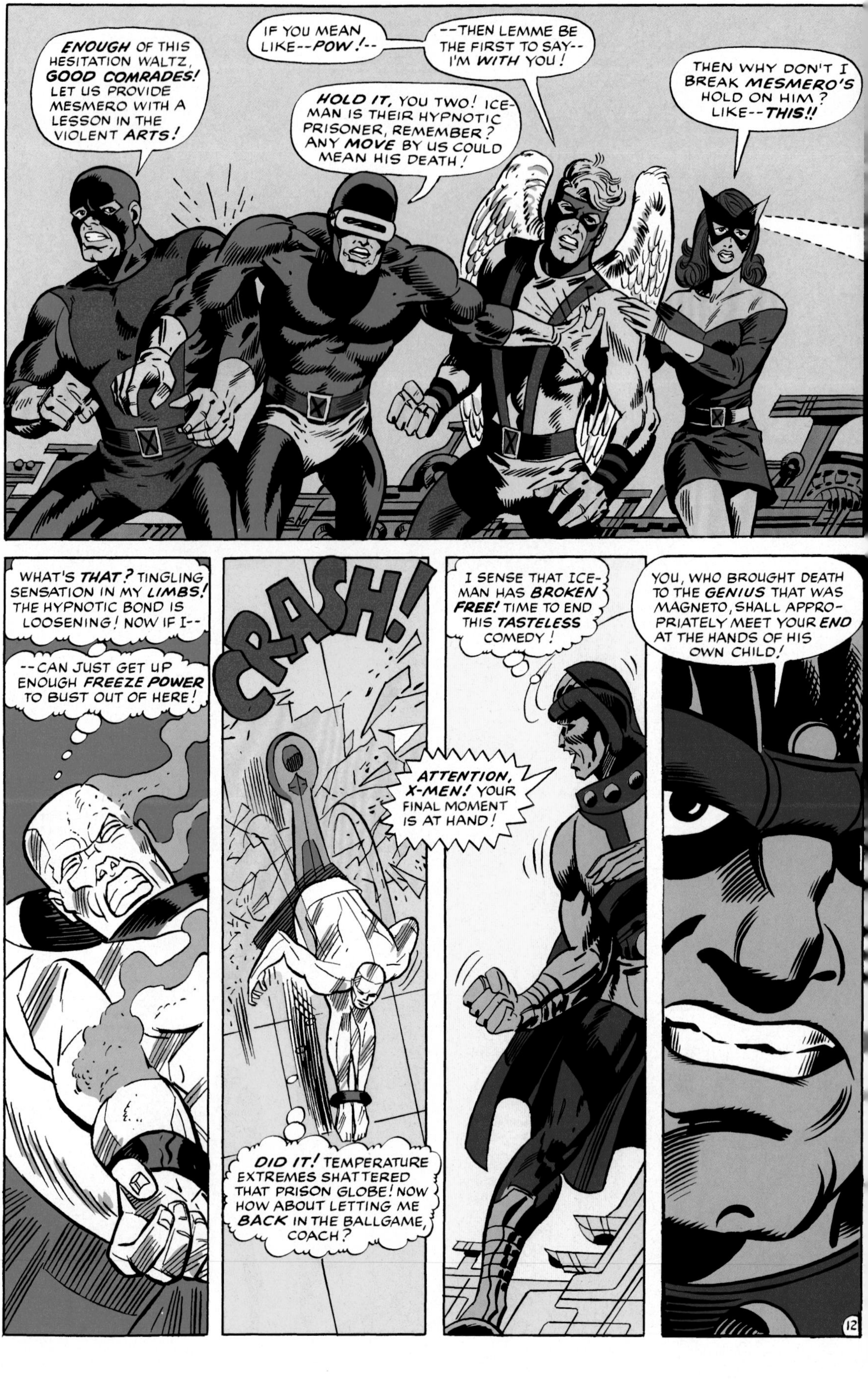

ENOUGH OF THIS HESITATION WALTZ, GOOD COMRADES! LET US PROVIDE MESMERO WITH A LESSON IN THE VIOLENT ARTS!
IF YOU MEAN LIKE--POW!--
--THEN LEMME BE THE FIRST TO SAY-- I'M WITH YOU!
HOLD IT, YOU TWO! ICE-MAN IS THEIR HYPNOTIC PRISONER, REMEMBER? ANY MOVE BY US COULD MEAN HIS DEATH!
THEN WHY DON'T I BREAK MESMERO'S HOLD ON HIM? LIKE--THIS!!
WHAT'S THAT? TINGLING SENSATION IN MY LIMBS! THE HYPNOTIC BOND IS LOOSENING! NOW IF I--
--CAN JUST GET UP ENOUGH FREEZE POWER TO BUST OUT OF HERE!
CRASH!
ATTENTION, X-MEN! YOUR FINAL MOMENT IS AT HAND!
DID IT! TEMPERATURE EXTREMES SHATTERED THAT PRISON GLOBE! NOW HOW ABOUT LETTING ME BACK IN THE BALLGAME, COACH?
I SENSE THAT ICE-MAN HAS BROKEN FREE! TIME TO END THIS TASTELESS COMEDY!
YOU, WHO BROUGHT DEATH TO THE GENIUS THAT WAS MAGNETO, SHALL APPROPRIATELY MEET YOUR END AT THE HANDS OF HIS OWN CHILD!
12

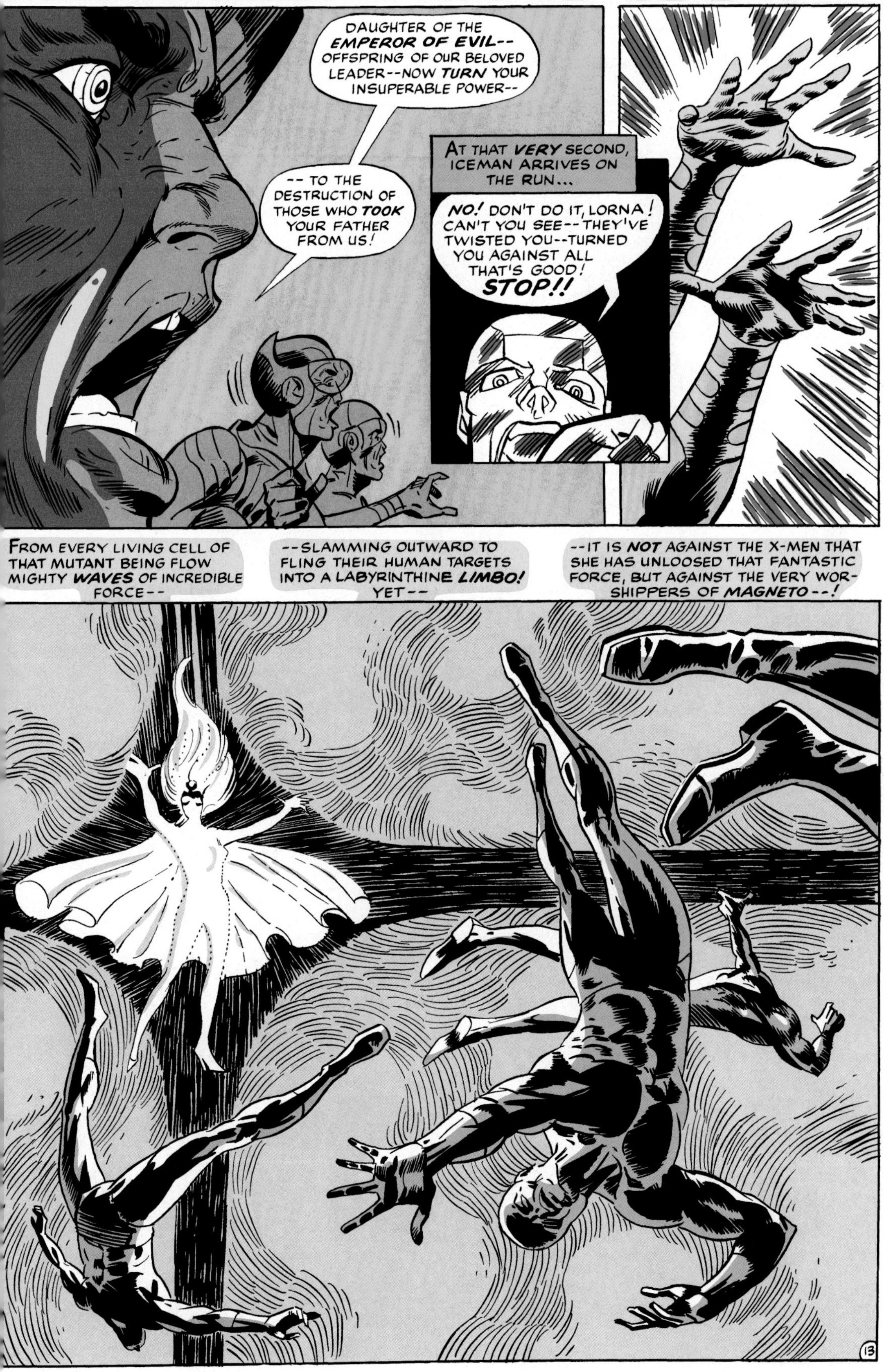
DAUGHTER OF THE EMPEROR OF EVIL-- OFFSPRING OF OUR BELOVED LEADER--NOW TURN YOUR INSUPERABLE POWER--
-- TO THE DESTRUCTION OF THOSE WHO TOOK YOUR FATHER FROM US!
AT THAT VERY SECOND, ICEMAN ARRIVES ON THE RUN...
NO! DON'T DO IT, LORNA! CAN'T YOU SEE--THEY'VE TWISTED YOU--TURNED YOU AGAINST ALL THAT'S GOOD! STOP!!
FROM EVERY LIVING CELL OF THAT MUTANT BEING FLOW MIGHTY WAVES OF INCREDIBLE FORCE--
--SLAMMING OUTWARD TO FLING THEIR HUMAN TARGETS INTO A LABYRINTHINE LIMBO! YET--
--IT IS NOT AGAINST THE X-MEN THAT SHE HAS UNLOOSED THAT FANTASTIC FORCE, BUT AGAINST THE VERY WOR-SHIPPERS OF MAGNETO--!
13

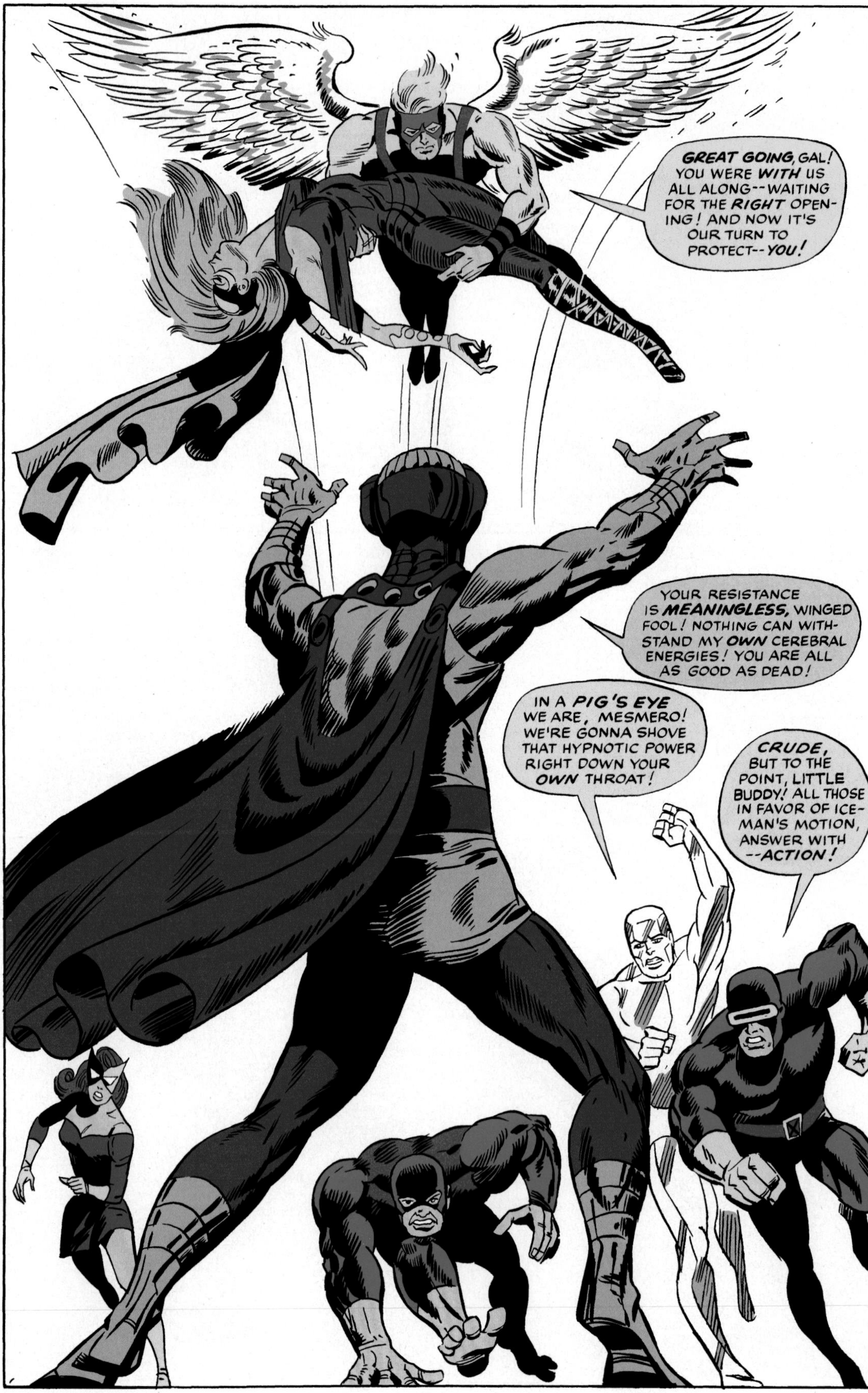

GREAT GOING, GAL! YOU WERE WITH US ALL ALONG--WAITING FOR THE RIGHT OPENING! AND NOW IT'S OUR TURN TO PROTECT--YOU!
YOUR RESISTANCE IS MEANINGLESS, WINGED FOOL! NOTHING CAN WITHSTAND MY OWN CEREBRAL ENERGIES! YOU ARE ALL AS GOOD AS DEAD!
IN A PIG'S EYE WE ARE, MESMERO! WE'RE GONNA SHOVE THAT HYPNOTIC POWER RIGHT DOWN YOUR OWN THROAT!
CRUDE, BUT TO THE POINT, LITTLE BUDDY! ALL THOSE IN FAVOR OF ICE-MAN'S MOTION, ANSWER WITH --ACTION!
14

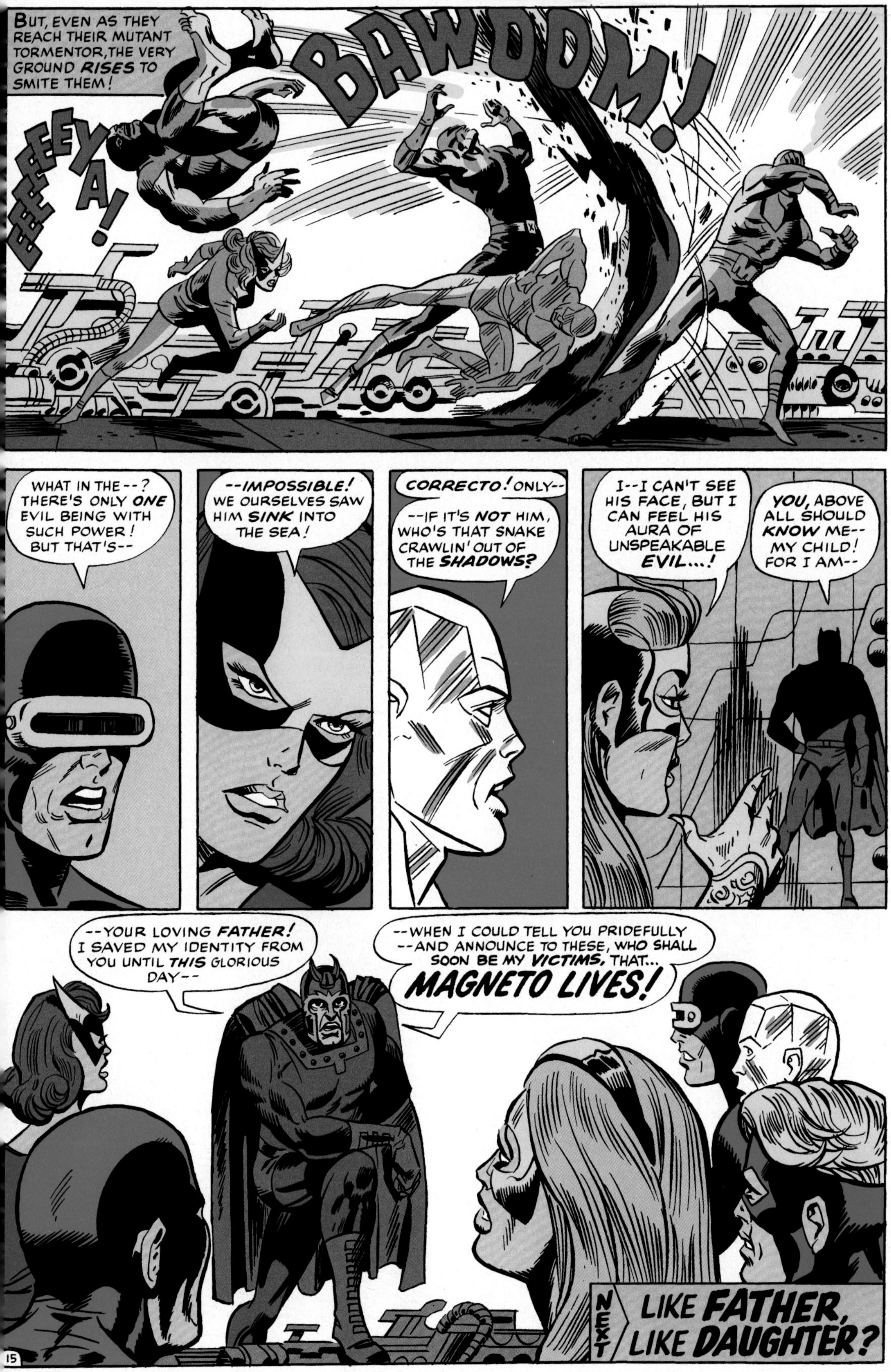

BUT, EVEN AS THEY REACH THEIR MUTANT TORMENTOR, THE VERY GROUND RISES TO SMITE THEM!
BAWOOM!
EEEEEEEYA!
WHAT IN THE--? THERE'S ONLY ONE EVIL BEING WITH SUCH POWER! BUT THAT'S--
--IMPOSSIBLE! WE OURSELVES SAW HIM SINK INTO THE SEA!
CORRECTO! ONLY--
--IF IT'S NOT HIM, WHO'S THAT SNAKE CRAWLIN' OUT OF THE SHADOWS?
I--I CAN'T SEE HIS FACE, BUT I CAN FEEL HIS AURA OF UNSPEAKABLE EVIL...!
YOU, ABOVE ALL SHOULD KNOW ME--MY CHILD! FOR I AM--
--YOUR LOVING FATHER! I SAVED MY IDENTITY FROM YOU UNTIL THIS GLORIOUS DAY--
--WHEN I COULD TELL YOU PRIDEFULLY --AND ANNOUNCE TO THESE, WHO SHALL SOON BE MY VICTIMS, THAT... MAGNETO LIVES!
NEXT LIKE FATHER, LIKE DAUGHTER?
15

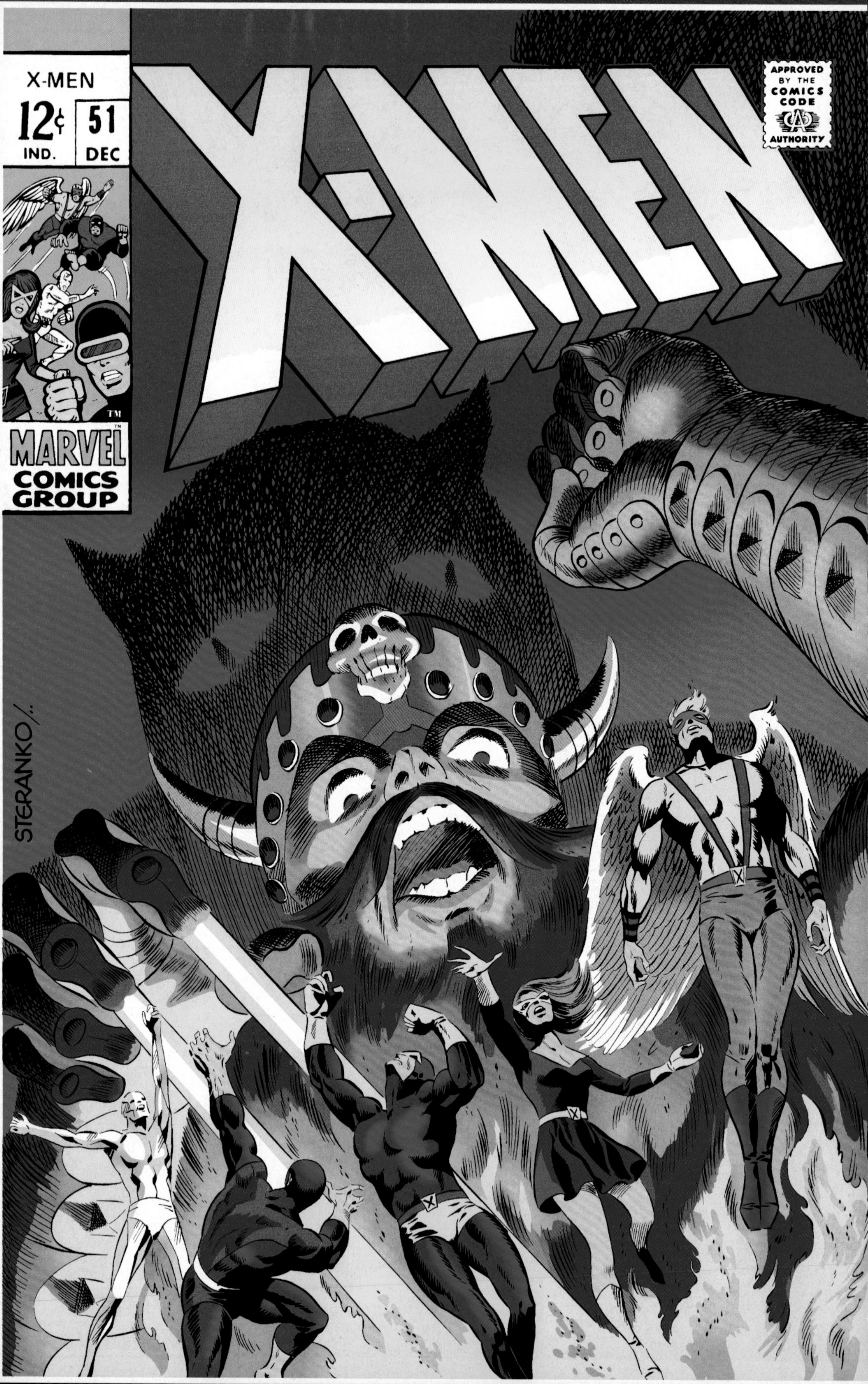

X-MEN
12¢
51
IND.
DEC
X-MEN
APPROVED BY THE COMICS CODE AUTHORITY
MARVEL COMICS GROUP
STERANKO

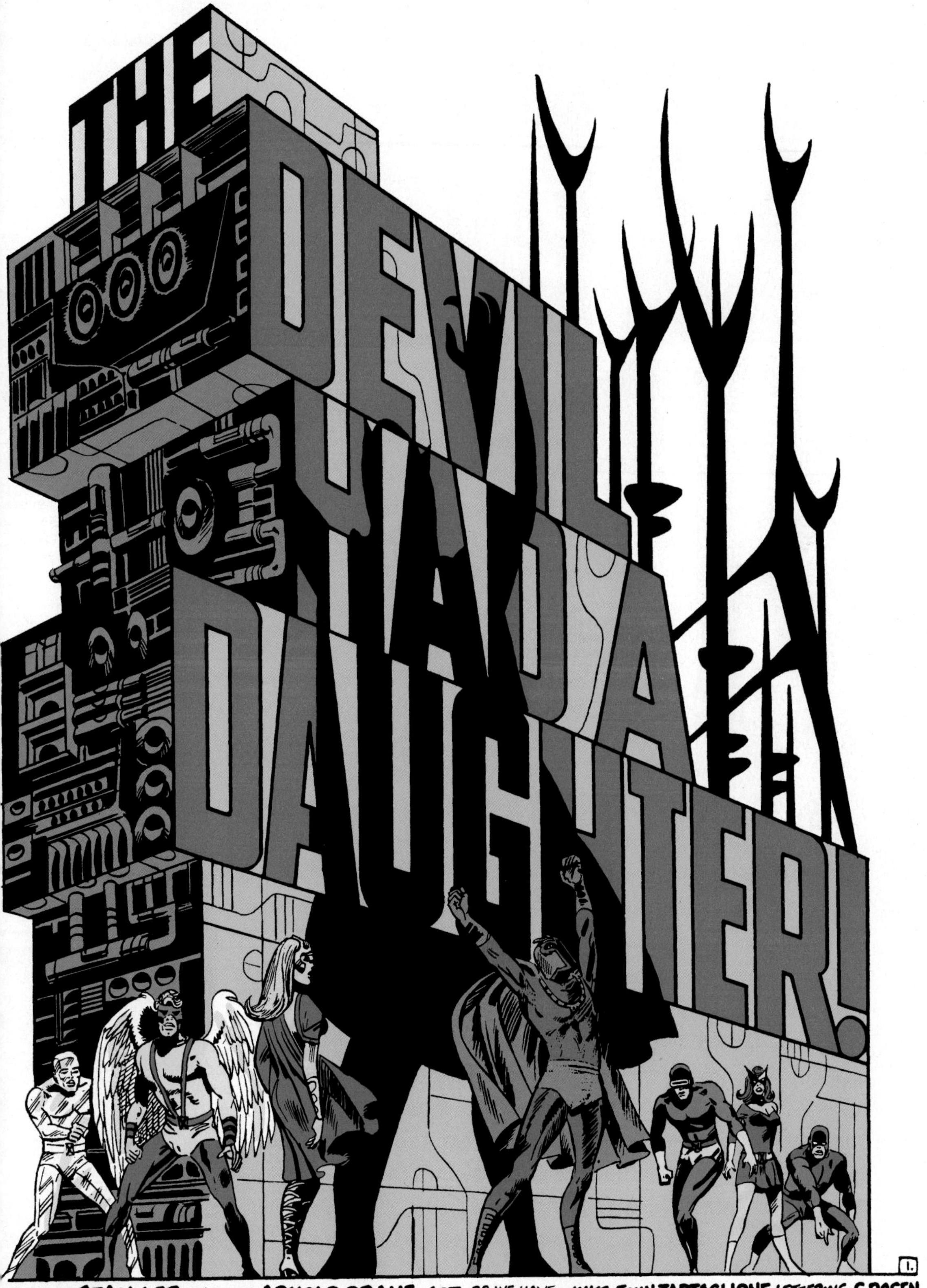
THE DEVIL HAD A DAUGHTER!
1.
EDITOR•STAN LEE WRITER•ARNOLD DRAKE ART• DO WE HAVE TO TELL YOU? INKS•JOHN TARTAGLIONE LETTERING•S.ROSEN

FROM THE GRAVE TO WHICH ALL HAD THOUGHT HIM CONSIGNED, MAGNETO HAS RETURNED...

YES! IT IS SO! THE GIRL IS FLESH OF *MY* FLESH...BLOOD OF *MY* BLOOD! HERS SHALL BE THE POWER AND GLORY KNOWN TO *NO* OTHER WOMAN! FOR...

SHE IS...THE *DAUGHTER OF MAGNETO!*

NOW, MY CHILD, *YOU* MUST MAKE YOUR CHOICE!

WILL YOU STAND BESIDE THESE *FOOLS* WHO ARE TOO BLIND OR TOO COWARDLY TO USE THE *INFINITE* POWER TO WHICH THEY, TOO, WERE BORN...

...A POWER BEYOND *ALL* OTHER MEN... A MIGHT DESTINED ONLY FOR *GODS?* OR...

..WILL YOU HEED THE CALL OF YOUR *OWN* BLOOD, AND ENTHRONED BESIDE ME, *RULE* ALL OF MANKIND?

THAT, FRIENDS, IS WHAT THEY CALL *STACKING* THE DECK! HE'S COMBINED THE *TWO* MOST POWERFUL HUMAN ELEMENTS!

VERILY! *FILIAL DUTY* AND THE INNER NEED FOR *POWER!* THE GIRL HAS *NO* OPTION BUT TO TURN AGAINST US!

SHE *COULD* HAVE A CHOICE...IF SHE KNEW THE TRUTH ABOUT MAGNETO! I'M NOT WILD ABOUT TELLING A GIRL THAT HER FATHER IS AN INSANE MASS *KILLER*...BUT IT HAS TO BE...EVEN THOUGH SHE'S *GOTTA* HATE ME FOR IT!

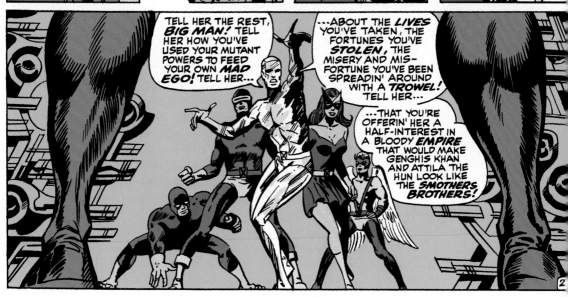

TELL HER THE REST, *BIG MAN!* TELL HER HOW YOU'VE USED YOUR MUTANT POWERS TO FEED YOUR OWN *MAD EGO!* TELL HER...

...ABOUT THE *LIVES* YOU'VE TAKEN, THE FORTUNES YOU'VE *STOLEN*, THE MISERY AND MISFORTUNE YOU'VE BEEN SPREADIN' AROUND WITH A *TROWEL!* TELL HER...

...THAT YOU'RE OFFERIN' HER A HALF-INTEREST IN A BLOODY *EMPIRE* THAT WOULD MAKE GENGHIS KHAN AND ATTILA THE HUN LOOK LIKE THE *SMOTHERS BROTHERS!*

2

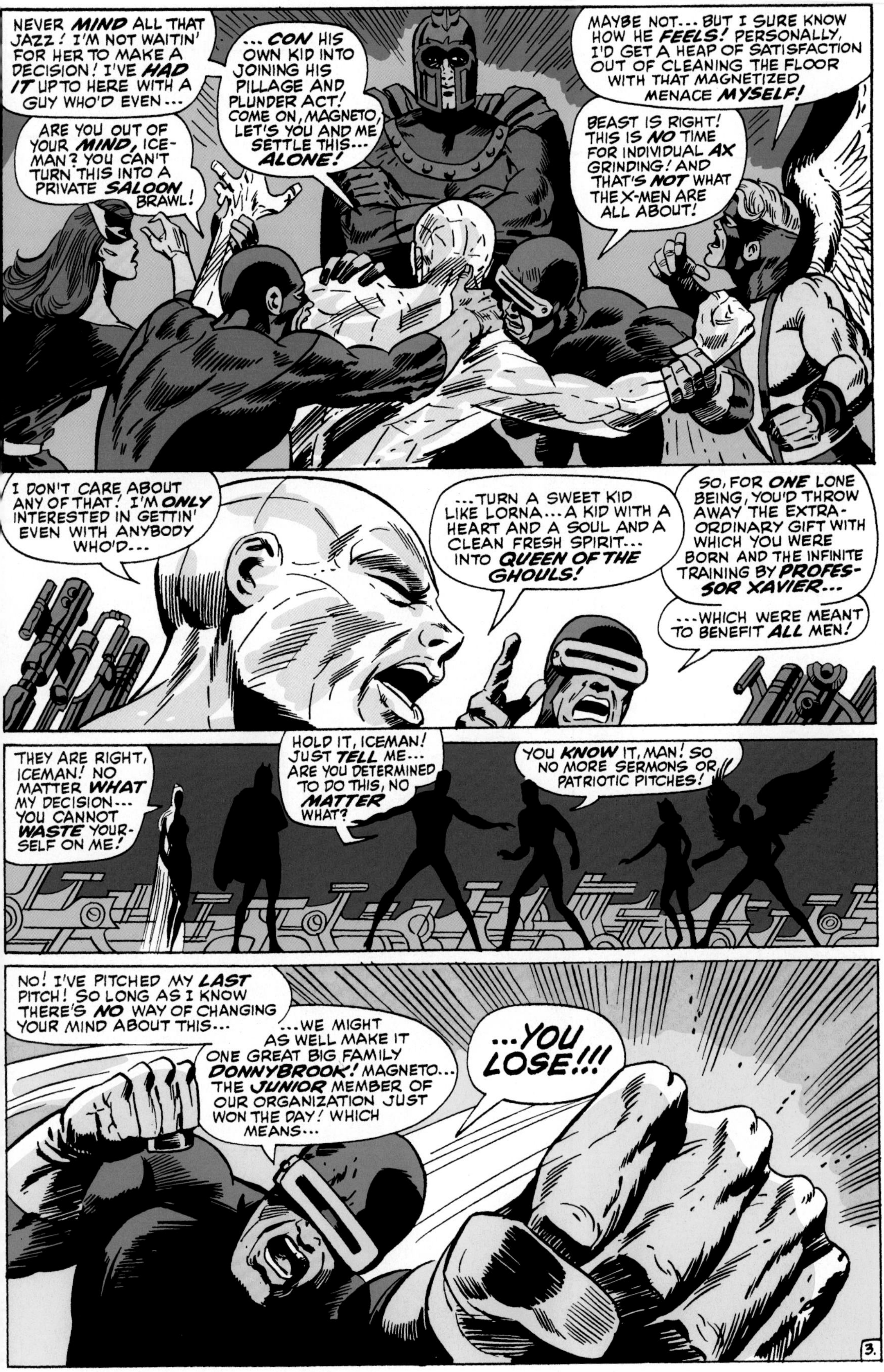

NEVER MIND ALL THAT JAZZ! I'M NOT WAITIN' FOR HER TO MAKE A DECISION! I'VE HAD IT UP TO HERE WITH A GUY WHO'D EVEN...
...CON HIS OWN KID INTO JOINING HIS PILLAGE AND PLUNDER ACT! COME ON, MAGNETO, LET'S YOU AND ME SETTLE THIS... ALONE!
ARE YOU OUT OF YOUR MIND, ICE-MAN? YOU CAN'T TURN THIS INTO A PRIVATE SALOON BRAWL!
MAYBE NOT... BUT I SURE KNOW HOW HE FEELS! PERSONALLY, I'D GET A HEAP OF SATISFACTION OUT OF CLEANING THE FLOOR WITH THAT MAGNETIZED MENACE MYSELF!
BEAST IS RIGHT! THIS IS NO TIME FOR INDIVIDUAL AX GRINDING! AND THAT'S NOT WHAT THE X-MEN ARE ALL ABOUT!
I DON'T CARE ABOUT ANY OF THAT! I'M ONLY INTERESTED IN GETTIN' EVEN WITH ANYBODY WHO'D---
...TURN A SWEET KID LIKE LORNA... A KID WITH A HEART AND A SOUL AND A CLEAN FRESH SPIRIT... INTO QUEEN OF THE GHOULS!
SO, FOR ONE LONE BEING, YOU'D THROW AWAY THE EXTRA-ORDINARY GIFT WITH WHICH YOU WERE BORN AND THE INFINITE TRAINING BY PROFES-SOR XAVIER...
...WHICH WERE MEANT TO BENEFIT ALL MEN!
THEY ARE RIGHT, ICEMAN! NO MATTER WHAT MY DECISION... YOU CANNOT WASTE YOUR-SELF ON ME!
HOLD IT, ICEMAN! JUST TELL ME... ARE YOU DETERMINED TO DO THIS, NO MATTER WHAT?
YOU KNOW IT, MAN! SO NO MORE SERMONS OR PATRIOTIC PITCHES!
NO! I'VE PITCHED MY LAST PITCH! SO LONG AS I KNOW THERE'S NO WAY OF CHANGING YOUR MIND ABOUT THIS...
...WE MIGHT AS WELL MAKE IT ONE GREAT BIG FAMILY DONNYBROOK! MAGNETO... THE JUNIOR MEMBER OF OUR ORGANIZATION JUST WON THE DAY! WHICH MEANS...
...YOU LOSE!!!

KRRR-NCH!

I DON'T KNOW HOW A *SUPER-ROGUE* LIKE YOU PRODUCED A TOP-DRAWER ITEM LIKE *LORNA*...BUT I'M GOING TO *TRY* NOT TO LET IT INFLUENCE ME! YOU'RE *STILL* NUMBER ONE ON MY...*RAT LIST!*

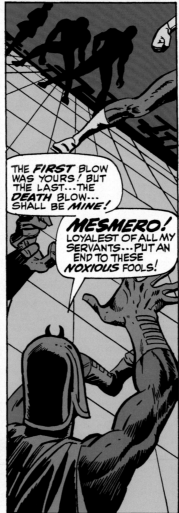

THE *FIRST* BLOW WAS YOURS! BUT THE LAST...THE *DEATH* BLOW... SHALL BE *MINE!*

MESMERO! LOYALEST OF ALL MY SERVANTS...PUT AN END TO THESE *NOXIOUS* FOOLS!

THERE IS A FORTUNE...AND MY UNDYING GRATITUDE... TO HIM WHO CLAIMS THEIR...*HEADS!*

4

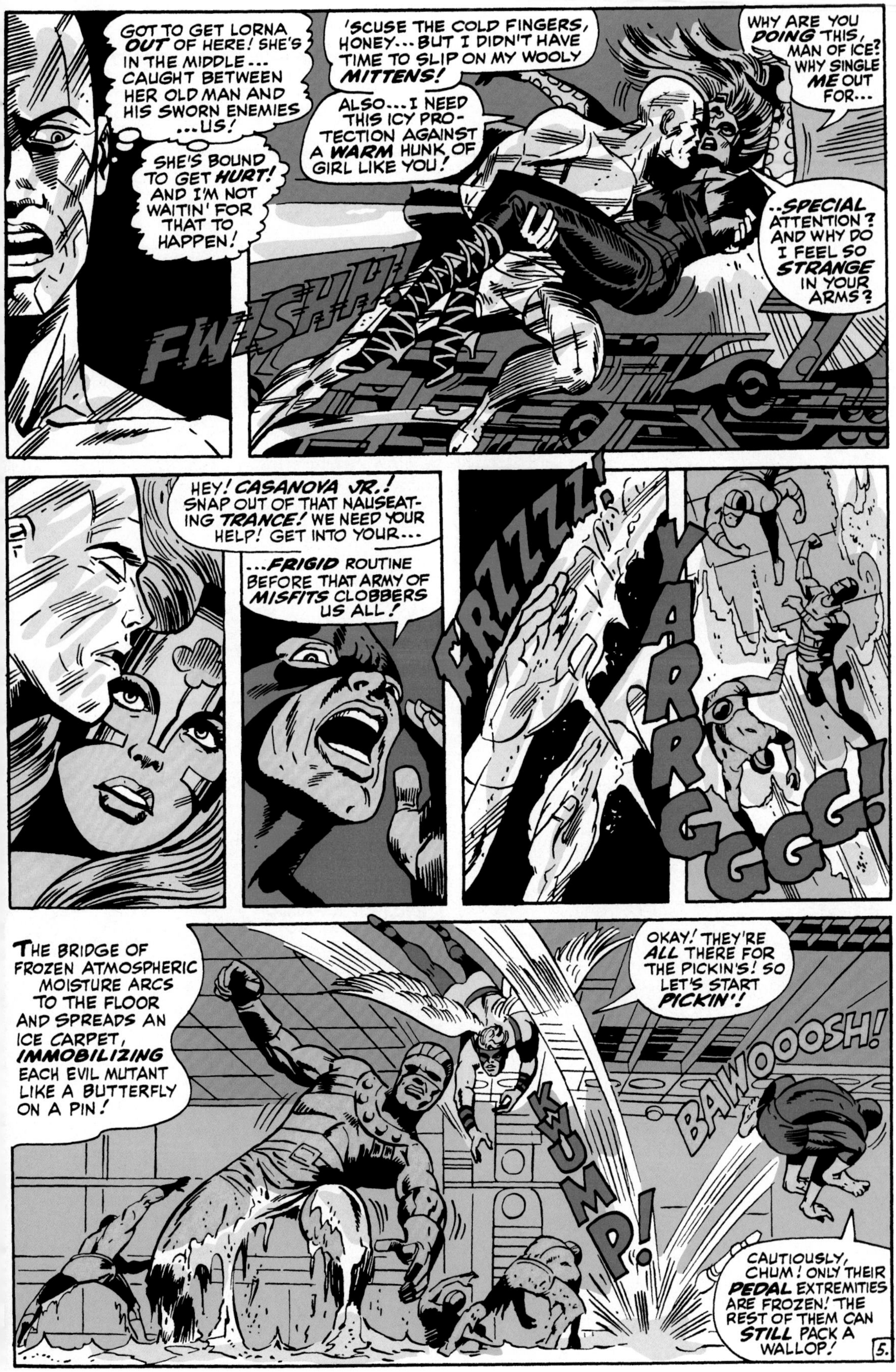
GOT TO GET LORNA OUT OF HERE! SHE'S IN THE MIDDLE... CAUGHT BETWEEN HER OLD MAN AND HIS SWORN ENEMIES ...US!
SHE'S BOUND TO GET HURT! AND I'M NOT WAITIN' FOR THAT TO HAPPEN!
'SCUSE THE COLD FINGERS, HONEY... BUT I DIDN'T HAVE TIME TO SLIP ON MY WOOLY MITTENS!
ALSO... I NEED THIS ICY PROTECTION AGAINST A WARM HUNK OF GIRL LIKE YOU!
WHY ARE YOU DOING THIS, MAN OF ICE? WHY SINGLE ME OUT FOR...
..SPECIAL ATTENTION? AND WHY DO I FEEL SO STRANGE IN YOUR ARMS?
FWISHHH
HEY! CASANOVA JR.! SNAP OUT OF THAT NAUSEATING TRANCE! WE NEED YOUR HELP! GET INTO YOUR...
...FRIGID ROUTINE BEFORE THAT ARMY OF MISFITS CLOBBERS US ALL!
FRZZZZZ!
YARRGGGG!
THE BRIDGE OF FROZEN ATMOSPHERIC MOISTURE ARCS TO THE FLOOR AND SPREADS AN ICE CARPET, IMMOBILIZING EACH EVIL MUTANT LIKE A BUTTERFLY ON A PIN!
OKAY! THEY'RE ALL THERE FOR THE PICKIN'S! SO LET'S START PICKIN'!
KWUMP!
BAWOOOSH!
CAUTIOUSLY, CHUM! ONLY THEIR PEDAL EXTREMITIES ARE FROZEN! THE REST OF THEM CAN STILL PACK A WALLOP!
5.

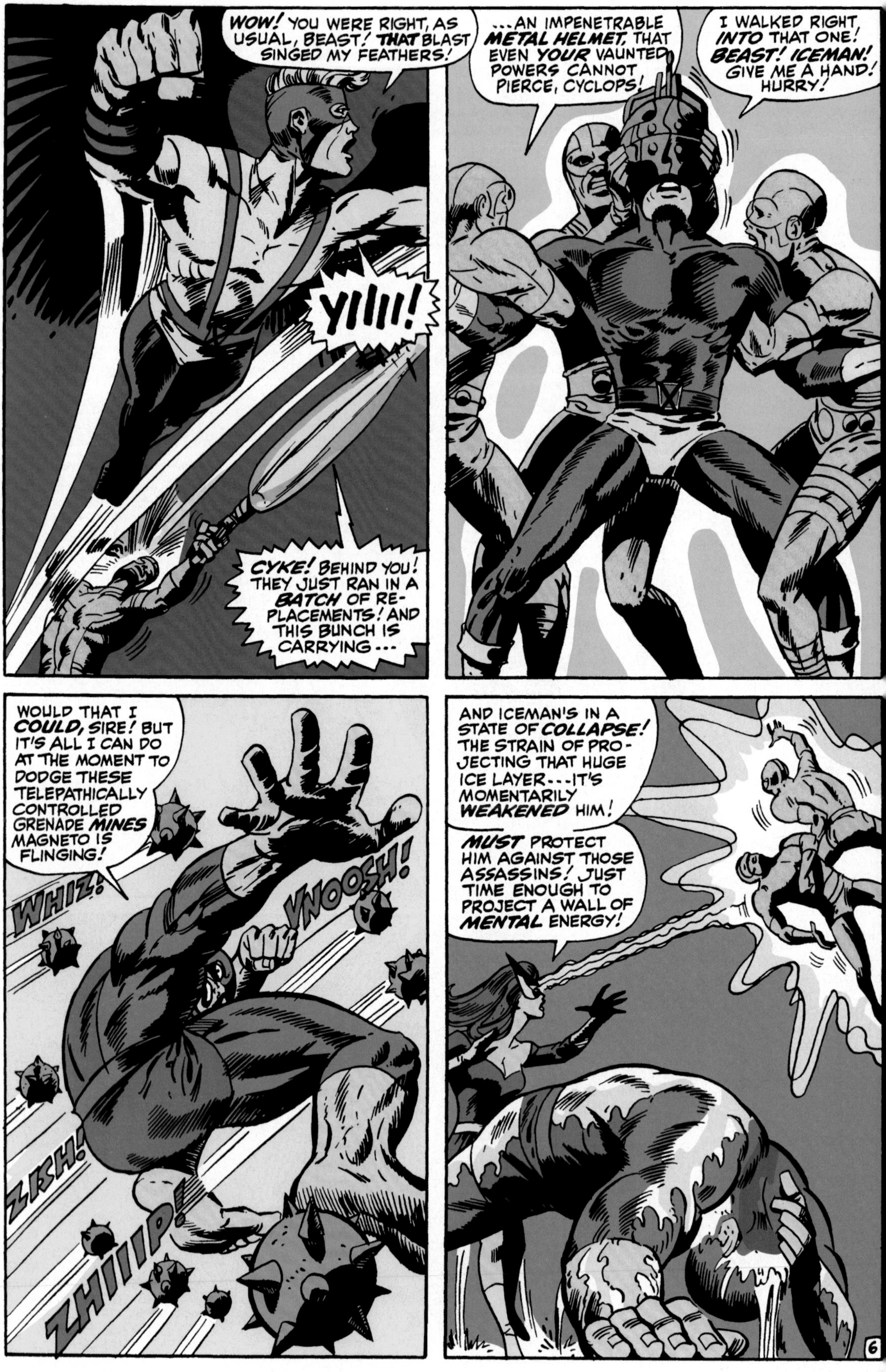

WOW! YOU WERE RIGHT, AS USUAL, BEAST! THAT BLAST SINGED MY FEATHERS!
YIIII!
CYKE! BEHIND YOU! THEY JUST RAN IN A BATCH OF RE-PLACEMENTS! AND THIS BUNCH IS CARRYING ---
...AN IMPENETRABLE METAL HELMET, THAT EVEN YOUR VAUNTED POWERS CANNOT PIERCE, CYCLOPS!
I WALKED RIGHT INTO THAT ONE! BEAST! ICEMAN! GIVE ME A HAND! HURRY!
WOULD THAT I COULD, SIRE! BUT IT'S ALL I CAN DO AT THE MOMENT TO DODGE THESE TELEPATHICALLY CONTROLLED GRENADE MINES MAGNETO IS FLINGING!
WHIZ!
VNOOSH!
ZISH!
ZHIIIP!
AND ICEMAN'S IN A STATE OF COLLAPSE! THE STRAIN OF PRO-JECTING THAT HUGE ICE LAYER---IT'S MOMENTARILY WEAKENED HIM!
MUST PROTECT HIM AGAINST THOSE ASSASSINS! JUST TIME ENOUGH TO PROJECT A WALL OF MENTAL ENERGY!

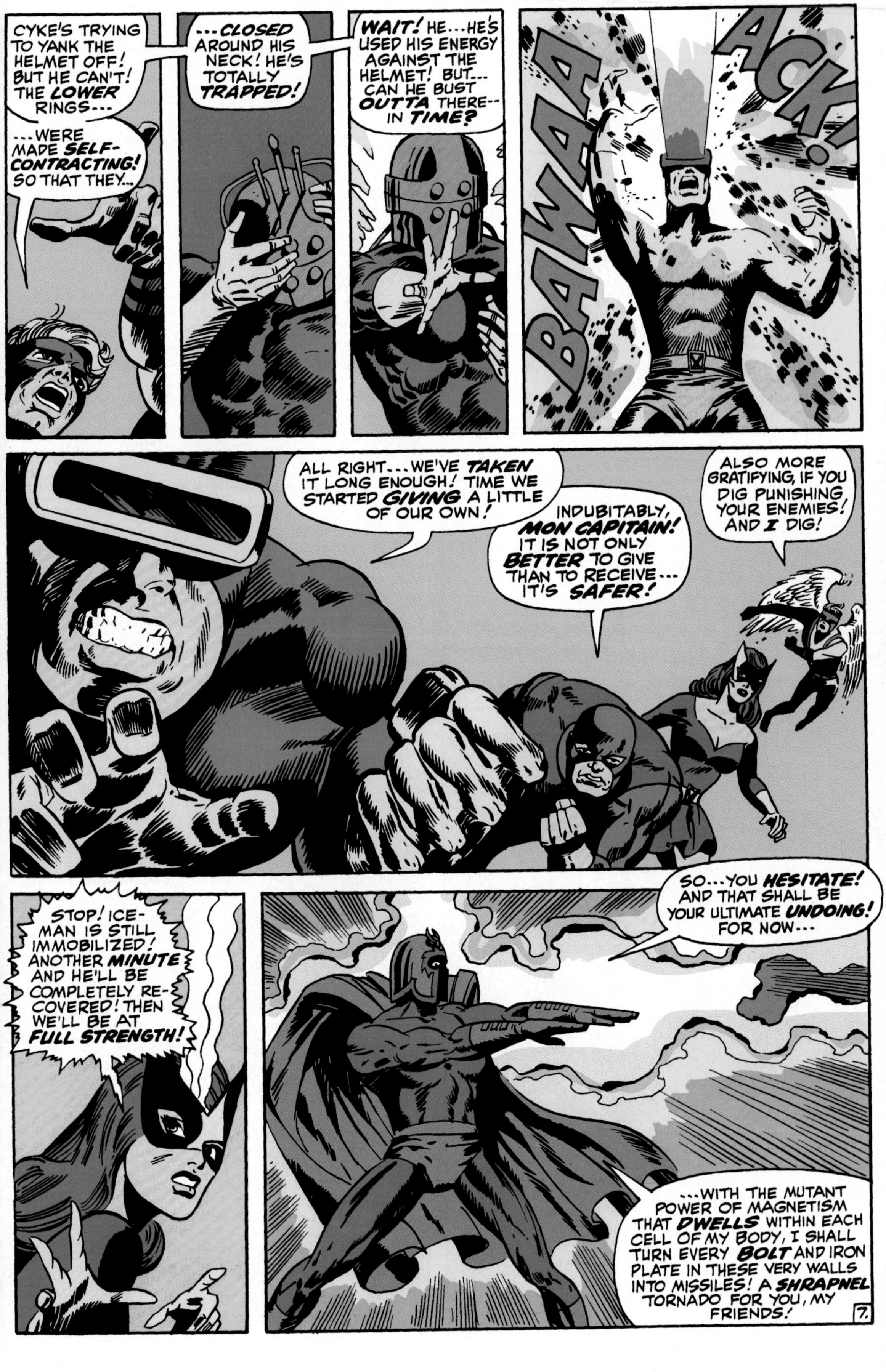
CYKE'S TRYING TO YANK THE HELMET OFF! BUT HE CAN'T! THE LOWER RINGS---
---WERE MADE SELF-CONTRACTING! SO THAT THEY...
...CLOSED AROUND HIS NECK! HE'S TOTALLY TRAPPED!
WAIT! HE...HE'S USED HIS ENERGY AGAINST THE HELMET! BUT... CAN HE BUST OUTTA THERE-- IN TIME?
BAWAACK!
ALL RIGHT...WE'VE TAKEN IT LONG ENOUGH! TIME WE STARTED GIVING A LITTLE OF OUR OWN!
INDUBITABLY, MON CAPITAIN! IT IS NOT ONLY BETTER TO GIVE THAN TO RECEIVE... IT'S SAFER!
ALSO MORE GRATIFYING, IF YOU DIG PUNISHING YOUR ENEMIES! AND I DIG!
STOP! ICE-MAN IS STILL IMMOBILIZED! ANOTHER MINUTE AND HE'LL BE COMPLETELY RE-COVERED! THEN WE'LL BE AT FULL STRENGTH!
SO...YOU HESITATE! AND THAT SHALL BE YOUR ULTIMATE UNDOING! FOR NOW...
...WITH THE MUTANT POWER OF MAGNETISM THAT DWELLS WITHIN EACH CELL OF MY BODY, I SHALL TURN EVERY BOLT AND IRON PLATE IN THESE VERY WALLS INTO MISSILES! A SHRAPNEL TORNADO FOR YOU, MY FRIENDS!
7.

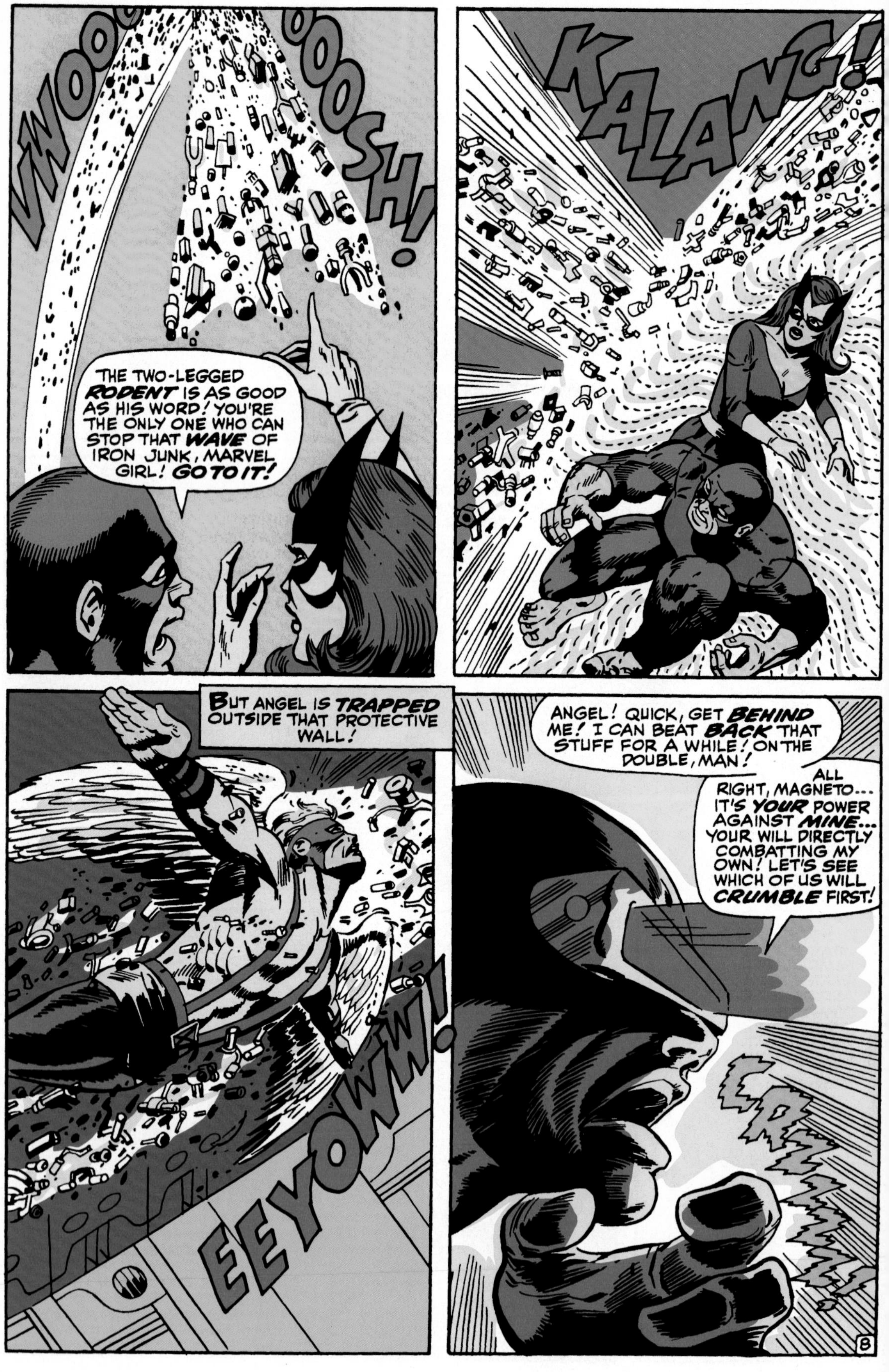
VWOOOOOOOSH!
THE TWO-LEGGED RODENT IS AS GOOD AS HIS WORD! YOU'RE THE ONLY ONE WHO CAN STOP THAT WAVE OF IRON JUNK, MARVEL GIRL! GO TO IT!
KALANG!
BUT ANGEL IS TRAPPED OUTSIDE THAT PROTECTIVE WALL!
EEYOWW!
ANGEL! QUICK, GET BEHIND ME! I CAN BEAT BACK THAT STUFF FOR A WHILE! ON THE DOUBLE, MAN!
ALL RIGHT, MAGNETO... IT'S YOUR POWER AGAINST MINE... YOUR WILL DIRECTLY COMBATTING MY OWN! LET'S SEE WHICH OF US WILL CRUMBLE FIRST!
CRMMM!
8

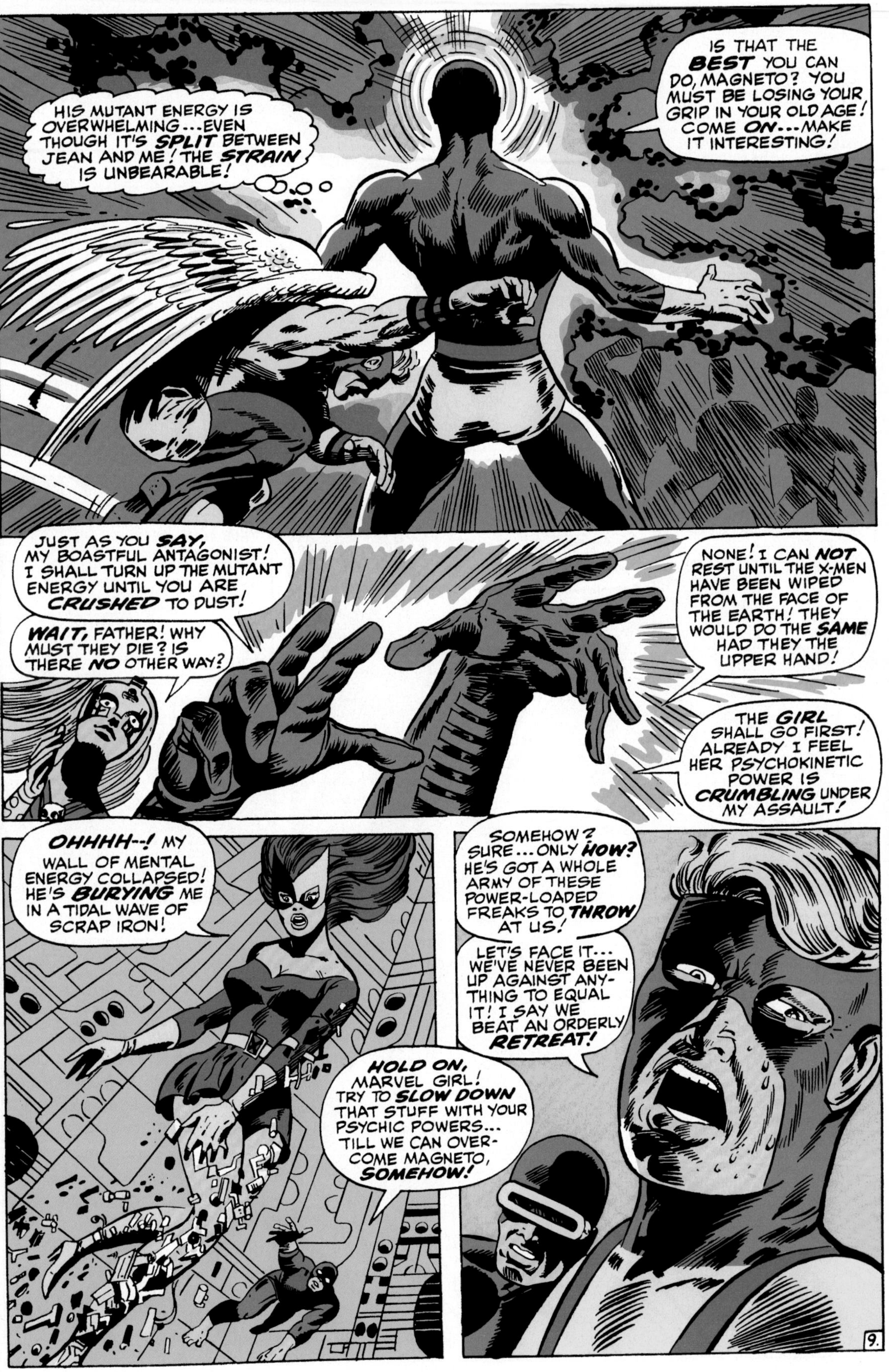

HIS MUTANT ENERGY IS OVERWHELMING... EVEN THOUGH IT'S SPLIT BETWEEN JEAN AND ME! THE STRAIN IS UNBEARABLE!
IS THAT THE BEST YOU CAN DO, MAGNETO? YOU MUST BE LOSING YOUR GRIP IN YOUR OLD AGE! COME ON... MAKE IT INTERESTING!
JUST AS YOU SAY, MY BOASTFUL ANTAGONIST! I SHALL TURN UP THE MUTANT ENERGY UNTIL YOU ARE CRUSHED TO DUST!
WAIT, FATHER! WHY MUST THEY DIE? IS THERE NO OTHER WAY?
NONE! I CAN NOT REST UNTIL THE X-MEN HAVE BEEN WIPED FROM THE FACE OF THE EARTH! THEY WOULD DO THE SAME HAD THEY THE UPPER HAND!
THE GIRL SHALL GO FIRST! ALREADY I FEEL HER PSYCHOKINETIC POWER IS CRUMBLING UNDER MY ASSAULT!
OHHHH--! MY WALL OF MENTAL ENERGY COLLAPSED! HE'S BURYING ME IN A TIDAL WAVE OF SCRAP IRON!
HOLD ON, MARVEL GIRL! TRY TO SLOW DOWN THAT STUFF WITH YOUR PSYCHIC POWERS... TILL WE CAN OVERCOME MAGNETO, SOMEHOW!
SOMEHOW? SURE... ONLY HOW? HE'S GOT A WHOLE ARMY OF THESE POWER-LOADED FREAKS TO THROW AT US!
LET'S FACE IT... WE'VE NEVER BEEN UP AGAINST ANYTHING TO EQUAL IT! I SAY WE BEAT AN ORDERLY RETREAT!
9.

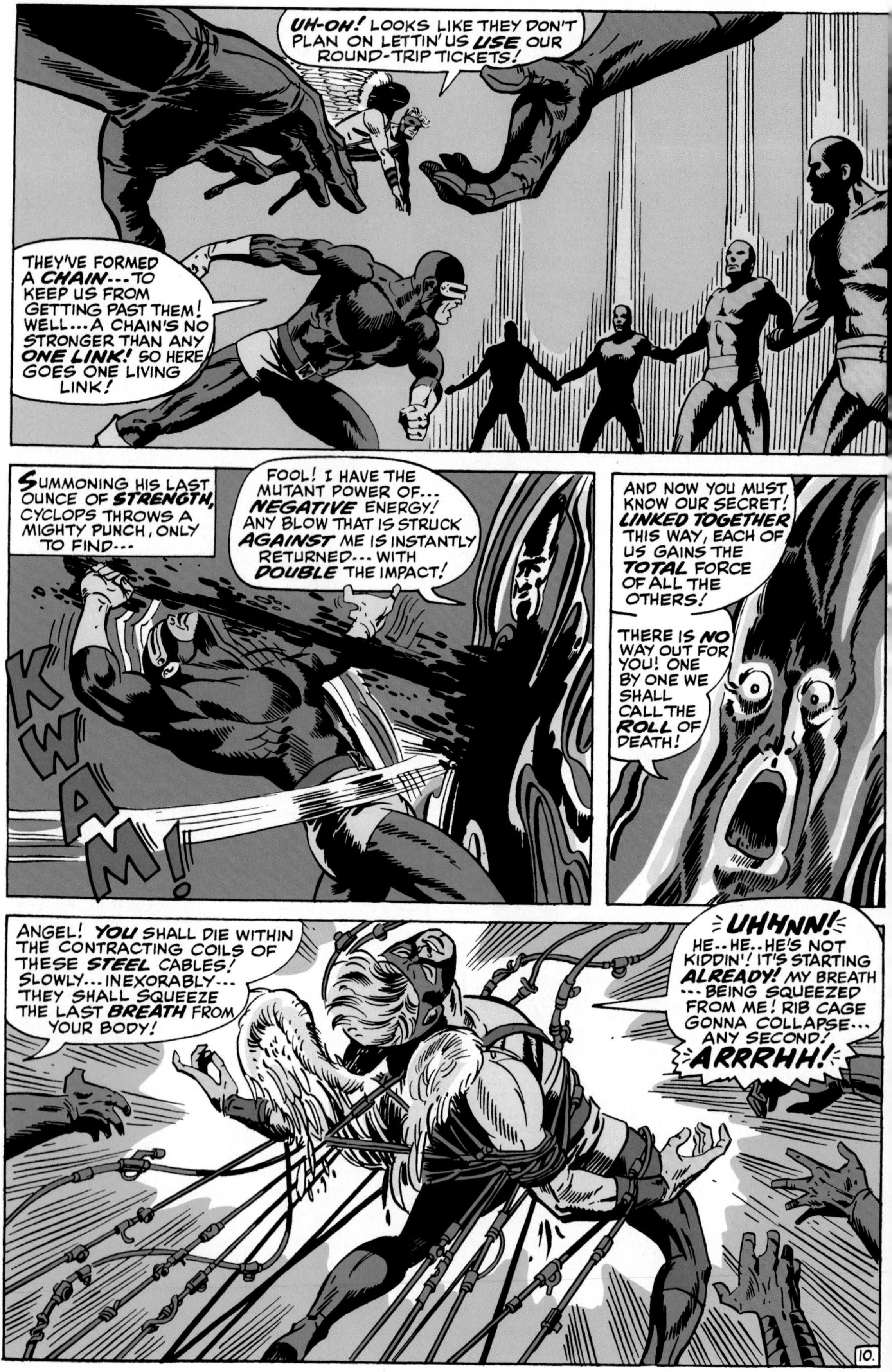

UH-OH! LOOKS LIKE THEY DON'T PLAN ON LETTIN' US USE OUR ROUND-TRIP TICKETS!
THEY'VE FORMED A CHAIN--- TO KEEP US FROM GETTING PAST THEM! WELL... A CHAIN'S NO STRONGER THAN ANY ONE LINK! SO HERE GOES ONE LIVING LINK!
SUMMONING HIS LAST OUNCE OF STRENGTH, CYCLOPS THROWS A MIGHTY PUNCH, ONLY TO FIND---
FOOL! I HAVE THE MUTANT POWER OF... NEGATIVE ENERGY! ANY BLOW THAT IS STRUCK AGAINST ME IS INSTANTLY RETURNED--- WITH DOUBLE THE IMPACT!
KWAM!
AND NOW YOU MUST KNOW OUR SECRET! LINKED TOGETHER THIS WAY, EACH OF US GAINS THE TOTAL FORCE OF ALL THE OTHERS!
THERE IS NO WAY OUT FOR YOU! ONE BY ONE WE SHALL CALL THE ROLL OF DEATH!
ANGEL! YOU SHALL DIE WITHIN THE CONTRACTING COILS OF THESE STEEL CABLES! SLOWLY... INEXORABLY--- THEY SHALL SQUEEZE THE LAST BREATH FROM YOUR BODY!
UHHNN! HE.. HE.. HE'S NOT KIDDIN'! IT'S STARTING ALREADY! MY BREATH --- BEING SQUEEZED FROM ME! RIB CAGE GONNA COLLAPSE... ANY SECOND! ARRRHH!
10.

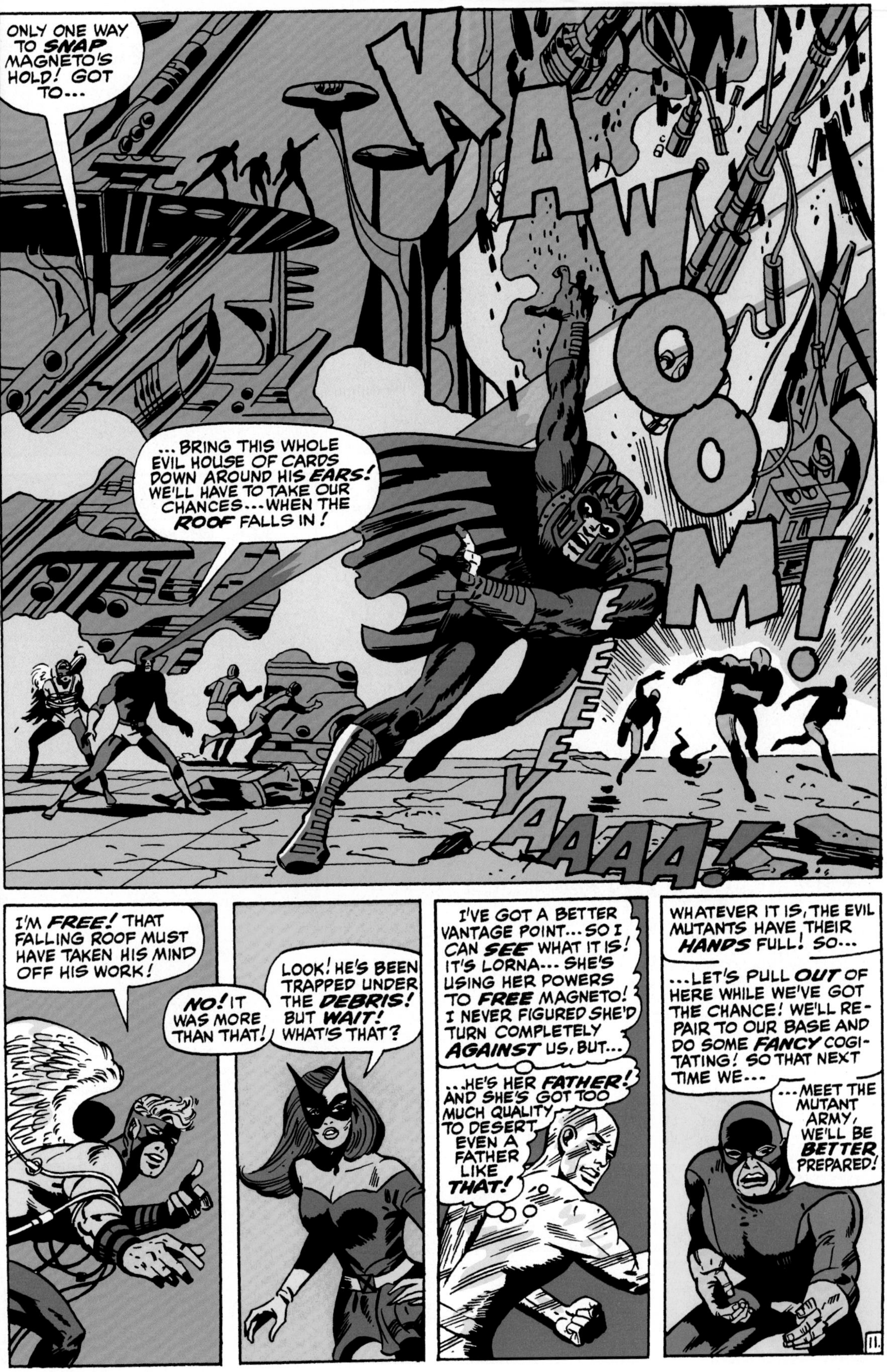

ONLY ONE WAY TO SNAP MAGNETO'S HOLD! GOT TO...
KAWOOOM!
...BRING THIS WHOLE EVIL HOUSE OF CARDS DOWN AROUND HIS EARS! WE'LL HAVE TO TAKE OUR CHANCES...WHEN THE ROOF FALLS IN!
EEEEEEYAAAAA!
I'M FREE! THAT FALLING ROOF MUST HAVE TAKEN HIS MIND OFF HIS WORK!
NO! IT WAS MORE THAN THAT!
LOOK! HE'S BEEN TRAPPED UNDER THE DEBRIS! BUT WAIT! WHAT'S THAT?
I'VE GOT A BETTER VANTAGE POINT...SO I CAN SEE WHAT IT IS! IT'S LORNA... SHE'S USING HER POWERS TO FREE MAGNETO! I NEVER FIGURED SHE'D TURN COMPLETELY AGAINST US, BUT...
...HE'S HER FATHER! AND SHE'S GOT TOO MUCH QUALITY TO DESERT EVEN A FATHER LIKE THAT!
WHATEVER IT IS, THE EVIL MUTANTS HAVE THEIR HANDS FULL! SO...
...LET'S PULL OUT OF HERE WHILE WE'VE GOT THE CHANCE! WE'LL RE-PAIR TO OUR BASE AND DO SOME FANCY COGI-TATING! SO THAT NEXT TIME WE...
...MEET THE MUTANT ARMY, WE'LL BE BETTER PREPARED!
11.

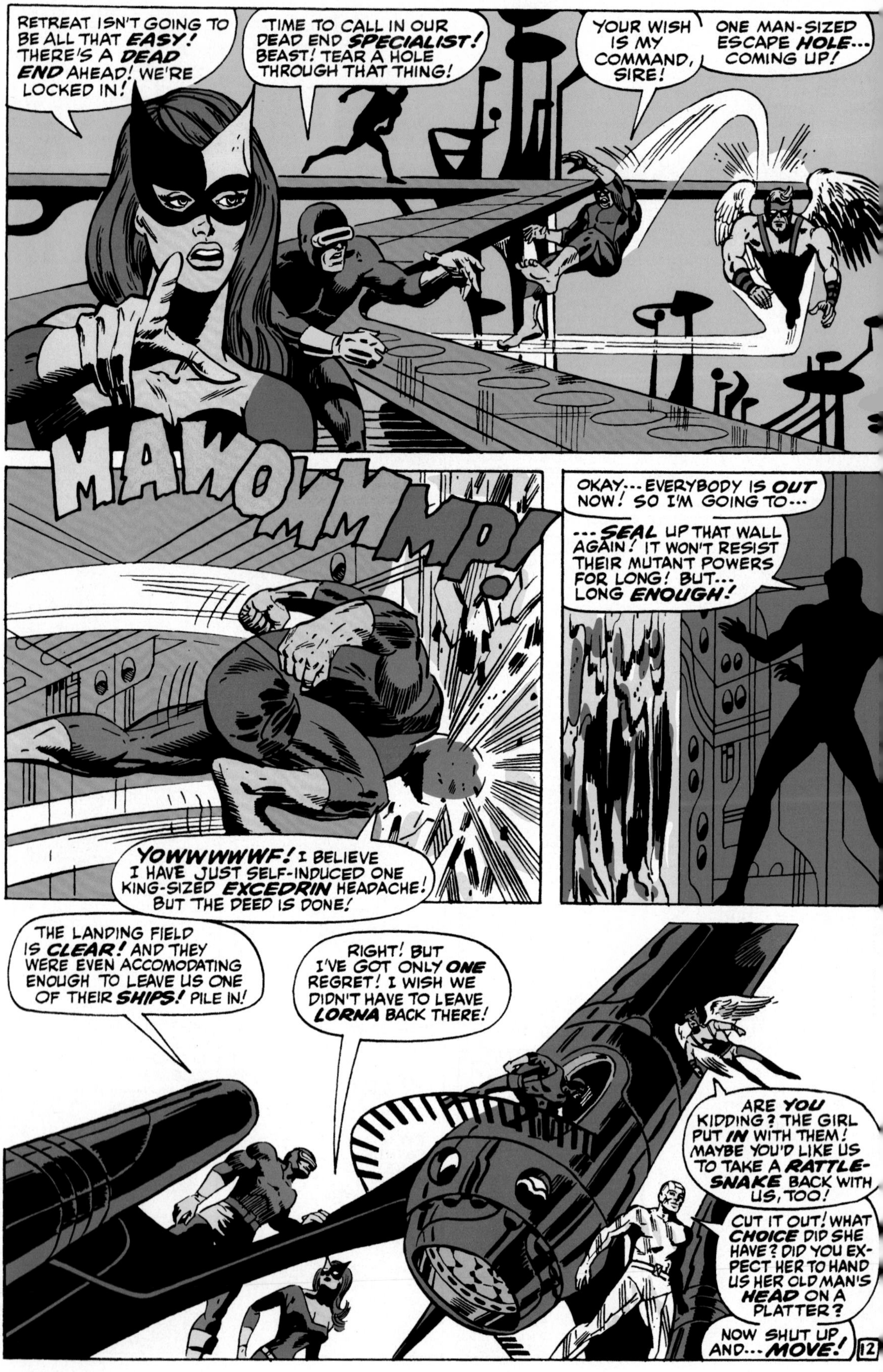
RETREAT ISN'T GOING TO BE ALL THAT EASY! THERE'S A DEAD END AHEAD! WE'RE LOCKED IN!
TIME TO CALL IN OUR DEAD END SPECIALIST! BEAST! TEAR A HOLE THROUGH THAT THING!
YOUR WISH IS MY COMMAND, SIRE!
ONE MAN-SIZED ESCAPE HOLE... COMING UP!
MAWOMMMP!
YOWWWWWF! I BELIEVE I HAVE JUST SELF-INDUCED ONE KING-SIZED EXCEDRIN HEADACHE! BUT THE DEED IS DONE!
OKAY... EVERYBODY IS OUT NOW! SO I'M GOING TO...
...SEAL UP THAT WALL AGAIN! IT WON'T RESIST THEIR MUTANT POWERS FOR LONG! BUT... LONG ENOUGH!
THE LANDING FIELD IS CLEAR! AND THEY WERE EVEN ACCOMODATING ENOUGH TO LEAVE US ONE OF THEIR SHIPS! PILE IN!
RIGHT! BUT I'VE GOT ONLY ONE REGRET! I WISH WE DIDN'T HAVE TO LEAVE LORNA BACK THERE!
ARE YOU KIDDING? THE GIRL PUT IN WITH THEM! MAYBE YOU'D LIKE US TO TAKE A RATTLE-SNAKE BACK WITH US, TOO!
CUT IT OUT! WHAT CHOICE DID SHE HAVE? DID YOU EXPECT HER TO HAND US HER OLD MAN'S HEAD ON A PLATTER?
NOW SHUT UP, AND... MOVE!

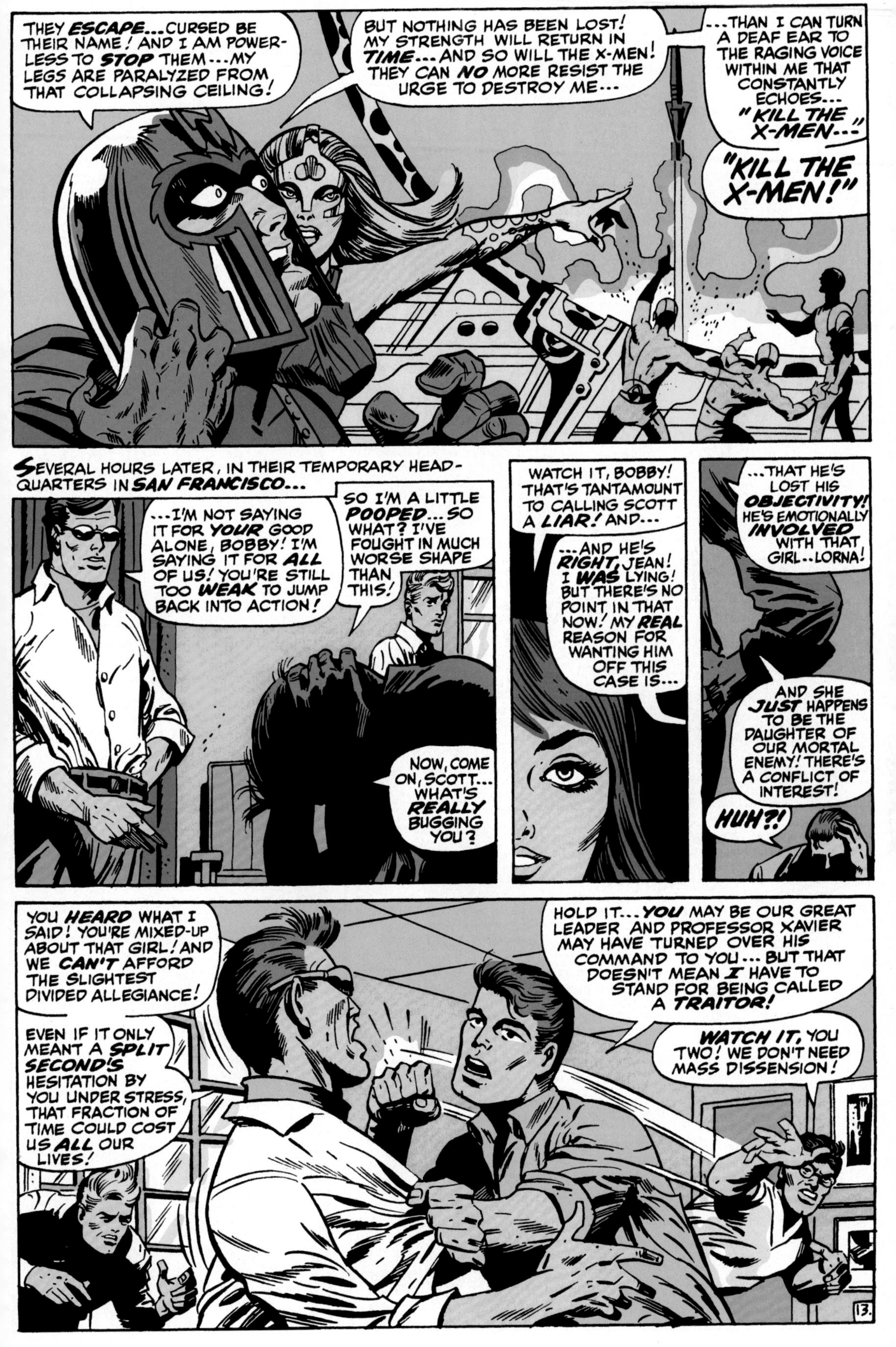

THEY ESCAPE... CURSED BE THEIR NAME! AND I AM POWERLESS TO STOP THEM... MY LEGS ARE PARALYZED FROM THAT COLLAPSING CEILING!
BUT NOTHING HAS BEEN LOST! MY STRENGTH WILL RETURN IN TIME... AND SO WILL THE X-MEN! THEY CAN NO MORE RESIST THE URGE TO DESTROY ME---
...THAN I CAN TURN A DEAF EAR TO THE RAGING VOICE WITHIN ME THAT CONSTANTLY ECHOES... "KILL THE X-MEN--!"
"KILL THE X-MEN!"
SEVERAL HOURS LATER, IN THEIR TEMPORARY HEAD-QUARTERS IN SAN FRANCISCO...
...I'M NOT SAYING IT FOR YOUR GOOD ALONE, BOBBY! I'M SAYING IT FOR ALL OF US! YOU'RE STILL TOO WEAK TO JUMP BACK INTO ACTION!
SO I'M A LITTLE POOPED... SO WHAT? I'VE FOUGHT IN MUCH WORSE SHAPE THAN THIS!
NOW, COME ON, SCOTT... WHAT'S REALLY BUGGING YOU?
WATCH IT, BOBBY! THAT'S TANTAMOUNT TO CALLING SCOTT A LIAR! AND...
...AND HE'S RIGHT, JEAN! I WAS LYING! BUT THERE'S NO POINT IN THAT NOW! MY REAL REASON FOR WANTING HIM OFF THIS CASE IS...
...THAT HE'S LOST HIS OBJECTIVITY! HE'S EMOTIONALLY INVOLVED WITH THAT GIRL.. LORNA!
AND SHE JUST HAPPENS TO BE THE DAUGHTER OF OUR MORTAL ENEMY! THERE'S A CONFLICT OF INTEREST!
HUH?!
YOU HEARD WHAT I SAID! YOU'RE MIXED-UP ABOUT THAT GIRL! AND WE CAN'T AFFORD THE SLIGHTEST DIVIDED ALLEGIANCE!
EVEN IF IT ONLY MEANT A SPLIT SECOND'S HESITATION BY YOU UNDER STRESS, THAT FRACTION OF TIME COULD COST US ALL OUR LIVES!
HOLD IT... YOU MAY BE OUR GREAT LEADER AND PROFESSOR XAVIER MAY HAVE TURNED OVER HIS COMMAND TO YOU... BUT THAT DOESN'T MEAN I HAVE TO STAND FOR BEING CALLED A TRAITOR!
WATCH IT, YOU TWO! WE DON'T NEED MASS DISSENSION!
13.

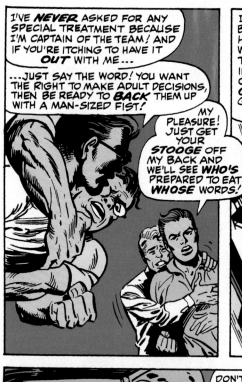

I'VE **NEVER** ASKED FOR ANY SPECIAL TREATMENT BECAUSE I'M CAPTAIN OF THE TEAM! AND IF YOU'RE ITCHING TO HAVE IT **OUT** WITH ME...

...JUST SAY THE WORD! YOU WANT THE RIGHT TO MAKE ADULT DECISIONS, THEN BE READY TO **BACK** THEM UP WITH A MAN-SIZED FIST!

MY PLEASURE! JUST GET YOUR **STOOGE** OFF MY BACK AND WE'LL SEE **WHO'S** PREPARED TO EAT **WHOSE** WORDS!

I WOULDN'T HAVE BELIEVED IT IF I HADN'T **HEARD** IT WITH MY OWN EARS! TWO X-MEN ACTING LIKE A PAIR OF THUGS IN A **GRADE-Z** GANGSTER MOVIE!

IS **THIS** WHAT WE GAVE OUR LIVES TO? IS THIS WHY WE SACRIFICED ANY NORMAL EXISTENCE WE MIGHT HAVE HAD TO BECOME THE **X-MEN**?

THE MONTHS AND MONTHS OF TENSION AND PAIN THAT WE UNDERTOOK TO **PERFECT** OUR MUTANT POWERS! THE DEVOTION THAT...

...PROFESSOR XAVIER LAVISHED ON US TO MAKE US THE BEST FIGHTING **TEAM** THAT EVER LIVED...!

--ALL THAT BLOWN TO **DUST** BY A PAIR OF HOT-HEADED FOOLS! IS **THAT** GOING TO BE YOUR GREATEST ACHIEVEMENT?

DON'T WHISTLE ME THE THE **STARS AND STRIPES FOREVER**! HE STARTED IT...

YOU WEREN'T LISTENING TO A **WORD** SHE SAID, WERE YOU? IT WENT IN ONE DUMB EAR...

...WITH THAT JAZZ ABOUT ME BEING A TRAITOR! BUT I'M GONNA FINISH IT! LIKE.. **NOW!**

--AND RIGHT OUT THE OTHER! WELL--**I** HEARD HER AND SHE'S RIGHT! THROWING PUNCHES AT EACH OTHER **ISN'T** GOING TO SOLVE ONE SOLITARY THING!

WELL **I'LL** BE..! YOU..YOU'RE CHICKEN! THAT'S WHAT YOU ARE! I'D **NEVER** HAVE BELIEVED IT!

YOU STILL DON'T GET IT, DO YOU, YOU WET-EARED PUP!

I **GET** IT, ALL RIGHT! OUR NOBLE LEADER HAS LOST HIS **COOL**! I'M GETTIN' OUT OF HERE BEFORE YOU BUST OUT IN **BIG** WET TEARS!

SLAM!

LET HIM GO! IT'S **BETTER** THIS WAY! HE'LL COOL OFF...

---IN TIME! AND BY THEN WE'LL BE **DONE** WITH MAGNETO!

THAT IS, IF MY PLAN DOESN'T RUN INTO ANY **SNAGS** ALONG THE WAY!

PLAN?! WHAT PLAN? HOW ABOUT LETTING THE **LOWLY** TROOPS IN ON THE **HIGH** COMMAND STRATEGY, GENERAL?

14

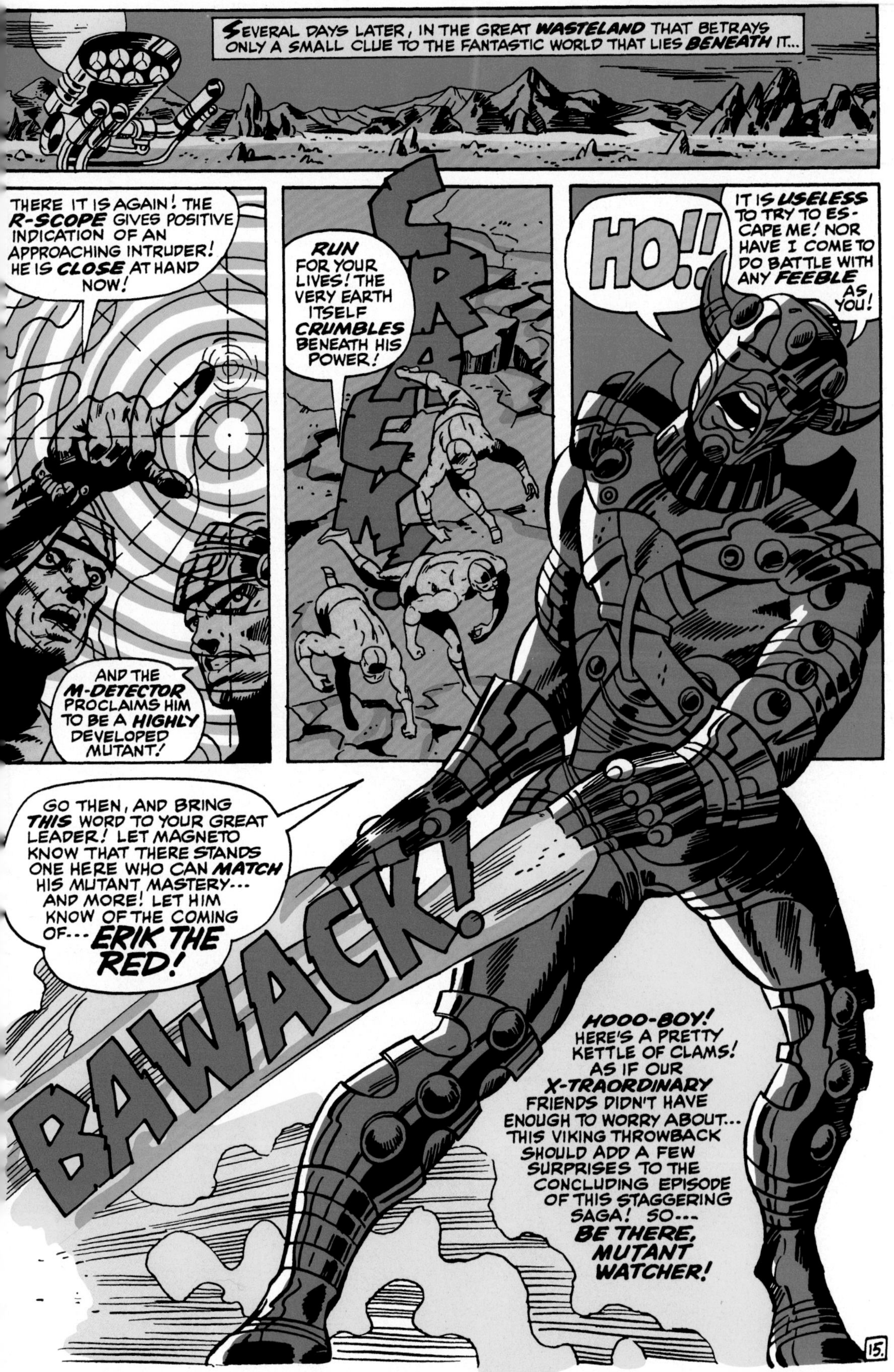
SEVERAL DAYS LATER, IN THE GREAT WASTELAND THAT BETRAYS ONLY A SMALL CLUE TO THE FANTASTIC WORLD THAT LIES BENEATH IT...
THERE IT IS AGAIN! THE R-SCOPE GIVES POSITIVE INDICATION OF AN APPROACHING INTRUDER! HE IS CLOSE AT HAND NOW!
AND THE M-DETECTOR PROCLAIMS HIM TO BE A HIGHLY DEVELOPED MUTANT!
CRACK
RUN FOR YOUR LIVES! THE VERY EARTH ITSELF CRUMBLES BENEATH HIS POWER!
HO!!
IT IS USELESS TO TRY TO ESCAPE ME! NOR HAVE I COME TO DO BATTLE WITH ANY FEEBLE AS YOU!
GO THEN, AND BRING THIS WORD TO YOUR GREAT LEADER! LET MAGNETO KNOW THAT THERE STANDS ONE HERE WHO CAN MATCH HIS MUTANT MASTERY... AND MORE! LET HIM KNOW OF THE COMING OF... ERIK THE RED!
BAWACK!
HOOO-BOY! HERE'S A PRETTY KETTLE OF CLAMS! AS IF OUR X-TRAORDINARY FRIENDS DIDN'T HAVE ENOUGH TO WORRY ABOUT... THIS VIKING THROWBACK SHOULD ADD A FEW SURPRISES TO THE CONCLUDING EPISODE OF THIS STAGGERING SAGA! SO... BE THERE, MUTANT WATCHER!
15.

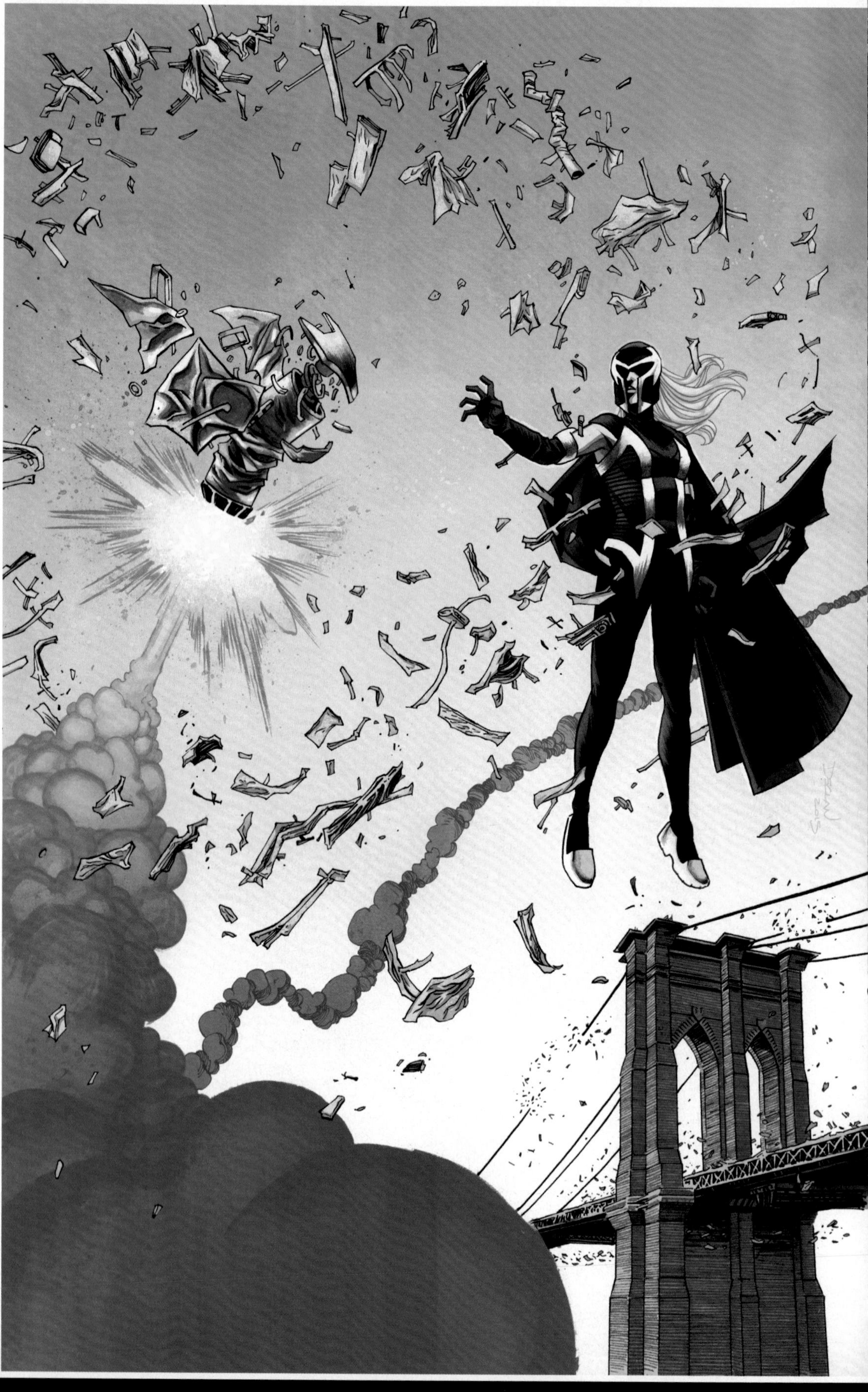

MAGNETO 19 Gwengneto Variant by Declan Shalvey

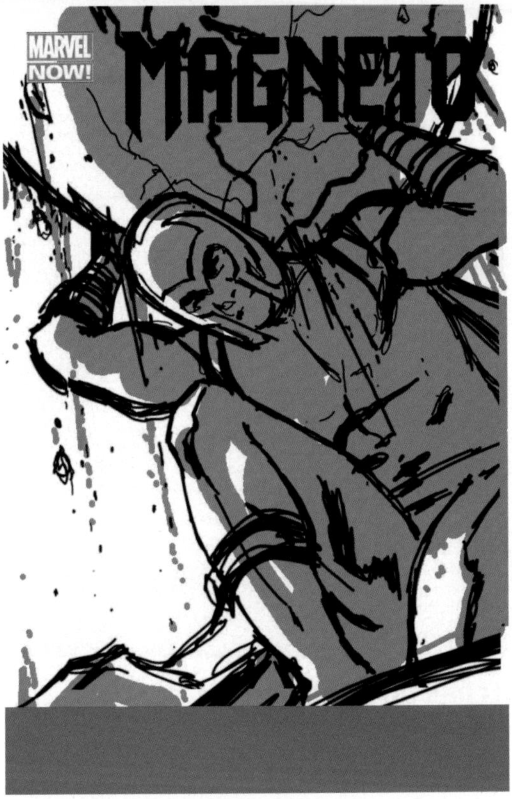
MARVEL
NOW!
MAGNETO

MAGNETO 18 Cover Sketch
by David Yardin

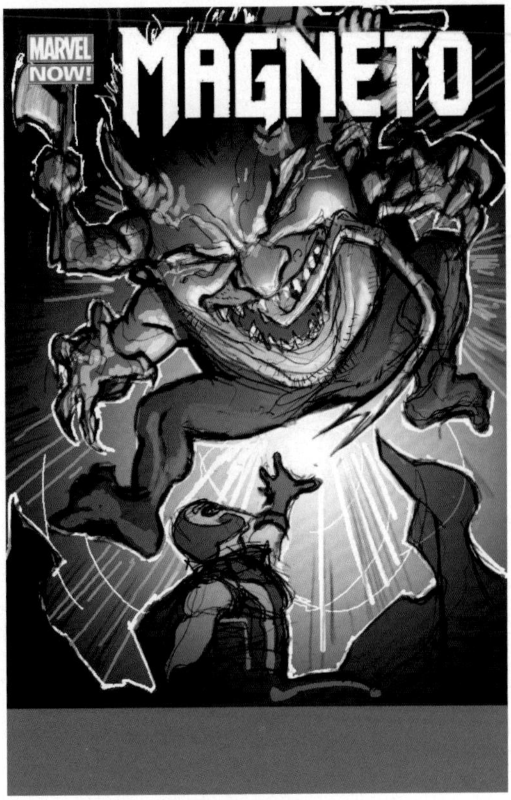
MARVEL
NOW!
MAGNETO

MAGNETO 19 Cover Sketch
by David Yardin

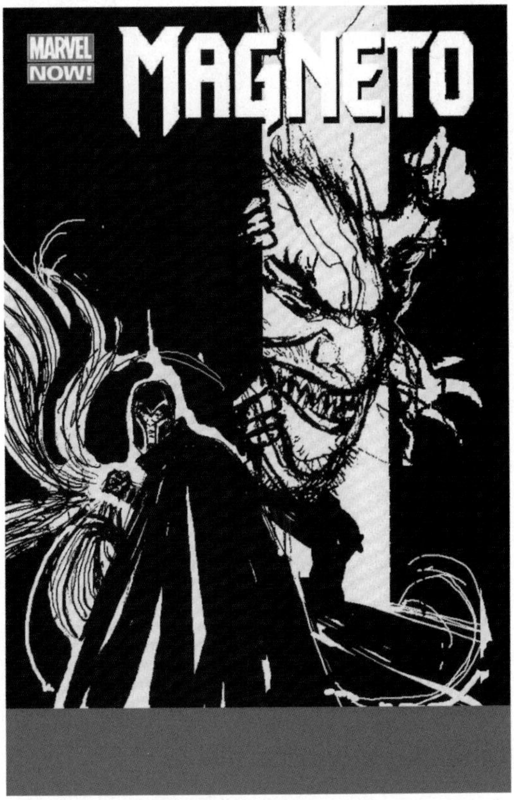
MARVEL
NOW!
MAGNETO

MAGNETO 19 Cover Sketch
by David Yardin

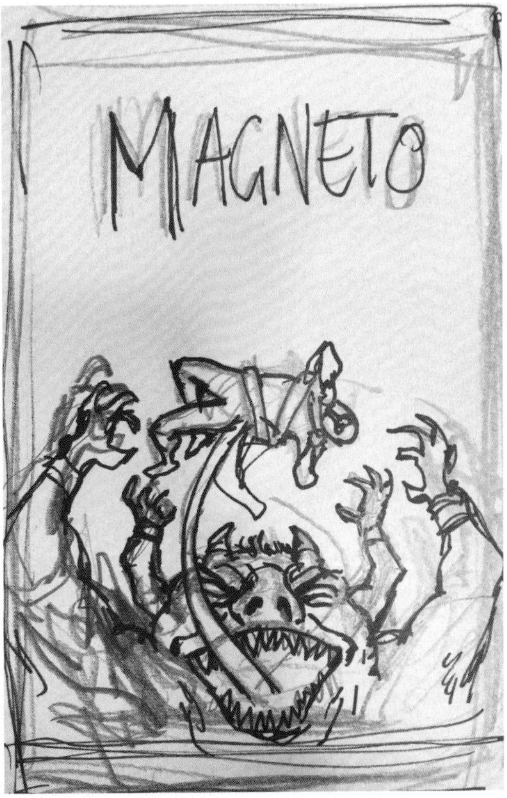
MAGNETO

MAGNETO 19 Cover Sketch
by David Yardin

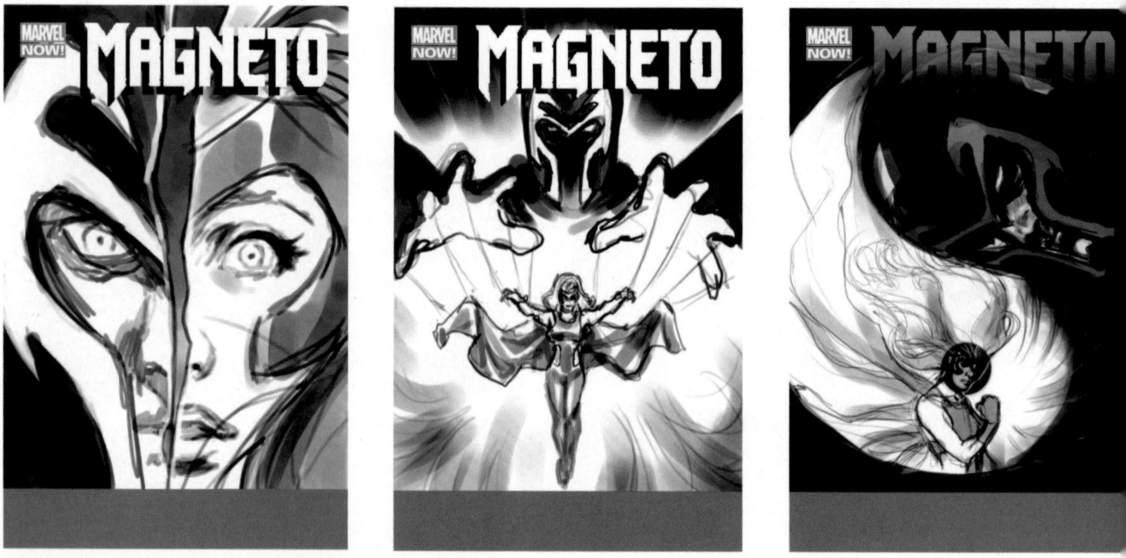
MARVEL NOW!
MAGNETO
MARVEL NOW!
MAGNETO
MARVEL NOW!
MAGNETO

MAGNETO 20 Cover Sketches by David Yardin

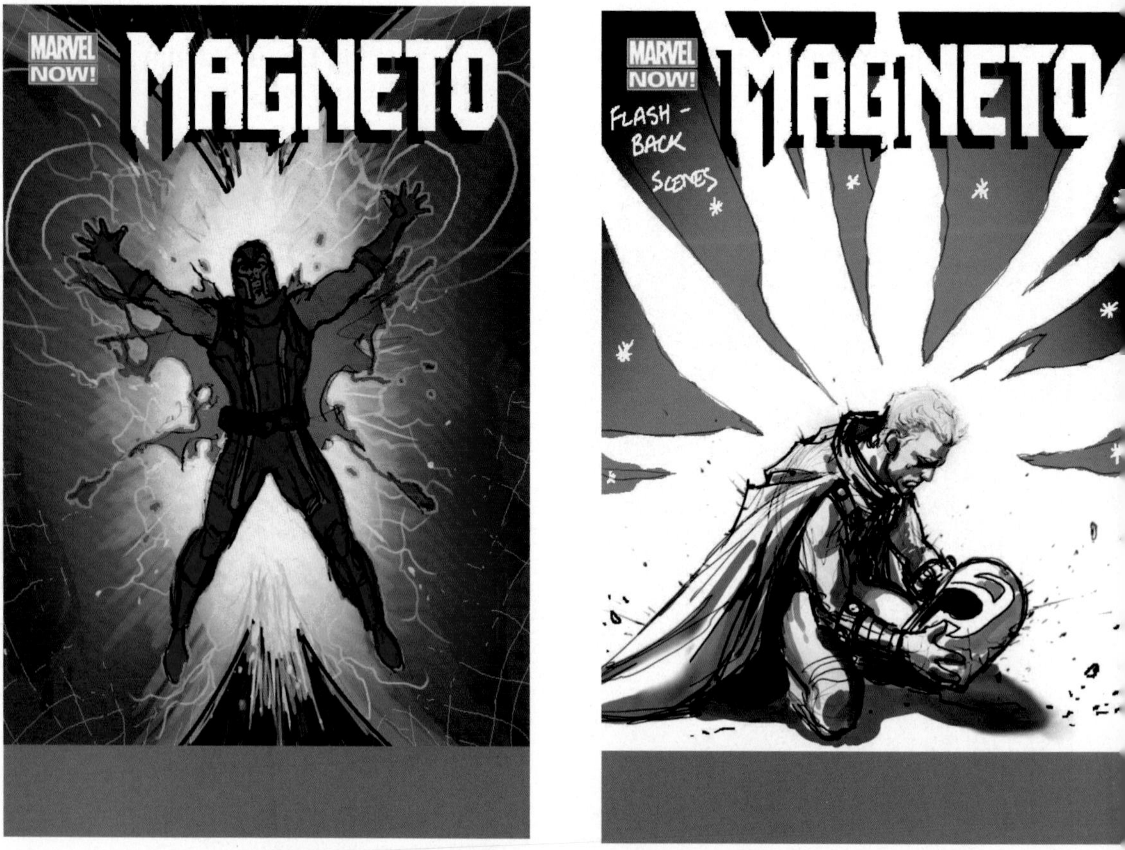
MARVEL NOW!
MAGNETO
MARVEL NOW!
MAGNETO
FLASH-BACK SCENES

MAGNETO 21 Cover Sketches by David Yardin

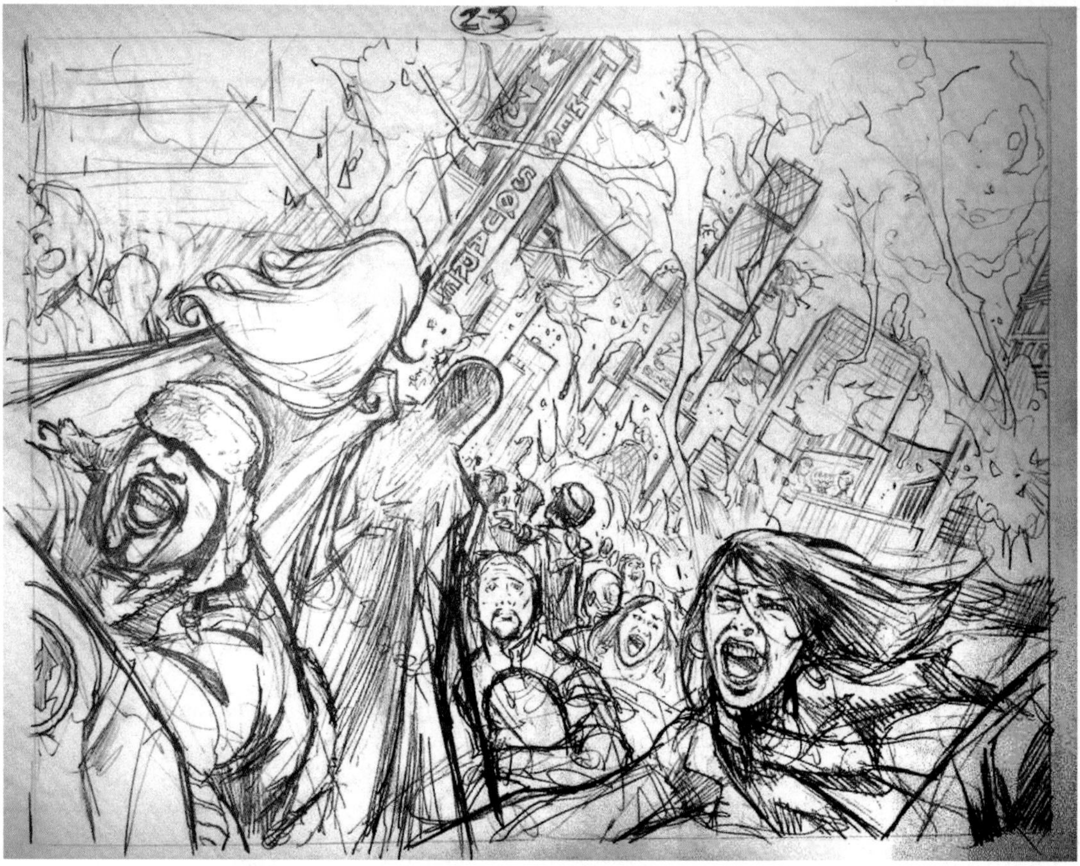

MAGNETO 18, Pages 2-3 Pencils by Paul Davidson

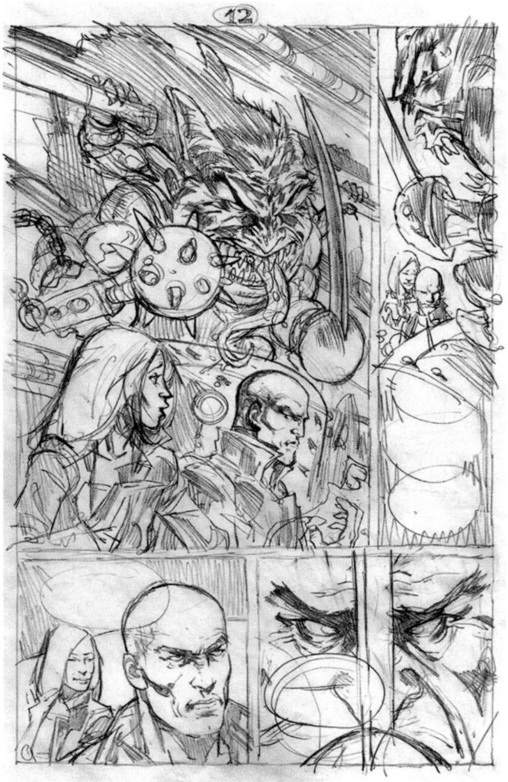

MAGNETO 19, Page 12
Pencils by Paul Davidson

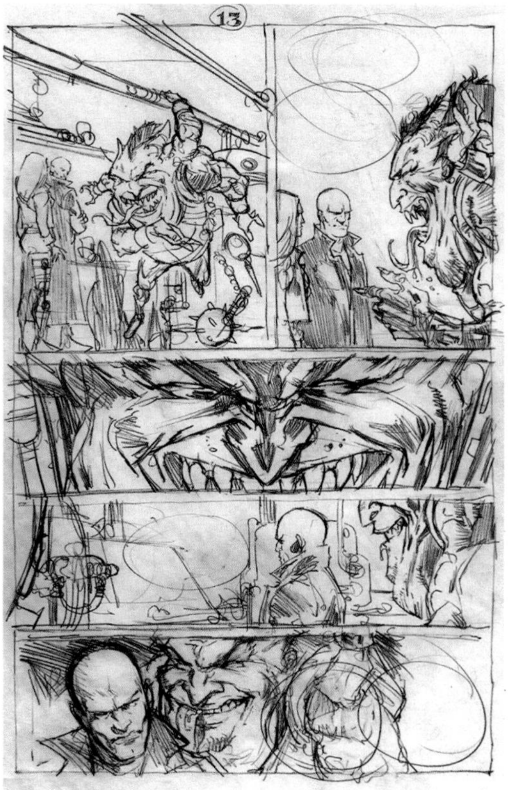

MAGNETO 19, Page 13
Pencils by Paul Davidson

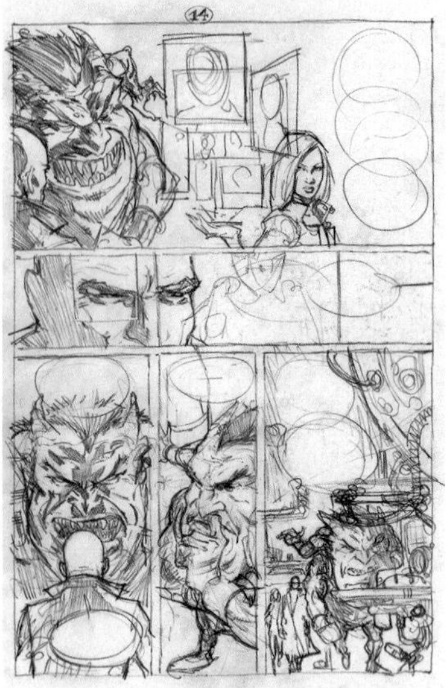

MAGNETO 19, Page 14
Pencils by Paul Davidson

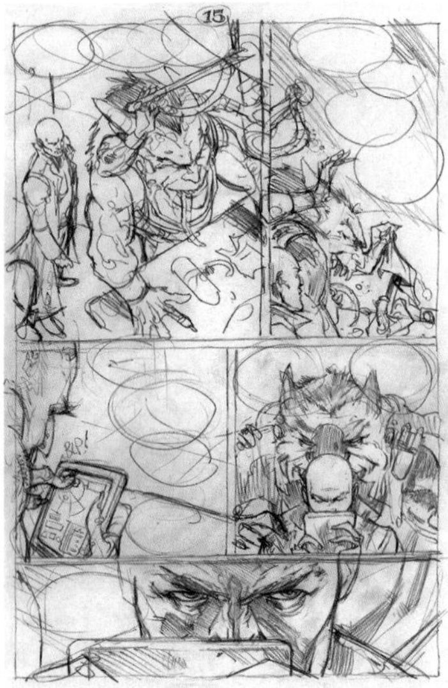

MAGNETO 19, Page 15
Pencils by Paul Davidson

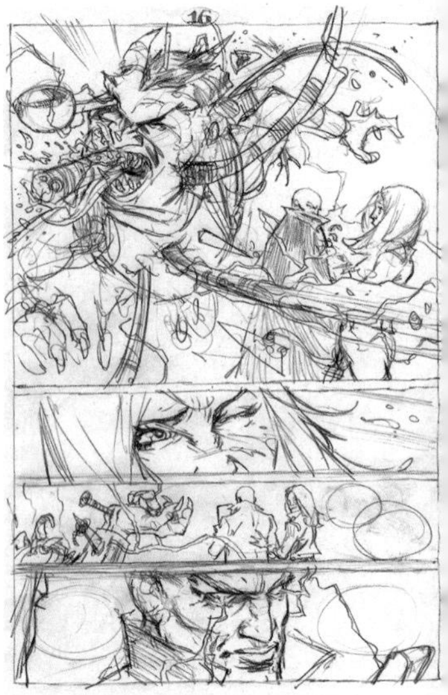

MAGNETO 19, Page 16
Pencils by Paul Davidson

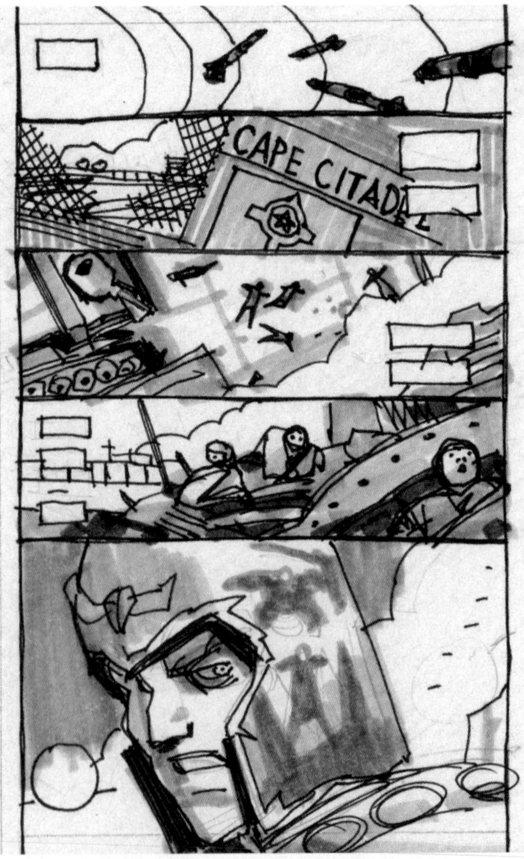
CAPE CITADEL

MAGNETO 21, Page 1 Layouts
by Gabriel Hernandez Walta

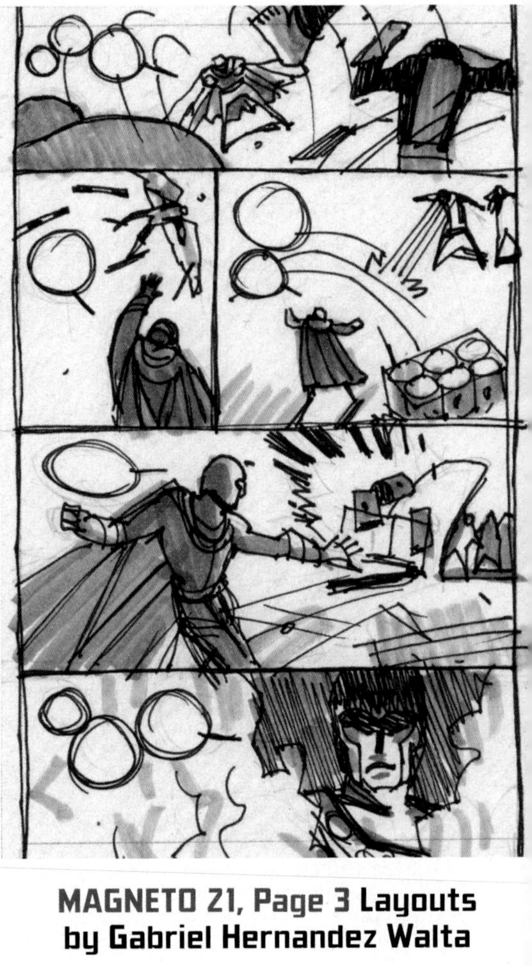

MAGNETO 21, Page 3 Layouts
by Gabriel Hernandez Walta